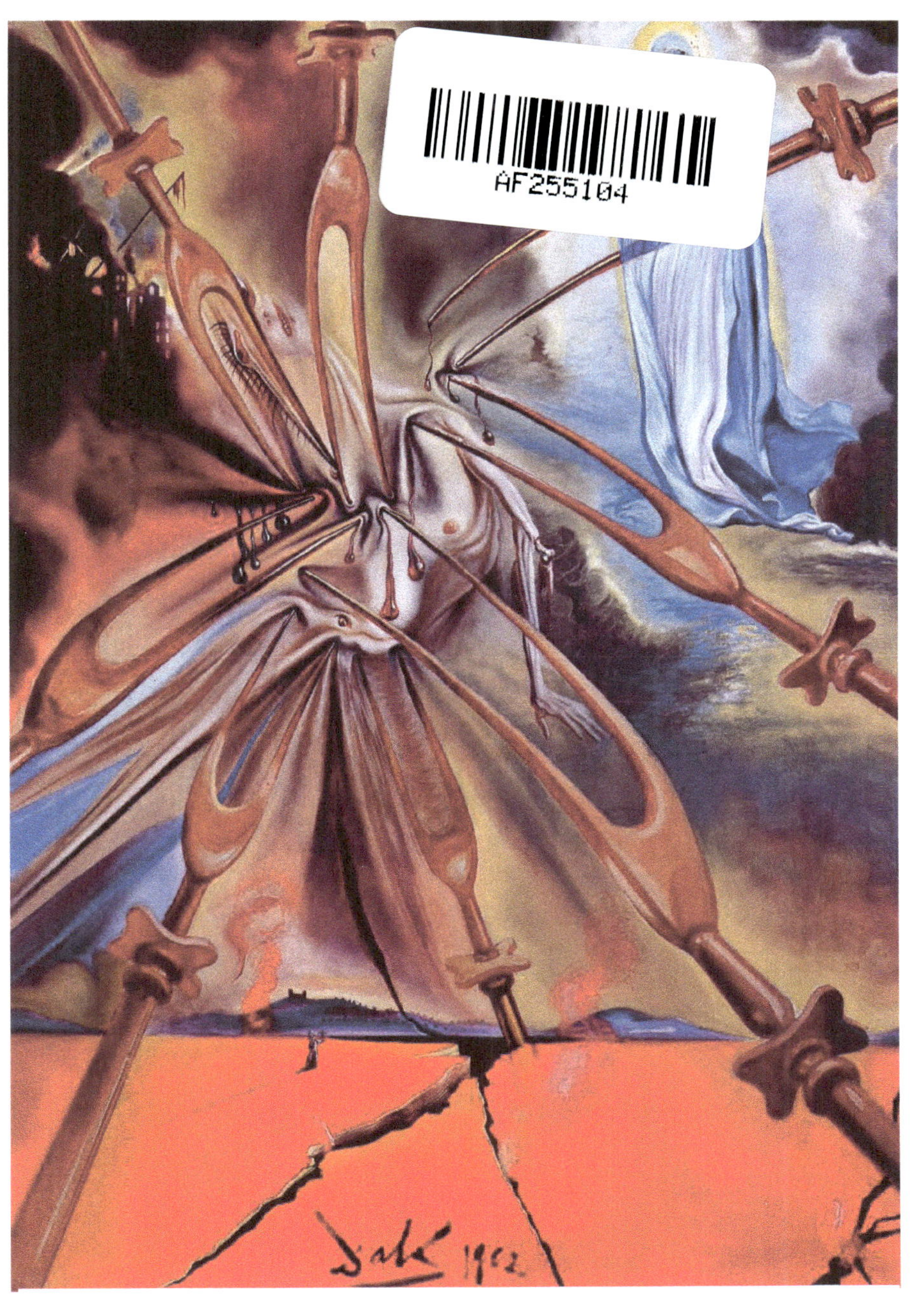

The Painting *Vision of Hell at Fátima* by Salvador Dalí, 1962.

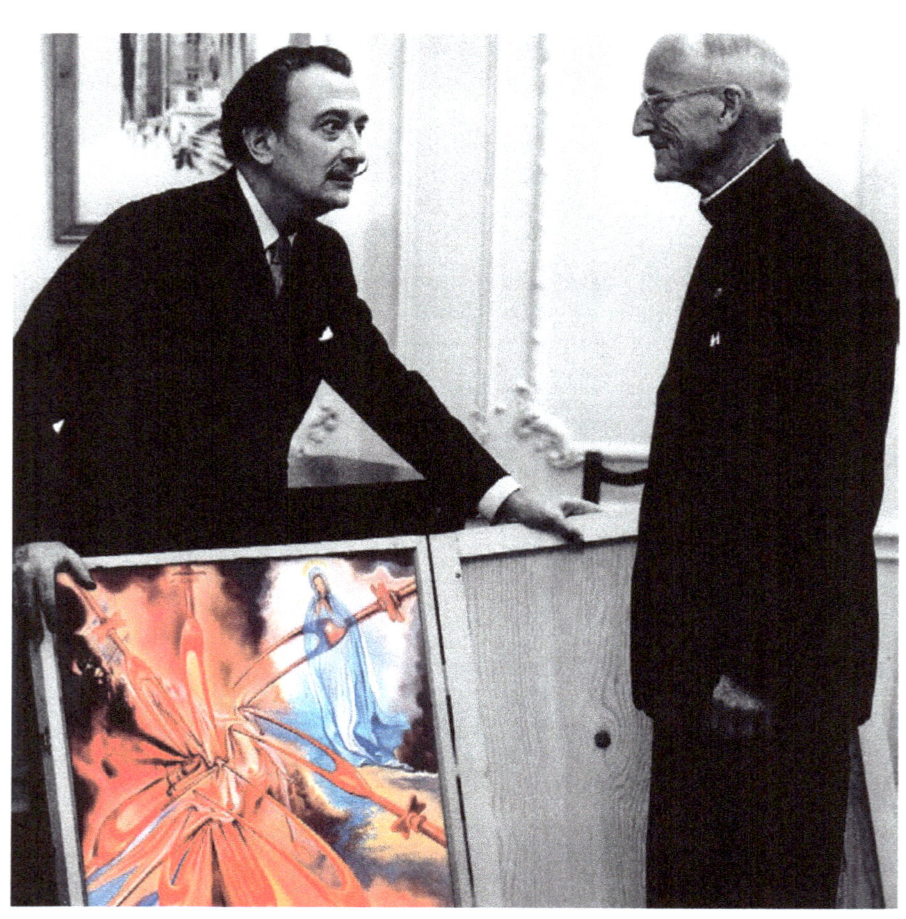

DALÍ'S FÁTIMA SECRET

A True Story of Salvador Dalí, the Apparitions of Fátima, and an American's Heavenly Inspiration from Hell.

By
Paul Perry

Foreword by
Carlos Evaristo
and
Introduction by
Nicholas Descharnes

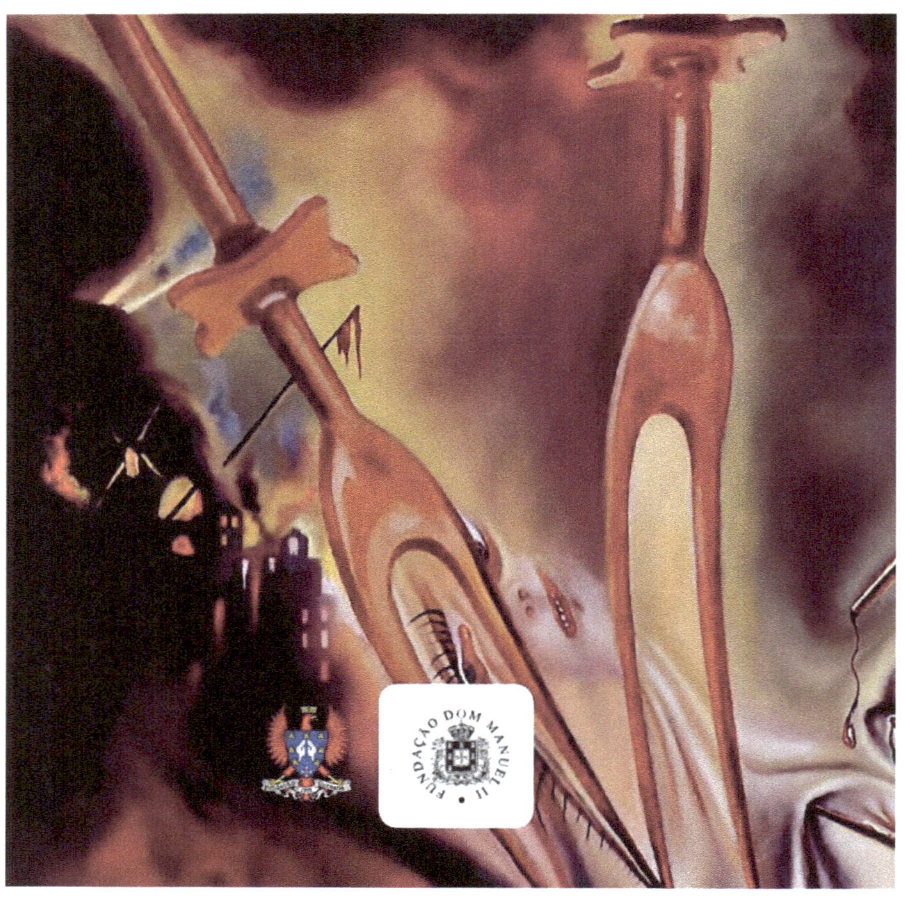

Copyright: Paul Perry 2020

Published by
SAKKARA Books

Archival Photos of Salvador Dalí: Robert Descharnes
Additional Archival Photos and Documents Courtesy: The Oureana
Historical Cultural Foundation, Ourém Castle, Portugal, The Blue Army
of Our Lady of Fátima, Washington, New Jersey

Sponsors
The Oureana Historical Cultural Foundation
The D. Manuel II Foundation
R.A.H.A. - Royal Archeological and Historical Association
International Crusade for Holy Relics Apostolate

Table of Contents

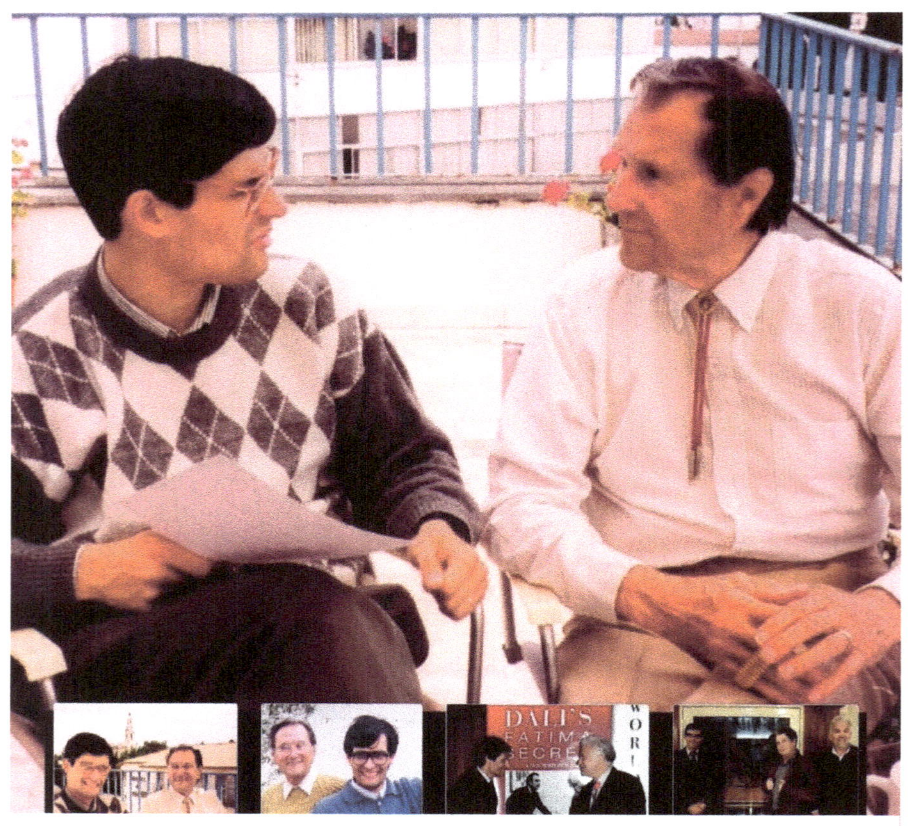

Main Photo: John Haffert and Carlos Evaristo in 1997 on the day of their visit to the Fátima Shrine to view the painting of The Vision of Hell on public display in Fátima. Additional Photos of John Haffert and Carlos Evaristo taken on the same date and shortly before Haffert's death in 2001. Carlos Evaristo greets author Paul Perry at the Fátima début of the Documentary "Dalí´s Greatest Secret" at the Domus Pacis in 2012. 50th Anniversary of the painting. Carlos Evaristo, Nicolas Decharnes and Author Paul Perry pose next to a copy of the painting exhibited today in the bullet proof case intended for the original in the lobby of the Domus Pacis in Fátima.

Foreword

A Secret Story Behind the Story of the Secrets

By
Carlos Evaristo
President of the Oureana Historical Cultural Foundation

This book is about the secret behind a secret, behind the Third Secret of Fátima. It tells the prophetic story of the horrific vision of July 13th 1917, a Divine Revelation that gave three illiterate shepherd children from a remote mountain village in Portugal, an overpowering glimpse of Hell and a moving surreal portrait of world events that were to come, involving Russia, Communism, wars, martyrdom and Pope John Paul II, all related to the struggle between good and evil and Our Lady's defense against militant atheism and religious persecution.

Although it is a bold affirmation to make, I think it is safe to conclude that with the disclosure of the third part of the Fátima secret by the Vatican in the year 2000, Salvador Dalí´s Fátima Secret has become, in essence, the last of the Fátima Secrets.

In 1992 and '93 I had the rare pleasure of interviewing Sister Lucia, the last remaining person to have experienced the apparitions of Fátima that took place in 1917.

I call these interviews rare because they were just that. After seeing the apparitions that quite literally changed the world, Sister Lucia spent much of the remainder of her life as a cloistered nun, living in a monastery amongst other nuns, although she was regularly informed of the harsh realities of exterior life.

The interviews with Sister Lúcia were the most lengthy and

controversial conversations ever published with the Seer. They swept the Catholic and secular world and made the Vatican intervene.

They also introduced me to John Haffert, the then retired founder of the Blue Army, the largest Catholic Apostolate, a virtual nation of Marian Crusaders aimed at spreading the word of Fátima.

I think it's fair to say that the apparitions of Fátima would barely be remembered if not for Haffert. In starting the World Apostolate of Fátima, also known as The Blue Army, he mobilized 80 million people around the message of Fátima. He managed to do this using faith and his entrepreneurial skills.

Haffert built a hotel in Fátima, purchased passenger jets and filled them with "Marian Pilgrims" destined for the shrine, beautified the primitive city of Fátima, etc, etc. There were a lot of "etceteras" in Haffert's life, all aimed at making the Holy apparitions and the Holy children who saw them popular role models.

Although many of the more staid members of the church criticized Haffert's approach to conversion and spirituality, few dared challenge the opinion of Pope Pius XII, who so loved the marketing abilities of Haffert that he called him, "the greatest man in the world."

Haffert was immensely interested in the words of Sister Lucia. So when our interviews with her were published, Haffert befriended me. He had spoken to Sister Lucia himself over 50 years before, but he wanted to know what new information - if any - Heaven's spokesperson had revealed to us about the Fátima apparitions and what lay in store for future.

Over time I was privileged to become two things that I'll always cherish: Sister Lucia's "unofficial" interpreter and unofficial confidant, and Haffert's "spiritual son."

Before the death of Haffert, I was appointed the president of The (Fátima) Oureana Historical Cultural Foundation for Religious Research. This incredible foundation is much more than a collection of the impressive property that it holds in Fátima and Ourém Castle. The Foundation is a treasure storehouse of information contained in tens of thousands of rare books, manuscripts, relics and photographs that make up its archive. Subsequently, I have become the custodian of these precious objects, many of them containing secrets of Fátima.

Among the secrets held are those related to Salvador Dalí, John Haffert, the seers of Fátima, and *The Vision of Hell*, the painting around which this book revolves.

The painting was the greatest investment ever made by a Catholic organization on what was to be a campaign poster aimed at saving all of the people in the world from Hell. It was to be a projected "passport" to the afterlife, conceived by two Americans who were firm believers in Heaven and its miracles. One man was John Haffert and the other a young Seminarian who believed he himself had been saved from the fires of Hell after reading the details of the visions as written by Sister Lucia.

The struggle of the sole surviving Fátima seer to save souls from Hell and Haffert's desire to help her is part of the secret told in this book.

This book removes the flamboyant theatrical mask of Salvador Dalí, the Master of Surrealism, exposing the fragile spiritual nudity of his tormented soul. This story exemplifies the personal spiritual struggle of one man.

The secrets revealed in this book come in part from John Haffert, who told them to me in a series of various written and taped conversations. Some of these revelations from Haffert came in 1997, exactly 80 years after the Fátima apparitions on the precise spot where the three children had the vision of Hell apparition. It was there he became emotional over the spiritual transformation that took place in the world. It was also there where he told me much of the story behind Salvador Dalí's painting.

"When Dalí was brought here he stood in awe," said Haffert. "Then he turned to me and said, 'This is where the Virgin Mary opened the earth so the children could see Hell.'"

Other events inspired other memories for Haffert. The accidental rediscovery of the painting under the bed of a religious sister at the Blue Army headquarters in New Jersey, prompted the founder of the apostolate to share with me much of the story you read here. He even produced a napkin used by Dalí from the St. Regis Hotel in New York. On it was written in faded and blotched ink were the terms of a contract drawn up in Haffert's own handwriting and signed by Dalí.

At one point over dinner he performed a demonstration of how *The Vision of Hell* was created by Dalí. He ordered roast chicken and a plate of escargot. Then with the sharp prongs of the escargot forks, proceeded to disassemble the meal in front of him, poking and prodding at his menu selection while he explained the how and why of the mysterious painting.

Of course this book doesn't consist only of my memories. To tell the entire story required dogged international reporting, even convincing the Blue Army in New Jersey to open a safe where letters pertaining to this story were found. That work, and the task of writing this book to reveal the full tale was that of Paul Perry, who has written several New York Times bestsellers. His discovery of long-lost photos and documents substantiated a story that was – until now – considered to be urban myth.

That the facts surrounding this story have been so difficult to find is no surprise. The late Robert Descharnes, Dalí's confidant and photographer for 40 years, never saw this painting nor did he hear Dalí speak of it. This was strange, said Descharnes, in an interview with Perry, because it was his job to photograph all of Dalí's paintings. Yet the painting has been authenticated and there is photographic proof from the Blue Army of Dalí presenting it to an official of that organization. Why the secrecy?

Robert Descharnes did not comment on this question before his death, but his son and business partner Nicolas Descharnes has a theory. "The Master believed himself redeemed through this work and considering himself nothing but God's brush," declared Descharnes.

In short, the work was not his, but rather God's! God was the true author!

Now, through the final disclosure of this story there is a chance that the surreal painting by Salvador Dalí of the Vision of Hell at Fátima will finally live up to its original expectations. May it be a beacon for all in their own personal quest for understanding on the path to Conversion and the Afterlife. May God grant that this be the mission for the future of *The Vision of Hell*, well beyond the forthcoming 100th anniversary of the apparitions of Fátima.

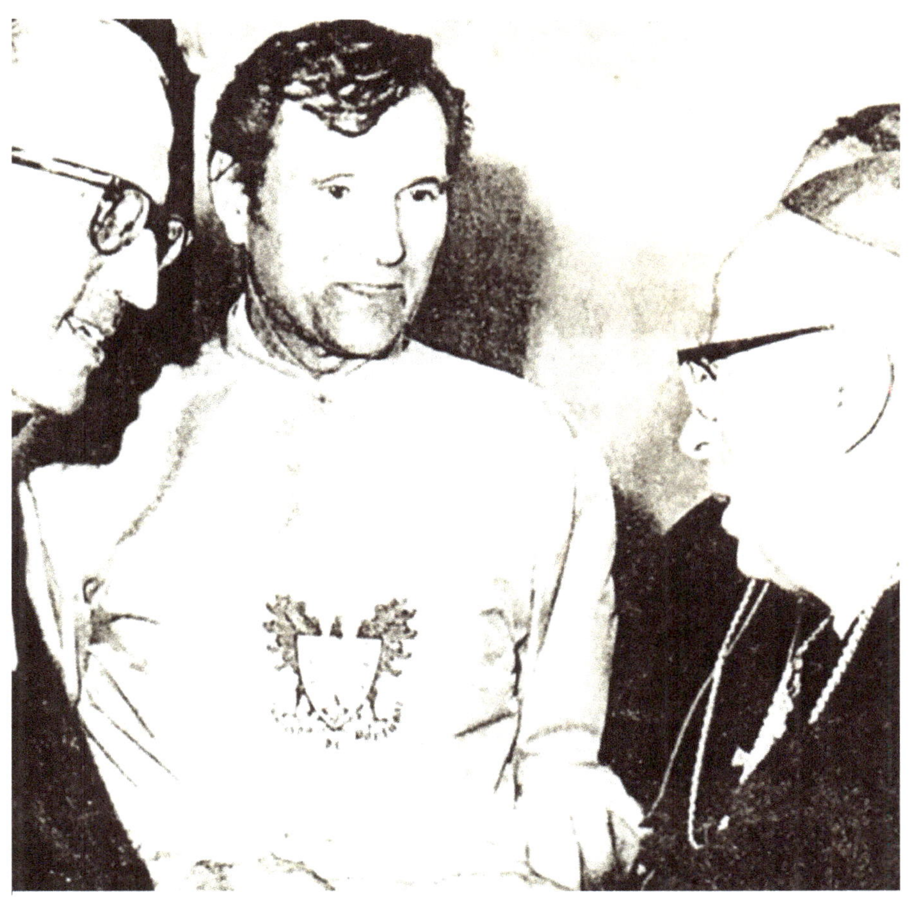

John Haffert with the President of TAP Air Portugal and Bishop D. João Pereira Venâncio of Leiria - Fátima at the inauguration of the Medieval Banquet Program in Ourém Castle on August 15th, 1971.

An Introduction to "Dalí's Fátima Secret"

By
Nicolas Descharnes
Descharnes & Descharnes
World Expert in the Works of Salvador Dalí

"Nicolas? It's Sotheby's Paris, Urgent!" I pick up the handset to my phone. Perhaps it is a new unknown canvas in the United States. As the global experts on the work of Salvador Dalí, we are privileged to be at ringside when a new painting "surfaces" following a death and the marketing of an unknown piece. Why the US necessarily? The Dalí-Gala couple stayed there from 1940 to 1948. They lived in part on the sponsorship of portraits.

"An American author writing a book on Dalí wants to contact you for an Introduction. What would be the price?" Surprised by the question of money, and wondering about the identity of the author, I answered: "Regarding the price, I have no idea now for an Introduction, we are naturally open to the idea. But who is it?" - "An American author. Do you authorize me to submit your email?" - "Of course!"

A few days later I received an email from a certain Paul Perry. I read it to my father Robert Descharnes whose answer was immediate: "I have to read the book" We were in 2011, Robert was still alive. He would leave us on February 15th, 2014. I answered Perry and he sent me the text, suspecting that it is not in its final version. He did not ask me for assurance of confidentiality considering the manuscript of a book is commercially sensitive before publication. This was undeniable proof of confidence, trust, and especially for a writer who has written five *New York Times* bestsellers.

In the middle of processing hundreds of emails we receive every day, I managed to find time to print the book Perry had sent and place a copy of it at Robert's bedside. My father had been friend of the late Salvador Dalí, and had met him in 1950 and attended to him up until his death in 1989. Robert lost his father when he was only two years old after an injury in the first World War. Dalí was like the father he had not had. He did not hesitate to risk his life to save that of Salvador Dalí in 1984 when a fire broke out in his bedroom at Pubol Castle in Spain.

The text was a moment that Robert slowly progressed at. I gathered he did not try harder because the text was in English. So I added to my various qualifications (manager, photographer, writer, editor, model, etc.) to that of reporter and bound myself to the text on behalf of my mentor.

My native language is not English, so I immediately imagined a very long and tedious time. The first part of the book tells the story of the 1917 apparitions in Fátima. This account is an absolute must for a proper understanding of the issues: mainly the existence of Hell. It is tedious, but soon, it is drawn by events.

Having set the scene, we discover the extraordinary personality of John Haffert, head of the Blue Army (The World Apostolate of Fátima) dedicated to the dissemination of the Message of Fátima, to whom we must pay tribute, and something that the reader will appreciate given this wonderful human testimony of remission.

So I finished the book at a rate increasing in the second part where there appears in an unusual devolution, a second character we will call Brother Michael since both Haffert, Dalí and Paul Perry who had met him promised he would remain anonymous even after 59 years. Both men were believers of modern-day Visions and how "effective" they can serve the cause of the Apparitions of the Blessed Virgin at Fátima. From 1917 to the 60s, it takes energy to keep unfailing hope.

But what hope? The main message is the existence of Hell. A constructive threat? The other key is the right word to disclose of Russia becoming the Communist atheist USSR stifling religion. I was finally convinced, thanks to this book that the Fátima children's visions are a reality. Why doubt the good word? This is probably because of religious paintings combining science. Dalí happened to try to rally the believers by using a cosmic mysticism.

Finally, after a multiple calendar exchange, I got to schedule a meeting with Paul Perry. We met in Tampa, Florida for breakfast at the hotel in the airport. "I would have so loved to meet Mr. Haffert", I said. "Me too!", he replied. Paul has a calm face, only his lips express any expression, so it seems he bathes in natural serenity. We talked about the events of Fátima and the fact that these Apparitions are somewhat forgotten today. We discussed Haffert and Brother Michael, men so beneficial to the prosperity of the religious institution of the Blue Army.

We spoke until half past four when we were interrupted by my next appointment. We could have spent all day talking. Gradually throughout our discussion, we felt increasingly close in search of the vision of Lucia, the shepherd girl and main witness, alongside her cousins Jacinta and Francisco, but mostly we spoke of the work Salvador Dalí painted in honor of the event. It seems to me that we were both convinced that our meeting was not accidental and that we were destined to meet again, in the same quest of mysticism throughout history.

The book was unfinished, the investigation had to continue. A safe was opened for the first time in many decades revealing never before published documents and photos. We then met at Fátima, in March of 2011, to the start filming a documentary on the subject called "Dalí's Greatest Secret" The book would slumber for a few years as interviews accumulated. Naturally, we visited Ourém overlooked by a medieval castle on a hilltop that can be contemplated from Fátima. Legend has it that a Moorish princess, kidnapped and married to a Christian knight committed suicide desperately awaiting the return of her husband who had gone off to war. Her name was Fátima. We encountered "accidentally" the historian and archaeologist Carlos Evaristo, right arm of the late John Haffert and who served as translator for Fátima Seer Sister Lucia. From that meeting there sparked a friendship and we started a series of projects together on the Sacred Relics, Christopher Columbus, the Royal Lipsanotheca and Relic Kingdoms which are still relevant today. This is perfectly expressed and comes directly from the title of the famous painting by Dalí soft watches

1931: The Persistence of Memory. Thus, we are an international triangle that is not accidental.

Robert would confirm he had not seen Dalí paint the picture commissioned by John Haffert neither in Port Lligat, nor in Paris. Dalí kept this secret until its delivery in New York in 1962. The date of the Commission was already in 1959 when Dalí was first approached by royal and aristocratic friends of Haffert. History has it that Dalí made a first version, but not satisfied he destroyed it. Haffert claimed Dalí had told him he had done at least two if not more, struggling with a face to give Our Lady. Haffert claimed he settled on his own mother's.

Everyone was waiting for the revelation of the last Secret of Fátima by the Vatican in 1960. It did not take place. Dalí had to paint his picture in honor of an ultimate secret undisclosed. It would therefore represent different historical elements in a unique composition.

The organic form the center is tortured, distorted by eight snail forks. We distinguish the shape is human because it reveals an eye, mouth and breast. Drops of blood bead. To view this malaise we shed tears like Dalí himself. The upper right shows a scene of desolation. The ruins of a burned city. The destruction by Communism identified by the menacing satellite Sputnik. Just below we distinguish an elongated silhouette, a soul suspended between Heaven and Earth. The soil is red and smoke escapes giant cracks reflecting heat from the bowels of the Earth, Hell. Haffert had claimed Dalí's left side of his face, the Sinister Side, with raised eyebrow and pointed mustache can be seen in the puffs of smoke coming from Hell.

In the distance you can see a mountain with the Castle of Ourém. This is the element that identifies the location in the painting. Dalí tries to make us perceive the unbearable Vision of Hell that Lucia lived. The Virgin, Our Lady of Fátima, is shown at the top right with the protective blue mantle. The glow of her Immaculate Heart is very realistic compared to a classical figurative representation with light rays. Her light is the central point of the appearance to which our eyes are drawn. It balances the composition with pressure points created by the forks to the left. The Virgin is immaterial in a halo of light that partially clears the fork height, giant torturer of souls. Dalí chose this particular culinary instrument, it is realistically in a classical composition with a land area, ethereal area and several scenes in the same class as the paintings of El Greco. During his meeting with Haffert in New York, he explained to him that he would use said specific utensils for the flesh snail content in the shell to devils is like a soul that they must eradicate. In this case, when the snail is cooked, its flesh is black. It is a being whose exoskeleton and protects it. The other animal that is a Dalí icon of the same nature, is the lobster. But its use by Dalí is more complex, because there are antennae and claws. He "cooked" his classical composition that was fought in 1962 in New York.

Dalí left the old continent to come to America when the Nazis invaded France during the summer of 1940. I dated his spiritual conversion traditionally to that year. He began writing his autobiography which appeared in 1942. The word "Catholic" is omnipresent throughout the structure. He said that religions are spiritual architecture but that the best spiritual architecture is Catholic. He would say he had no Faith, but all his work from that time says otherwise.

In 1940 he wrote a mystery project, the data pieces before the courts and cathedrals in medieval times. A young polytheistic priest would sacrifice for the conversion of his followers to Christianity, convinced by the beautiful singing of a procession. He would kill a Minotaur off stage, representing the surrealists, but well dressed, he would be killed, hence the sacrifice for the conversion of his followers to the Catholic monotheism. The funeral of the young priest takes place before the Escorial. The play would never be achieved, as it was deemed too religious. It continues with a second piece in 1942 that also did not see the light of day.

Did Dalí deliberately conceal his religion in his statements and behavior in order to preserve his painting career and to continue its propaganda? In 1951 he wrote in his Mystical Manifesto "Ecstasy is the incorruptible mold." The use of this term connects us to God by his work in religious texts. He cites the very believer Gaudí as another Catalan genius devoted to building his Sagrada Familia.

His conversion he kept a secret as also he kept secret his daily religious practices and attendance of Mass. Since the painting of *The Vision of Hell* his Catholic Religious art dominated his creativity. Catholic references abound in his work. One was particularly touched by the purity and brightness of the face of the Lord: "Christ del Vallès" painted in 1962, the Tinell exhibition in Barcelona to help victims of a disaster at the time. The fullness of Christ's face is an ecstasy reflects the Faith of Dalí. That same year he presented his painting *The Vision of Hell* to Monsignor Colgan of the Blue Army.

Nicolas Descharnes, May 2016

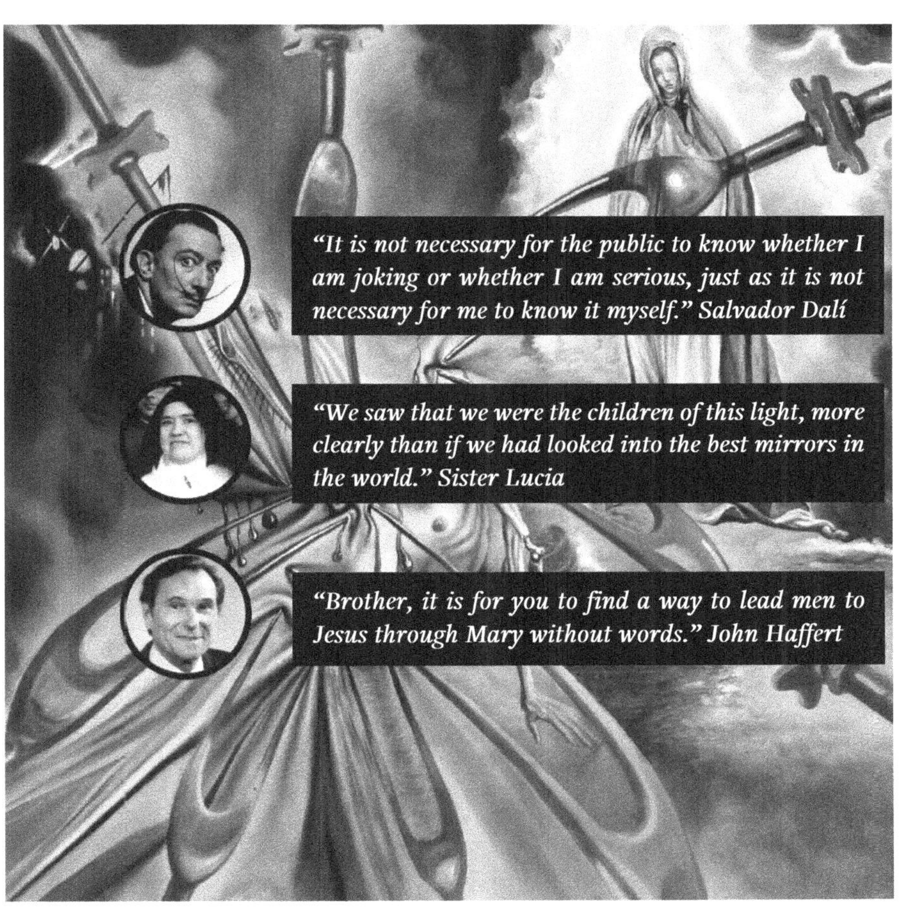

"It is not necessary for the public to know whether I am joking or whether I am serious, just as it is not necessary for me to know it myself." Salvador Dalí
"We saw that we were the children of this light, more clearly than if we had looked into the best mirrors in the world." Sister Lucia
"Brother, it is for you to find a way to lead men to Jesus through Mary without words." John Haffert

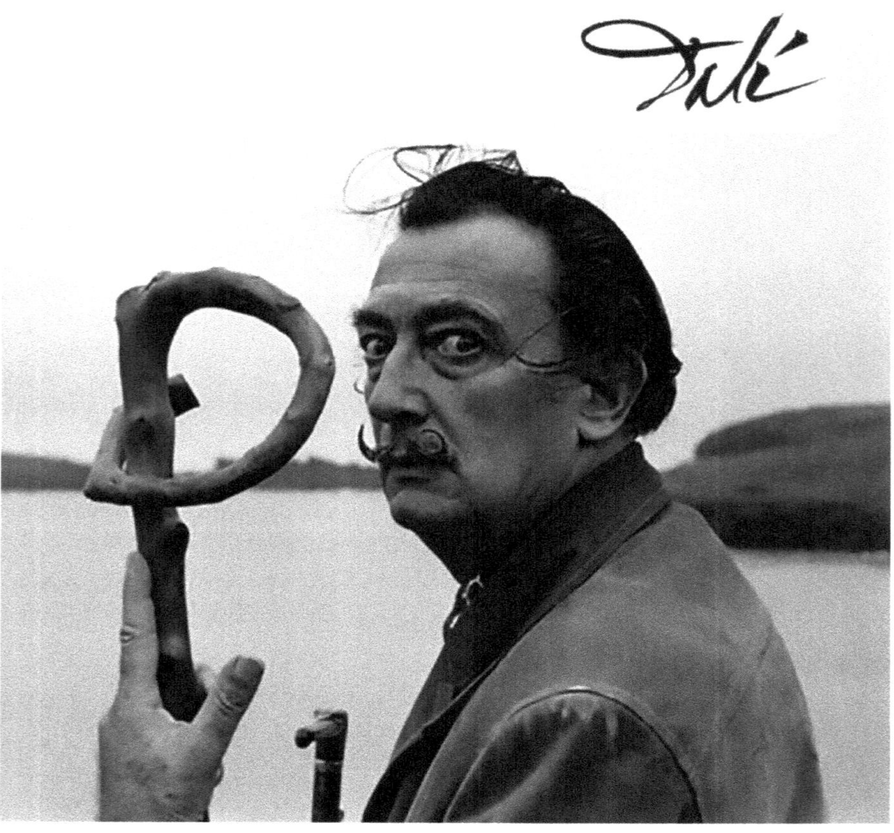

Salvador Dalí photographed by Robert Decharnes holding two of his emblematic walking sticks or canes. The smaller cane Dalí used at the meeting with John Haffert at the Saint Regis Hotel in New York to show the price per canvas. "$30,000, the size of my cane. $15,000, half the size of my cane."

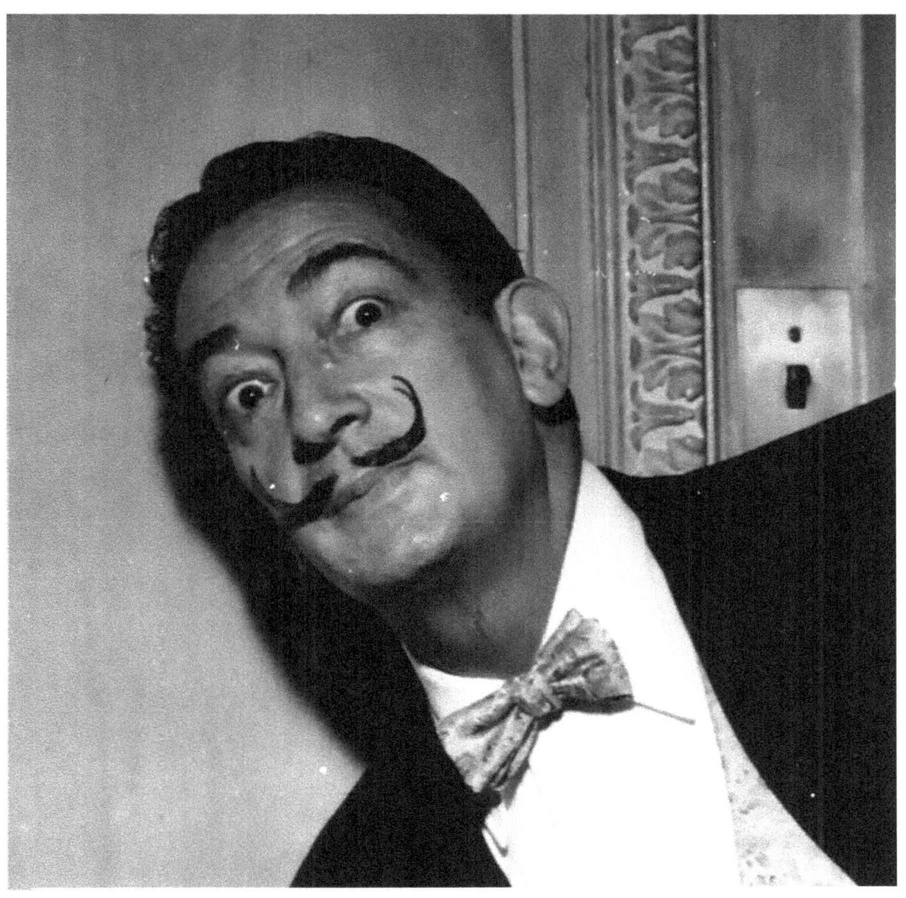

The flamboyant Salvador Dalí all dressed up for a Gala event in one of his theatrical poses at his home away from home; the Saint Regis Hotel.

1

"Seeking heaven"

At the age of 37, Salvador Dalí stripped naked in front of a wardrobe mirror at the estate of a friend in Bowling Green, Virginia. It was time, he declared, to see what effect the years had had on his body.

This wasn't the first time Dalí had closely considered a mirror reflection of his nude, corporeal self. As a child, Dalí frequently stood naked before a mirror and clenched his penis between his thighs so he looked as much as possible like a little girl. It was that act, wrote Dalí, that led to his desire to be "like a beautiful woman," a statement he followed quickly with a disclaimer: "Let there be no misunderstanding on this point – I'm not a homosexual!"

But his self-examination on July 30, 1941 was not about sexual preference. It was about mortality.

Dalí and Gala, his flamboyant wife, had escaped from Europe just shortly before the Nazis stormed France.

Their departure from their home continent had not been without the chaos of ego-driven events that always seemed to swirl around the Dalís. First, the founder of surrealism, Andre Breton, considered Dalí's approach to painting to be too commercial and contrived for the artist to be officially called a "surrealist." In what resembled a corporate board meeting, Breton and other top surrealists came together in Paris and voted him out of the surrealist movement.

Looking back, such a schism certainly could have been predicted. The young Spaniard had virtually stolen the surrealistic movement from the serious Breton. A psychiatrist, Breton founded surrealism on the techniques of free association of the mind, or "automatism," which followers believed to be "the royal road to the understanding of the unconscious."

Dalí embraced surrealism as soon as he moved to Paris in 1929. And by 1931 he captured the movement perfectly in The Persistence of Memory, a painting of clocks melting against a Spanish landscape that is replete with a huddle of ants and a man in dapper dress. To this day, Dalí's melting clocks are the iconic image of surrealism, considered by one critic to be "one of the strangest statements in art of man's obsession with the nature of time."

Dalí says he created the painting in one of those timeless moments of automatism. Eating Camembert cheese alone at his dinner table, Dalí said that he began meditating on the softness of the cheese. Then, in what seemed like a waking dream, he went to look at the work on his easel, a landscape of Port Lligat, his home in Spain. At first, Dalí said the soft cheese reminded him of the body of Christ, because "the body of Jesus is the same as cheese. This is not only Dalí (the artists always spoke of himself in the third person); the first man who talked about this was Saint Augustine, who once compared the body of Christ to mountains of cheese."

Dalí pondered that image until, "In a flash," he saw the cheese turn into melted clocks. Within two hours he had placed three timepieces on the tiny canvas, each with their hands stopped at different positions. Did these different times have something to do with the man in the painting? Dalí did not know. Dalí did not question the mysteries that came from his mind. That was what surrealism was all about, the dictation of thought in the absence of all control exercised by reason. In other words, Dalí entered the dream-state to find his most vivid and puzzling material. The reliance on this dream-state was so prevalent that even Sigmund Freud was in awe. As the father of psychiatry said to the admiring artist, "It is not the unconscious I seek in your pictures, but the conscious."

By the time Freud made that proclamation in 1938, Dalí had already been expelled from the Surrealist movement. Breton, the founder and spokesman of the movement, claimed Dalí's work was too "thought out" and commercial and therefore was no longer of interest to Surrealists. Dalí, on the other hand, declared the card-carrying members of the group to be dogmatic and humorless, ossified by a manifesto that did not allow true exploration of the psyche. As he explained in his own writing: "The secret lies in lucidly keeping a steady course between the waves of madness and the straight lines of logic. Genius consists of being able to live while going constantly from one frontier to another, grasping handfuls of the treasures of mystery that one then, like an athlete, holds at arm's length to make them shine."

Being expelled from the Surrealist movement was okay with Dalí. Indeed, being expelled from institutions seemed to be a proud part of the artist's life up to this point. He did not hesitate to tell any who asked that he had been expelled from elementary school for incorrigibility, and that he had been tossed out of the Escuela Nacional de Bellas Artes de San Fernando, Madrid's preeminent art college, for militant nonconformity. Like other great artists and performers from this period, Dalí clearly did not want to belong to an institution that would have him as a member.

It is no wonder that he considered the Surrealist movement to be devoid of "spiritual content" and said he felt no remorse when Breton drummed him out of their ranks. Instead he founded his own school, one called "paranoiac-critical method," that allowed him to "overcome the materialist and atheist elements in Surrealism and to incorporate its sources of inspiration in Spanish mysticism, giving it a Christian and mystical content." Time Magazine described this new method best when they called it "an attempt to enter a kind of delirium while keeping a part of the mind detached, alert to the imperatives of the rational world."

+ + +

With money borrowed from friend Pablo Picasso, the Dalís boarded the S.S. Excambion in Lisbon and arrived in the United States in May of 1941.

Now, safely ensconced at Hampton Manor, the 486 acre estate of Paris friend Caresse Crosby, inventor of the backless brassiere and owner of Washington, DC's only modern art gallery, Dalí could relax enough to explore the effects of time and stress on his body.

Alone in one of the estate's 30 bedrooms, Dalí removed his clothing and stepped boldly to the ward-robe mirror. He could see himself from head-to-toe, and if there was anything he didn't like in what he saw he did not let on. Later he wrote that his body exactly resembled that of his adolescence, except for a stomach that had grown bigger. His hair was still black as ebony, and his feet "have not yet known the degrading stigma of a single corn."

Pleased with what he saw, he began to address his mental state.

"I am not on the eve of a voyage to China, nor am I about to get a divorce; neither am I thinking of committing suicide, nor of jumping over a cliff clutching the warm placenta of a silk parachute to attempt to be reborn; I have no desire to fight a duel with anyone or with anything; I want only two things: first, to love Gala, my wife; and second, that other inescapable thing, so difficult and so little desired – to grow old."

It seemed like a short list of wants for a man so voracious as Salvador Dalí. But now, living at the edge of a war such as the world had never known, perhaps Dalí had scaled back his material expectations. He had studied theology and the "special sciences" of the past 100 years and knew them well, he declared. This examination of the sciences led to an increased level of spiritualism in Dalí's life, as well as a stronger belief in religion, a belief that was still challenged heavily by doubt. This belief and doubt showed in the symbolism used in his paintings. He sometimes said that the crutches he used in his paintings were a symbol of death and resurrection. Later he would deny such religious symbolism, saying that the crutches were really related to a fear of impotency, an affliction he denied but discussed frequently. At times he considered his work to be a mixture of Freudian and Christian influences. At other times he denied the Christian aspects, considering himself to be a scientist with a paintbrush.

Still, for the most part, he seemed aware that a deep well of unfulfilled spirituality ruled his life. "One thing is certain: nothing, absolutely nothing, in the philosophic, esthetic, morphological, biological or moral discoveries of our epoch denies religion," he wrote in his first autobiography, The Secret Life of Salvador Dalí. "On the contrary, the architecture of the temple of the special sciences has all its windows open to heaven."

But still, as Dalí sat naked at his desk on that summer day in 1941, the surrealist felt an emptiness in his search for divinity. He wrote:

"Heaven is what I have been seeking all along and through the density of confused and demoniac flesh of my life – heaven!. . . And what is heaven? Where is it to be found? Heaven is to be found, neither above nor below, neither to

*the right nor to the left, heaven is to be found exactly in the
center of the bosom of the man who has faith!"*

His brief essay on his search for heaven ended with this poignant irony.

*"At this moment I do not yet have faith, and I fear I shall
die without heaven."*

+ + +

Fear and fascination…in so many ways Dalí was a man driven by the two horsemen of motivation. He feared sex (to the chagrin of his sex appreciative wife) yet he was fascinated by it. He was germophobic yet at the same time was fascinated by excrement. He feared death immensely yet told interviewer Mike Wallace that "death is free of eroticism and is a sublime and beautiful experience." He feared change yet was always changing, sometimes at such a rapid rate that he created inventions that would not show up in the marketplace for years after they had already appeared in his artwork. The next time you see artificial fingernails, transparent mannequins for store windows, or running shoes with springs in the heels, think of Dalí, who included these objects in his paintings before they became products. And he feared the future, yet could always hear its breathing behind him as he painted more and more of it into his futuristic work.

By the late 1940's, Dalí's future was in America. For the time being, Europe held nothing for him. Not only had he been dismissed from the surrealist movement, World War II was on the brink of starting. War was no place for an artist like Dalí, whose repertoire of paintings included The Enigma of Hitler, a dark announcement that a medieval period of National Socialism was going to spread its shadow over Europe through the leadership of the German ruler. And then there was the simple fact that America had not yet discovered Dalí, where Europe had already formed its opinion of him. Dalí felt that the sense of anticipation was missing in his European audience and he was looking for new and unchallenged eyes to greet his work.

"I had a growing desire to feel myself in contact with a 'new flesh,' with a new country," he wrote in his autobiography, The Secret Life. "(One) that had not been touched by the decomposition of Post-War Europe. America! I wanted to go over there and see what it was like."

He went on.

"America was different. Our kind of esthetic civil war had not yet touched that country except in a purely informative way. And often what with us had tragic undertones assumed at most an aspect of entertainment in America. Cubism had never had a real influence, and in America it had been rightly considered as an indispensable experiment which should properly be filed among the official archives of history. Thus, taking no sides, far from the battle, having nothing to gain and nothing to lose or to combat, they could be lucid and see spontaneously what had the most impression upon them among all things that were happening in Europe. And what was going to make the most impression on them was precisely myself, the most partisan, the most violent, the most imperialistic, the most delirious, the most fanatical of all. Europeans are mistaken in considering American incapable of poetic and intellectual intuition. It is obviously not by tradition that they are able to avoid mistakes, or by a perpetual sharpening of "taste." No, American does not choose with the atavistic prudence of an experience which she has not had, or with the refined speculation of a decadent brain which it does not possess, or even with the sentimental effusion of its heart which is too young...

"No, American chooses better and more surely than it would with all these things combined. America chooses with all the unfathomable and elementary force of her unique and intact biology. She knows, as does no one else, what she lacks, what she does not have. And all that America "did not have" on the spiritual plane I was going to bring to her, materialized in the integral and delirious mixture of my paranoiac work, in order that she might thus see and touch everything with the hands of liberty."

Now that Dalí was in America, he set out to make himself famous and to form strong opinions about this country that would support his next phase of work.

The ever-outrageous Dalí became an instant hit with the press. In one scene written by New York art dealer Julien Levy in his book *Memoir of an Art Gallery*, Dalí is presented at Levy's gallery to a number of newspapermen who don't understand surrealism and certainly don't understand Dalí. But the Spanish artist understood them, at least the nature of their business, and knew exactly what to do. wrote Levy:

> *"Dalí was indeed a sight for newsmongering eyes, again his paintings were attached to him and he attached to them. "they want to see some of your work," I explained. "These are the gentlemen of the Press and, I hissed in French, "they can take or leave you." He got the idea at once, untangled himself from his harness and began stripping the paper from the largest and most unwieldy of the paintings. "This is important," I said, "let me tell you a little about Surrealism." I gave a brief lecture and when they asked Dalí which was his favorite picture he answered, "The portrait of my wife." "Yes," I agreed, "you see he has painted her with lamb chops on her shoulder." "Lamb chops?" they roared. That did it! The pencils began to move, the cameras to click."*

Press coverage led to greater fame that led to more offers. The Bonwit-Teller Department Store asked Dalí to dress two of their Fifth Avenue windows. Dalí quickly accepted but with one condition: he be allowed to present whatever came into his head.

Bonwit-Teller accepted and soon found that they had a horror show on their hands. Dalí had found mannequins from the 1900s that were covered with dust and cobwebs. "Be sure not to let anyone touch the dust," he told his assistant. "It is their chief beauty."

He positioned the filthy mannequin as stepping into a water-filled bathtub trimmed with fur. Inside, coming up from the water, were two arms holding up a mirror. His goal with this display was to evoke the Narcissus myth, he said.

In the other window he positioned the head of a buffalo carrying a bloody pigeon in his mouth. The feet of the bed on display were made of buffalo feet, and the black satin bedsheets were visibly burnt and the pillow on which the mannequin laid her head was made of burning coals. Next to the bed sat a mannequin dressed in dark clothing to represent the "phantom of sleep."

Dalí called this window display a "manifesto of elementary surrealist poetry."

The next day Dalí and Gala walked by the store and were shocked to see that his display had been completely changed. Conventional mannequins replaced the ancient dusty ones, and the buffalo head, bed and the sleeping occupant were gone. What still remained was the water-filled bathtub and a sign proudly announcing that the great surrealist, Salvador Dalí, had designed the window display.

Dalí stormed the upstairs management offices of the department store where he was kept waiting in a stark corridor for fifteen minutes. Finally, a smiling man came out to ask what he could do for Dalí.

Dalí carefully explained that the window dressings were no longer his and that he wanted his name removed from the windows. The man, the fresh smile still on his clean-shaven face, told Dalí that they had paid for the use of his name and therefore his name would remain. As an afterthought, the department store minion told Dalí that he was glad to meet the great artist.

Dalí excused himself and went downstairs where he stormed boldly across the department store's main floor and into the window display. Outside dozens of pedestrians watched in awe as the famous Spaniard struggled to tip over the bathtub, which he did, driving it through the plate glass window.

The crowd shouted as Dalí followed the shattered glass out onto Fifth Avenue and down the street where he was courteously arrested by a plainclothes policeman.

The event at Bonwit-Teller brought more press and more press brought another disappointing commission, this one from a corporation that wanted him to design a pavilion at the site of the World's Fair entitled The Dream of Venus. The contract promised "complete imaginative freedom," but it did not deliver. When the company insisted upon putting fish tails on the swimming costumes, Dalí cut them off with scissors and quit. He later wrote a manifesto on the event entitled Declaration of Independence of the Imagination and of the Rights of Man to His Own Madness, in which he renamed the project The Nightmare of Venus.

Like the surreal poet he was, Dalí compiled his impressions of New York, pulling images from his subconscious and writing them on paper. What he provided was a Whitman-esque picture of New York as the gateway to America, one with dazzling beauty and deep funk. Here is a portion of his prose poem:

"...the poetry of New York was not what they had tried in Europe to tell us it was. The poetry of New York does not lie in the pseudo-esthetics of the rectilinear and sterilized rigidity of Rockefeller Center. The poetry of New York is not that of a lamentable Frigidaire in which the abominable European esthetes would have like to shut up the inedible remains of their young and modern plastics! No!"

The poetry of New York is old and violent as the world; it is the poetry that has always been. Its strength, like that of all other existing poetry, likes in the most gelatinous and paradoxical aspects of the delirious flesh of its reality. Each evening the skyscrapers of New York assume the anthropomorphic shapes of multiple gigantic Millet's Angeluses of the tertiary period, motionless and ready to perform the sexual act and to devour one another, like swarms of praying mantes before copulation. It is the unspent sanguinary desire that illuminates them and makes all the central heating and the central poetry circulate within their ferruginous bone-structure of vegetable diplococcus.

And so on. Dalí was getting his fix on America as well as his own future plans, which involved a return to traditional ideals with the Dalían twist.

"My surrealist glory was worthless," he wrote in *The Secret Life*. "I must incorporate surrealism in tradition. My imagination must become classic again. I had before me a work to accomplish for which the rest of my life would not suffice. Gala made me believe in this mission. Instead of stagnating in the anecdotic mirage of my success, I had now to begin to fight for a thing that was 'important.' This important thing was to render the experience of my life 'classic,' to endow it with a form, a cosmogony, a synthesis, an architecture of eternity."

By now Dalí was a great believer in science. He described himself in 1935 as a fish swimming between "the cold water of art and the warm water of science." Booted out of the surrealist movement, Dalí found himself drifting to where the founders of surrealism always said he would go, toward religion. To their great dismay, he made several statements about the power of religion in his life, including this one to a Spanish journalist: "Reason forces me to be Catholic. And just as many people have attained to religious truth via physics, I hope to attain to it via metaphysics and art. Believe me, this is one of my deepest urges."

Despite criticism from the surrealist hierarchy, Dalí moved forward and never looked back. The dropping of the atomic bomb in Japan in 1945 caused a melding of art, science and religion in Dalí's mind. At mid-career he changed horses, combining Renaissance-style painting with the traditional imagery of Christian faith. Art critics called these the "two chief taboos of modern art," but Dalí didn't care. He called the work of modern artists soul-less and unfocused, and declared that the work of his contemporaries might as well be painted with their own excrement because, "their material comes so directly from the tube of their biology without mixing in it even a bit of their heart and soul."[1]

As the egotistical and brilliant are wont to do, Dalí put pen to paper and began to write about this new mysticism that sprang from the dropping of the atom bombs over Japan.

> *"The explosion of the atom bomb on 6 August 1945 sent a seismic shock through me," he wrote in his Mystical Manifesto. "Since then, the atom has been central to my thinking. Many of the scenes I have painted in this period express the immense fear that took hold of me when I heard of the explosion of the bomb. I used my paranoic-critical method to analyse the world. I want to perceive and understand the hidden powers and laws of things, in order to have them in my power. A brilliant inspiration shows me that I have an unusual weapon at my disposal to help me penetrate to the core of reality: mysticism – that is to say,*

---

[1] Italian artist Piero Manzoni followed Dalí's advice, canning his own excrement under the label "Artist's Shit," which eventually were sold to the Tate Modern Museum in London for 22,300 pounds in government funds!

the profound intuitive knowledge of what is, direct communication with the all, absolute vision by the grace of Truth, by the grace of God. More powerful than cyclotrons and cybernetic calculators, I can penetrate to the mysteries of the real in a moment... Mine the ecstasy! I cry. The ecstasy of God and Man. Mine the perfection, the beauty, that I might gaze into its eyes! Death to academicism, to the bureaucratic rules of art, to decorative plagiarism, to the witless incoherence of African art! Mine, St. Teresa of Avila!... In this state of intense prophecy it became clear to me that means of pictorial expression achieved their greatest perfection and effectiveness in the Renaissance, and that the decadence of modern painting was a consequence of skepticism and lack of faith, the result of mechanistic materialism. By reviving Spanish mysticism, I, Dalí, shall use my work to demonstrate the unity of the universe, by showing the spirituality of all substance."

Dalí carefully outlined how he proposed to accomplish the mystical canvas.

"I decided to turn my attention to the pictorial solution of quantum theory, and invented quantum realism in order to master gravity... I visually dematerialized matter; then I spiritualized it in order to be able to create energy. The object is a living being, thanks to the energy that it contains and radiates, thanks to the density of the matter it consists of. Every one of my subjects is also mineral with its place in the pulse beat of the world, and a living piece of uranium. In my paintings I have succeeded in giving space substance... I maintain with full conviction that heaven is located in the breast of the faithful. My mysticism is not only religious, but also nuclear and hallucinogenic. I discovered the self-same truth in gold, in painting soft watches, and in my visions of the railway station at Perpignan. I believe in magic and in my fate."

It was during this period of Nuclear Mysticism that many critics and buyers stopped paying attention to Dalí. Religion and the renaissance were disliked by critics and historians who always wanted art to be pushing into the future and who, frankly, had a disdain for anything religious. They let their feelings be known in merciless attacks on his religious art.

John Canaday of the *New York Times* wrote this indignant screed about a Dalí exhibit:

> *"I suppose that no man has the right to say of another that his stated conversion to religion is an opportunistic pose. But certainly one has the right to say what one thinks when faced by Dalí's intrusive and embarrassing holy pictures, the crucifixion in the Metropolitan Museum and the Last Supper in the National Gallery in Washington... They seem to me to be blatant expressions of morbid eroticism, in which the artist had abused the right of sanctuary to the point of sacrilege."*

Hilton Kramer called Dalí's new work "complete rubbish," the "ostentatious display of old master ambition degenerated into the purest Kitsch."

Attacks were especially vicious from Andre Breton, the father of surrealism, who wrote: "Dalí, who disappeared around 1935 and has been replaced by the personality who is better known by the name Avida Dollars, a society portrait painter who recently returned to the bosom of the Catholic church and to the 'artistic ideal of the Renaissance', and who nowadays quotes letters of congratulation and the approval of the Pope."

But for others who were interested in a new age approach to religious art, Dalí was breaking new and exciting ground. Father Bruno Froissart wrote: "Salvador Dalí has told me that nothing has as stimulating an effect on him as the idea of the angel. Dalí wanted to paint heaven, to penetrate the heavens in order to communicate with God. For him, God is an intangible idea, impossible to render in concrete terms. Dalí is of the opinion that He is perhaps the substance being sought by nuclear physics. He does not see God as cosmic; as he said to me, that would be limiting. He sees this as a thought process contradictory within itself, one which cannot be summarized in a uniform concept of structure. At heart a Catalonian, Dalí needs tactile forms, and 'that applies to angels, too'... if he has been preoccupied with the Assumption of the Virgin Mary, for some time now, it is, as he explains, because she went to heaven 'by the power of the angels'... Dalí conceives protons and neutrons as 'angelic elements'; for, as he puts it, in the heavenly bodies there are 'leftovers of substance, because certain beings strike me as being so close to angels, such as Raphael or St. John of the Cross."

Chester Dale, a noted American collector of impressionists and modern French paintings, was "bowled over" by Dalí's *Corpus Hypercubus*, when it saw it at the Carstair's Gallery. "I can't explain it except in one way – when it hits me, it hits me hard. It's a very honest picture, very great." Multi-millionaire Huntington Hartford felt the same way about Dalí's nuclear mysticism. When he saw *The Discovery of America by Christopher Columbus*, he said that it "exceeded my greatest expectations" and purchased it for his Gallery of Modern Art for a whopping $250,000.

Dalí loved Nuclear Mysticism and the new direction it offered for his work. Once again he was unique, surpassing surrealism, which had been taken over, in his words, by bureaucrats. He was also controversial again. When *Christ of St. John of the Cross* was purchased in 1952 by the Glasgow Art Museum, there was a public outcry at the purchase price of L8,200. Visitors were hostile at the perspective of the painting, which shows the crucifixion from above. One angry patron even charged forward with a knife and slashed it when the painting first went on display. Still, the museum reported an increase in entry fees and gift shop sales of the reproduction that nearly equaled the price of the painting in only a few years.

In America, the hanging of *The Last Supper* at the National Gallery in Washington led Harvard theologian Paul Tillich to declare it a collection of the worst elements in religion. He even went so far as to compare the rendering of Jesus in the painting to that of "an athlete on an American baseball team." Congressman Frank Thompson, Jr., asked that the painting be removed from its central location in the museum, and perhaps even removed from the museum all together.

Yet despite the hue and cry over Dalí's new direction, his religious art became more and more popular. He had declared himself a reborn Catholic and modernized the icons of the faith and the faithful loved it. Dalí loved it too. As he told the faithful among his followers: "The progress of the sciences has been colossal. But from the spiritual point of view, we live in the lowest period of civilization. A divorce has come about between physics and metaphysics. We are living through an almost monstrous progress of specialization, without any synthesis."

+ + +

For many in the Catholic faith, Dalí would be that synthesis. Yet at this point in Dalí's life, 1959, it was hard to believe that his work would be linked to a modern religious event that took place 42 years earlier in the obscure town of Fátima, Portugal. Yet within the year, Dalí would be pulled into the dream world of an obscure Catholic organization – some might call it a cult – that would have him translate a visionary encounter with the Virgin Mary that changed the world.

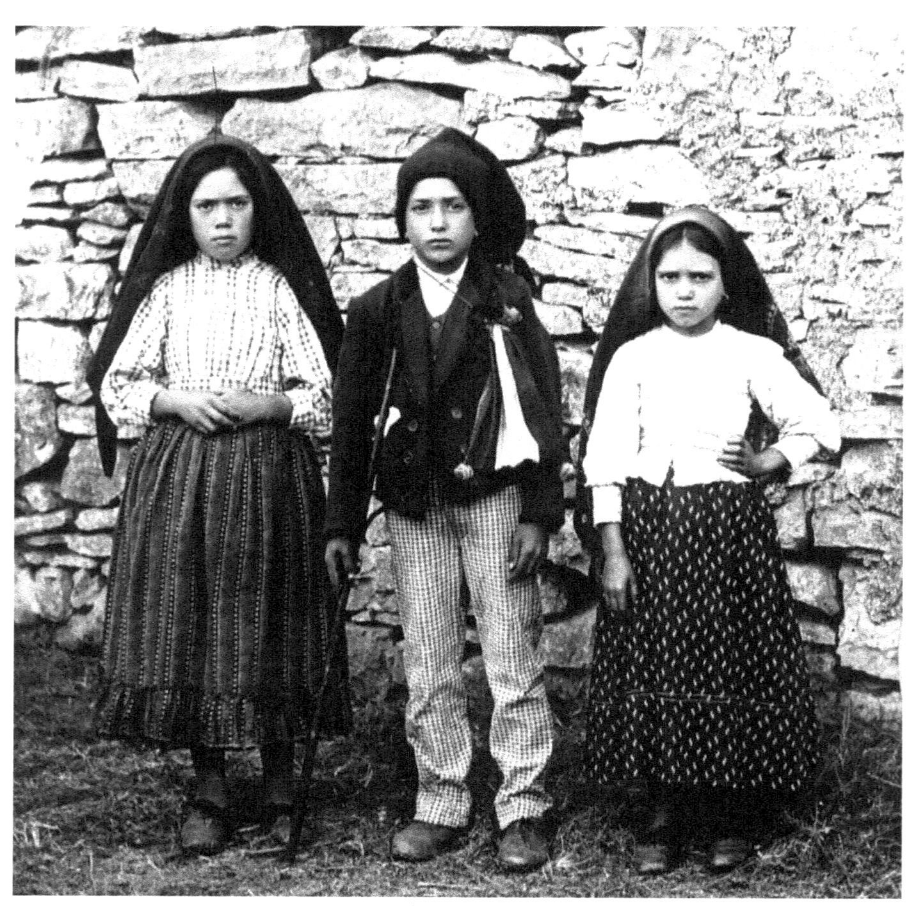

The three Seers of Fátima, Lúcia dos Santos, Francisco Marto and Jacinta Marto, photographed on October 13th, 1917 by Photojournalist Joshua Benoliel of the "O Secúlo" Lisbon Daily Newspaper. This photo was first published on October 29th, 1917 in the Magazine "O Século Ilustrado."

2

A Bright Flash of Light

The date was May 13, 1917, and the three children – Lucia, Jacinta and Francisco – were driving their family sheep to a grazing area called Cova da Iria near the town of Fátima in Portugal. They had done this hundreds of times before and were lulled by the daily routine and the lunch that they had just eaten before moving the sheep to this spot.

Suddenly a bright flash of light brought them out of their stupor. They scanned the sky. There was no reason to suspect a rainstorm. There were no clouds, only the clear blue heavens and the hot sun beating down. Still Lucia decided to play it safe. She speculated that the weather was about to change and insisted that they all return home.

Then a second flash of light took place. They all turned quickly and were frozen by the apparition that they saw on top of an oak tree.

"There was an oak tree and a Lady dressed completely in white, brighter than the sun, was floating above its top," recounted Lucia years later. "She had rays of light around her, like you see when the sun shines through a glass filled with water, but much brighter. We stood still, shocked by what we saw. We were so close that we were inside the circle of light that radiated out from her. She was less than five feet away."

A more complete description came later. The Lady seemed to be about 18 years of age. She was about four feet tall and had dark eyes that were accentuated by the pure white dress that was tied at the neck with a golden ribbon. The dress went down to her feet and a white cloak covered her head. Her hands were folded in front of her and held a rosary of shining white beads that were joined at the bottom by a silver cross. A bright light surrounded her head, framing a face of extraordinary sadness.

"Don't be afraid, I won't hurt you," she said to the children.

"Where are you from?" asked Lucia.

"I'm from heaven," said the vision.

"And what are you doing in this world?" asked Lucia.

"I am here to ask you to come to this place on the thirteenth of every month, during the next six months, at the same time as today. Then I'll tell you who I am and what I want. After that I'll come here once more for the seventh time."

Lucia had questions that couldn't wait.

"Will I go to heaven?" she asked.

"Certainly."

"And Jacinta?"

"Yes, she will too."

"And Francisco?"

"Yes, he will also. But he must pray a lot of rosaries before that."

"Can you tell me if the war will go on for a long time or will it come to an end soon?"

"I cannot tell you that now, just as I cannot tell you what I want." With that the Lady began asking questions of her own.

"Are you prepared to offer yourself to God, and accept all the sufferings He will send you to help make up for the sins of the world?"

"Yes, we are ready!" said Lucia, unaware that the other children could not hear the Lady that they saw.

"You will have to suffer a great deal," said the Lady. "But the grace of God will give you the strength to bear it."

As if to add an exclamation point, the Lady opened her hands and when she did a bright light shot out and bathed the children in light.

"We saw that we were the children of this light, more clearly than if we had looked into the best mirrors in the world," Lucia wrote later. The light humbled the trio and they knelt down and began to pray.

"Pray the rosary daily to end the war and bring peace to the world," said the Lady.

When the children looked up they could see the Lady rise slowly and move east, "the light all around her seemed to open a path for her through the sky."

When the Lady faded into the distance, the three children heard a dull explosive noise, "like a rocket exploding in the distance."

The encounter left the children silent. They gathered the sheep from a neighbor's field and began their walk back along the stony path to their home in Aljustrel, a tiny hamlet that was a part of the village of Fátima.

Jacinta was the first to speak.

"What a beautiful, beautiful Lady she was," said Jacinta over and over again as though she was in a trance.

It was only when Lucia began repeating the words she had heard from the Lady that she realized Francisco had heard nothing. He had seen the Lady's lips move, but heard no words. The 10-minute Apparition was a silent one for the young boy, which left him feeling slighted.

+ + +

Lucia decided that the three should keep news of the Apparition to themselves. This was not the first time they made this decision, a year earlier in the same area the children saw what they described as an angel. It came to them when they sought shelter from a rainstorm in a cave overlooking Aljustrel. They had just completed their lunch when a strong wind began shaking the olive trees below the cave's entrance. The children looked upward and saw the figure of a young boy against the sun. Lucia later said that he was "whiter than snow," and the brightness of the sun shown through him as though he was transparent. Lucia recalled the next moments.

"'Don't be afraid! I am the angel of peace. Pray with me.' He knelt on the ground and bent down till his forehead touched the earth. We did the same thing and prayed with him. Then he disappeared."

Although the children kept the event to themselves, they always felt magic in the air whenever they found themselves near the cave. Finally, in the summer of 1916, they decided to visit the cave once again. As they lay down to take an afternoon siesta, the angel appeared again. The children were stunned.

"What are you doing?" asked the angel. "Pray! Pray, pray! Pray without stopping, pray and offer sacrifices."

The children were confused.

"How do we offer sacrifices?" Lucia asked.

"Make sacrifices from your ordinary lives."

As would happen later, the two girls heard these words. Francisco was left with a silent vision. He could only rely on the account given to him by Lucia and then he didn't even fully understand the message.

Late in August, as the children were herding sheep on the mountain slopes overlooking Aljustrel, the angel appeared for a third time. He came as the children were offering their noon prayers. When they looked up, the angel was there, said Lucia. This time he was carrying a chalice, and above it was a consecrated host dripping with drops of blood. According to Lucia, the chalice stayed suspended in the air as the angel fell to his knees to pray.

"Then he stood up and took hold of the chalice and the host once more. He gave me the host and gave Jacinta and Francisco the contents of the chalice to drink. Then he knelt down again and prayed before he disappeared."

+ + +

Somehow the children had managed to keep these early visionary encounters to themselves. But this one would be different. Despite their vow of silence, Jacinta had barely returned home when she blurted out the story of the Lady's appearance.

The mother laughed at her daughter.

"Oh yes, you certainly did," she said. "And you are a saint now, for you can see the mother of God!"

Despite disappointment at her mother's response, Jacinta continued to press the issue. She continued to tell the story to her mother the rest of the day. And at the evening meal, she held her family spellbound with the story of the tiny Lady and her beautiful clothing that glowed as she spoke.

Her brothers ridiculed her almost to the point of tears until her father, Ti Marto, intervened. "Since the beginning of the world the Mother of God as appeared at different times and places," he said. "If this never happened, the world would be in a worse state than it is today. God is great. We don't understand everything He does, but may His will be done."

The family fell silent for the remainder of the meal. But it was obvious that Ti Marto had given this story a patriarchal seal of approval.

The next day Senhora Marto roamed the village, telling everyone who would listen of the miracle at Cova da Iria. One of those was Lucia's mother, Maria Rosa. She thought her daughter had either become mad, or worse, a liar. She cornered Lucia and insisted that she admit the incident was a lie. When Lucia refused, she dragged her to the village priest, Father Ferreira.

Father Ferreira was a stocky and imposing man, especially in an interrogation, as Lucia would find even more in the future. He questioned her hard about the Apparition, and despite a threat by her mother to be "shut up in a black hole" for the rest of her life, Lucia stuck to her story.

Stung by her mother's retribution, Lucia carried on with her young life. But by now, word had spread throughout the village, and everyone knew that the next Apparition was slated for June 13.

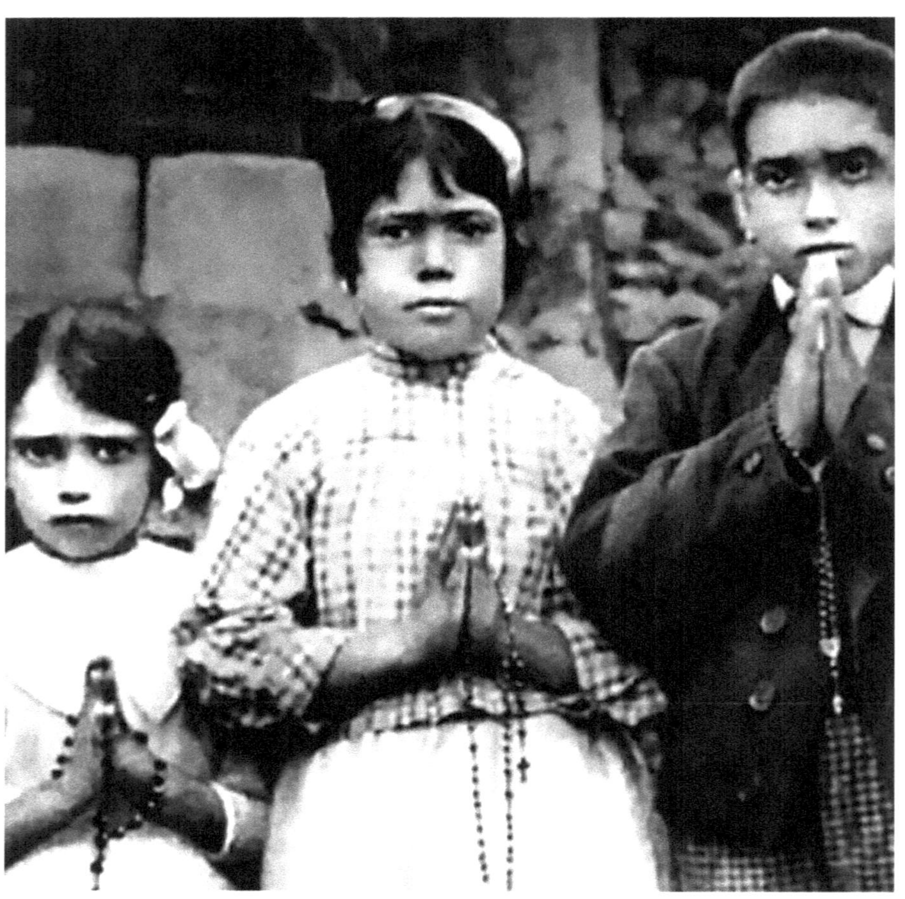

Photograph taken of the three Fátima Seers in 1917 following the Apparitions.

3

Word Spreads

To have a religious Apparition in 1917 Portugal was practically a political crime. All of Europe had begun to light up like a tinderbox in 1914 after a 19-year-old college student assassinated Archduke Franz Ferdinand of Austro-Hungary in Sarajevo. A short time later, Austria declared war on Serbia, which led Russia to mobilize her army in defense of her ally. Germany marched against France, causing Great Britain to march against Germany. And so it went until the war was on. After only one month, more than 600,000 German and French soldiers had lost their lives.

By May of 1917, World War I was in full sway. The United States had joined forces against Germany and Portugal was newly involved. The conflict was just beginning to wreak havoc into far-flung places like Fátima, an agrarian community already burdened by and perhaps more preoccupied with something they better understood, like the repercussions of drought.

At this time, the relationship between church and state in Europe was volatile. Throughout Europe, Christians were being targeted in ethnic cleansing campaigns. In Portugal, nuns and members of the clergy were persecuted and could be arrested for appearing publicly in their robes. All along the countryside, chapel doors were being sealed shut with nails.

Authoritarian regimes were gaining momentum in Portugal, Spain, and other parts of Europe. It was the beginning of an era when much of

Europe was uninterested in democracy and fed-up with the chockablock diversity of the empires. Each nation-state wanted its own identity, its own strength, and they struggled to get it. Portugal was in such a state of political turmoil that they had eight presidents, 44 governments and 20 revolutions between 1911 and 1926.

The era could be euphemized as one of "streamlining" forces and consolidation of power, where rules and orders were issued from the state and the state alone. Religion was seen as a competing entity – faith was foe.

So as the rumors of the coming Apparition swept Fátima, the children's parents felt the fear of possible government retribution. There were people in the town government who were members of a sect of Freemasonry that were vehemently anti-Catholics. And in addition there were Communists, followers of a fresh political dogma to the world scene that espoused distrust of all religions. Their leader, Vladimir Lenin, was in the process of leading a revolt against the czar of Russia and taking over the country. His successes had emboldened Communists around the world and now there was even a significant cadre of them in Fátima.

The children's parents were quite concerned.

Lucia's mother begged, cajoled and even insulted her daughter as a means of getting her to stay away from the Cova da Iria where the virgin had promised to appear. Lucia refused. Although she usually com-plied with her parent's wishes, the child insisted that she was under orders of a higher authority and that she would lead the other two children back to the cove.

On June 13, 1917, she did just that. It was the day of the Feast of Saint Anthony, in which a parade of local farmers passed through town and money and food were gathered for the poor. Despite this festival, about 50 people showed up at the oak tree in which the "White Lady" had appeared exactly one month before. At approximately 11 a.m., the children arrived alone. Their parents had decided not to come, afraid of the government and concerned that nothing might happen and they would be accused of perpetuating a hoax. The children quietly knelt down under the big oak tree near the one where the Lady had appeared and said their prayers. When they finished, they stood and faced the east, waiting for the vision to take place.

Only Lucia saw the flash above the tree. "The lightning has flashed already, the Lady is coming," quoted a letter that was written by one of the witnesses. Lucia ran quickly to the small oak tree where the Lady had appeared followed by the other children and then the 50 faithful.

"Soon more and more people came," said Senhora Maria dos Santos Carreira of Fátima, one of the witnesses to be later deposed. "Lucia stood about ten feet away from the tree and looked toward the east. It was very quiet. I asked her, 'Where is the tree where the Lady appeared?'

"'It's this one here,' she said, and went over and laid her hand on it. It was a pretty little tree about three feet tall with evenly growing branches. Lucia moved away from the tree, looked in the direction of Fátima, and then sat down in the shade of a fig tree nearby. The children joined her."

Lucia described what happened next: "After Jacinta, Francisco, and I recited the rosary, together with some other people, we saw the light that we call lightning again. Then the Lady was above the oak tree, the same way it all happened in May.

"'What do you want from me?' I asked.

"'I want all three of you to recite the prayers of the rosary every day and I want you to learn to read and write. After that I'll tell you what I really want.'

"When I asked her to heal a certain sick person, she answered, 'If he opens his heart to Jesus Christ, he will be cured within a year.'

"'Please take us with you to heaven,' I said.

"'Yes, I shall take Jacinta and Francisco with me to heaven soon, but you have to stay here for a while longer. Jesus wants to make use of you to help people under-stand and love me.'

Lucia truly knew at this point that the other children could not hear the Lady. She had just proclaimed their pending deaths, and neither responded.

"Will I be left here alone?" asked Lucia.

"No, my child. Are you suffering very much? Don't let yourself be discouraged. I shall never leave you."

At that point, according to Lucia, the Lady opened her hands and the light came out of them again. This time Lucia saw Jacinta and Francisco in a beam of light going up to heaven. She saw herself bathed in a light pouring down on earth.

Although everyone heard Lucia's voice, some of the witnesses reported that they heard a buzzing or murmur that they thought could have been the voice of the Lady. In describing the voice, Maria dos Santos Carreira said it was, "as if I heard a voice from a great distance, something like the humming of a bee."

Many of the people heard a dull explosion – "underground thunder" one described it – when the Apparition disappeared. At that point, Lucia pointed toward the east and said, "Look, she's leaving!"

Did anyone see the Lady besides the children? Some said they did. Maria Carreira declared, "We saw only a little cloud above the tree, that rose up slowly and moved off toward the east. Some of us lost sight of it, but others said they could still see it, until finally it disappeared completely. . . Lucia said, 'Now we can't see her anymore. She has gone back to heaven and the door has closed.'"

There was more. The witnesses looked up in the tree and noticed that the branches were now bent toward the east, "as if the hem of her cloak had been drawn across them," said one of the witnesses.

The witnesses approached the tree and began plucking twigs.

"Only take the ones from the bottom," said Lucia. "don't take any that were in contact with the Lady." he witnesses walked off toward Fátima, reciting the prayers of the rosary, delighted to have observed the visionary encounter. The festival was in full-swing and the crowd wanted to know where these newcomers had been.

"(W)e told them that we had been at the Cova and how happy we were to have gone there," said Maria dos Santos. "Many of them were sad that they had missed something so very important, but by then it was too late."

The crowd absorbed the witnesses, and the witnesses spread word of what they had seen.

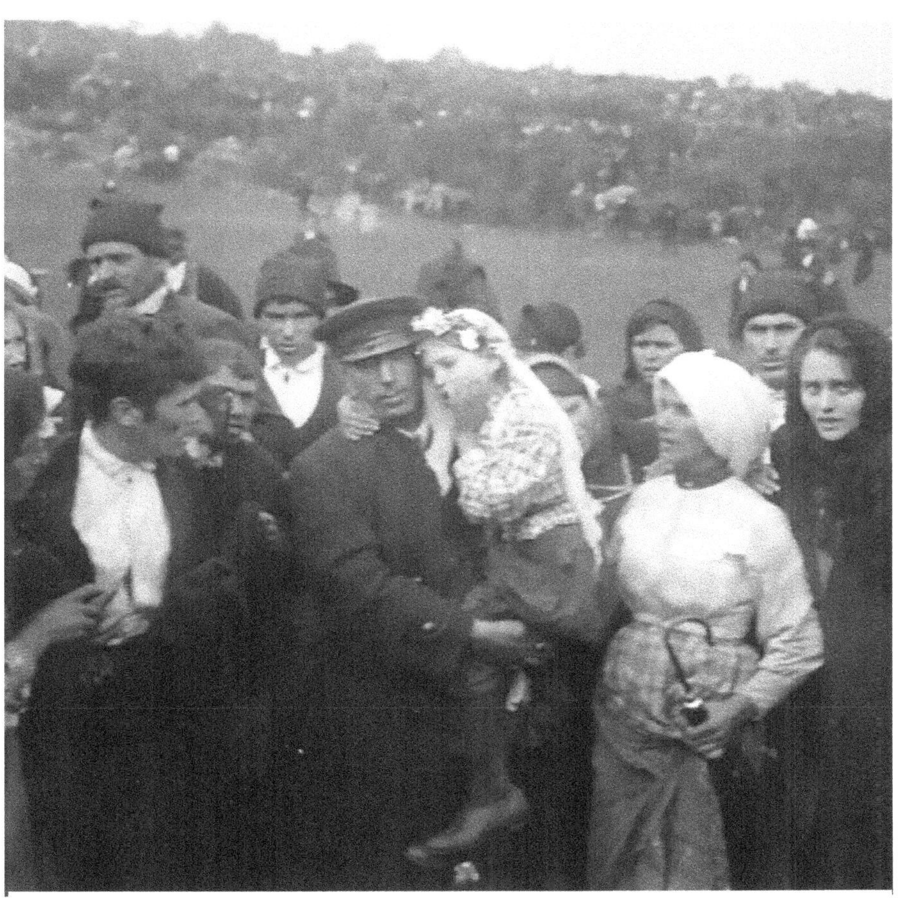

Photograph showing the little Seer Jacinta Marto wearing a garland crown and veil that one of the Pilgrims had made for her. She is being carried through the crowd by a devoted Soldier on October 13th, 1917.

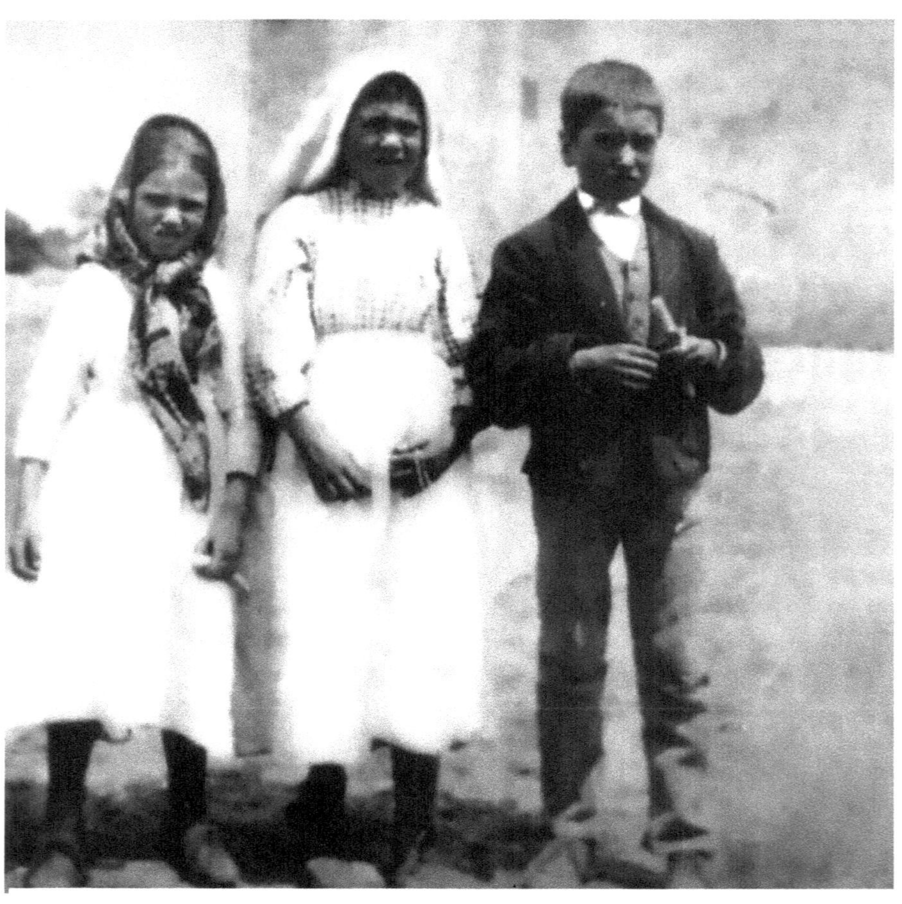

The horrified Seers Jacinta, Lúcia and Francisco photographed immediately after the July 13th, 1917 Apparition and Vision of Hell during which the Three Part Secret was confided to the three little Shepherds.

4

Revelations

The day after the June apparition, Lucia's mother took her to see Father Ferreira at the rectory in Fátima. He had become alarmed by what he was hearing and wanted to have a talk with the young girl. Lucia brought Jacinta and Francisco with her to the meeting.

The priest listened to the story of the children again, taking notes and at times looking irritated. At times he asked questions that the children couldn't, or wouldn't, answer. Finally the priest leaned back in his chair and made a proclamation that hurt Lucia deeply.

"It could be a trick of the devil. We will wait and see."

The comments of the priest cast doubt on veracity of the apparitions for Lucia. She began to think that she was possessed, a conduit for Satan, perhaps. Her cousins convinced her otherwise.

"That was certainly not the devil!" they said. "The devil is ugly and lives under the earth. The Lady was wonderfully beautiful and went up toward heaven."

Lucia thanked her cousins, but still had doubts about what she had seen and heard in the Cova. For the next several weeks the child had bad dreams, and fits of extreme depression. Sometimes her mother would say that on July 13, "the devil is sure to be there." Several times Lucia told Jacinta that she was tempt-ed to say that the whole thing had been a lie, just to heal her bad relationship with her mother. When she said that, little

Jacinta pushed her from another direction. "Don't do it," said Jacinta. "You know that lying is a sin!"

The pressure was so great on Lucia, that the night before the promised July 13 vision, she went to her two cousins and said that she was not going to accompany them to the Cova. Jacinta and Francisco were stunned but resolute. "we'll go," said Jacinta. "The Lady has ordered us to come."

The next day Lucia paid a visit to her cousins and found them at the foot of Jacinta's bed, praying and weeping. Neither child had the courage to go to the Cova without Lucia, said Jacinta, and they were praying for strength.

"I will go with you," said Lucia, who now felt it her destiny to return to the Cova.

At noon, the three children made their way to the Cova. They were not alone. Instead of 50 spectators like they had last time, the children found themselves pushing through a crowd of more than 3,000. Many of the people had come from neighboring villages and spent the night sleeping under the stars. Those who did busied themselves with the construction of a wooden arch and a cross to mark the site of the apparition.

The three children were recognized and were escorted to the front of the crowd by two men who kept the crowd at bay. When one of the men recognized Ti Marto, Jacinta's father, he ordered the crowd to part so he could join his daughter. The three children had plenty of support from the crowd, many of whom were now saying rosary and praying for the young seers. Still, Lucia would say later that the three had never before felt so alone.

Ti Marto went to his daughter's side, and as he did he noticed that Lucia had moved away from the other two children and was kneeling on the ground, saying the rosary.

"The crowd repeated the words after her," said Ti Marto, in a witness deposition that took place later. "When they finished, she jumped up so quickly, it was as if she was being pulled up by invisible hands. She looked to the east and called out, 'Close your umbrellas' – many people had them open for protection against the sun – 'Our Dear Lady is coming!' I strained my eyes but could see nothing. Then I saw what looked like a very small gray cloud above the oak tree. The heat had gone down and a pleasant breeze was blowing, not at all like it usually is in high summer.

"The people were so silent, I could have heard a needle hitting the ground. Then I heard a humming sound, but could not make out any words.

I imagine that's how a telephone sounds, although I've never spoken on the telephone in my life. I asked myself what it could be, and was it close, or far away? For me, these were signs that this was a miracle."

There were other reports of a tiny cloud above the tree, but that was the most that could be seen by the crowd. The children, however, were having a different experience. All three could see the Lady as they had before. Lucia was speechless, held spellbound by the beauty of seeing the Lady again.

"Lucia, say something," said Jacinta. "Can't you see that the lady is here and wants to talk to you?"

Lucia snapped out of it.

"What does Your Grace wish of me?" she asked.

"I want you to come here on the thirteenth of next month and to continue to pray the rosary every day, to bring peace to the world and the end of the war," Lucia later recalled the Lady saying.

Many of the pilgrims had asked Lucia to ask the Lady for help and healing. Lucia had her own request. She wanted the Lady to perform a miracle so that everyone would believe she had truly appeared to the children.

"Continue to come here every month, as I said," declared the Lady. "In October I will tell you who I am and what I wish and I will also perform a miracle, so that everyone who sees it will believe."

What seemed like the ending of this day's heavenly message was only the beginning. The Lady opened Her hands as she had before, only this time all Hell broke loose. Lucia recalled the first part of the vision that would become known as the Three Secrets of Fátima. This one has become known simply as "The Vision of Hell."

"A ray of light seemed to penetrate the earth and we saw a great sea of fire," said Lucia." And in that fire there were souls, like black embers floating in the wind. There were great clouds of smoke, and showering sparks everywhere with shrieks and groans of sorrow and despair that horrified us and made us tremble with fear.

"The devils looked like strange animals, terrible and disgusting, with the transparency of glowing coals. Frightened and begging for help, we raised our eyes to the Lady, who said to us with sadness but also great kindness, 'You saw Hell, where the souls of poor sinners go. To save the world God wants the world to turn to Me. If they do what I tell you, many souls will be saved and there will be peace."

What the saw was more horrible than any medieval artist could conjure. Lucia could never provide an account of the vision that did it justice. Rather, she seemed to freeze-up when the subject was broached and ultimately refused to talk about it because, as she declared many times, trying to remember brought back something she was trying to forget.

As the first part of the secret faded, the Lady revealed the second part, once again speaking only to Lucia who later revealed her comments in one of her memoirs.

"The war is going to end. But if people do not stop offending God, another even more terrible war will begin in the reign of (Pope) Pius XI. If you see the sky lit up by an unknown light, you'll know it's the sign given to you by God, and that he is about to punish the world for its crimes, by war, hunger, and persecutions against the Church and the pope.

"To prevent this I will come to ask for the consecration of Russia to My Immaculate Heart. If they listen to me, Russia will convert and there will be peace, if not, Russia will spread her errors throughout the world, starting wars and persecuting the Church. The good will be martyred. The Pope will suffer, and various nations will be annihilated.

"In the end I will triumph. The pope will bless Russia and she will convert and a period of peace will be granted to the world."

Then the Lady spoke to Lucia of another prophecy and the part of the vision that would become known as the Third Secret, one that was not revealed by the church for more than 80 years. The final part of the vision contained a prophesy similar to those in Sacred Scripture which do not describe "with photo-graphic clarity" the details of future events, wrote Cardinal Angelo Sodano of the third secret. As a result, this third Secret required symbolic interpretation, one that the church chose to do behind closed doors. One of the conclusions of Vatican ciphers is that the Third Secret predicted the assassination attempt of Pope John Paul, which, ironically, took place on May 13, 1981, the anniversary of the first Fátima Apparition.

The Third Secret may have been the most closely guarded secret in the Vatican, and as a result was surrounded by a great amount of public interest. It was therefore largely regarded as a disappointment when released by Cardinal Joseph Ratzinger (later elected Pope Benedict XVI) on June 26, 2000, it was regarded as a disappointment by some, and a premonition of symbolic importance by others. Here is the Third Secret in Lucia's own words:

"After the two parts which I have already explained, at the

left of Our Lady and a little above, we saw an Angel with a flaming sword in his left hand; flashing, it gave out flames that looked as though they would set the world on fire; but they died out in contact with the splendor that Our lady radiated towards him from her right hand: pointing to the earth with his right hand, the Angel cried out in a loud voice: 'Penance, penance, penance!. And we saw in an immense light that is God: 'something similar to how people appear in a mirror when they pass in front of it' a Bishop dressed in white 'we had the impression that it was the Holy Father.' Other Bishops, Priests, men and women Religious going up a steep mountain, at the top of which there was a big Cross of rough-hewn trunks as of a cork tree with the bark: before reaching there the Holy Father passed through a big city half in ruins and half trembling with halting step, afflicted with pain and sorrow, he prayed for the souls of the corpses he met on his way: having reached the top of the mountain, on his knees at the foot of the big Cross he was killed by a group of soldiers who fired bullets and arrows at him, and in the same way there died one after another the other Bishops, Priests, men and women Religious, and various lay people of different ranks and positions. Beneath the two arms of the Cross there were two Angeles each with a crystal aspersorium in his hand, in which they gathered up the blood of the Martyrs and with it sprinkled the souls that were making their way to God."

At the time of the Third Secret's public release in 2000, then Cardinal Ratzinger agreed with Cardinal Angelo Sodano when he called the vision a "synthesis of events" that were compressed against a background of future facts that "extend through time in an unspecified succession and duration."

"This compression of time and place in a single image is typical of such visions, which for the most part can be deciphered only in retrospect," wrote the future Pope. "The history of the entire century can be seen represented in this image. Just as the places of the earth are synthetically described in the two images of the mountain and the city, and are directed towards the cross, so too time is presented in a compressed way."

For Pope John Paul II, the interpretation was much more personal.

It represented himself walking through the ruins of Communism towards his own certain martyrdom. He had only been spared the prophetic outcome because of Our Lady's Maternal intercession who had defrayed the assassin's bullet from his heart.

From all accounts, Lucia would have liked to have this interpretation on that day thirteenth day of July when she witnessed the vision.

According to most accounts she looked puzzled at the secret she had just seen and heard, almost as though a very important person had just uttered urgent information in a language she barely understood.

In fact, many in Portugal were so uneducated in World affairs, that they understood the word "Russia," to be a wicked golden haired woman, perhaps a ruler, since in Portuguese the word is pronounced similarly to "Russa", meaning "blonde".

"Do you want anything more from me?" she asked the Lady.

"No, I want nothing more from you today," said the Lady, who then rose into the sky and faded into the east.

What happened next was heard by everyone and described by Ti Marto. "We heard a loud clap of thunder and the little wooden arch, which had two lanterns hanging on it, trembled as if there had been an earthquake. Lucia, who was still kneeling, sprang up quickly, pointed to the sky, and cried, 'There She goes! There She goes!'

"After a few moments she said, 'Now you can't see Her anymore.' This was enough proof for me." The crowd gathered around the children and peppered them with questions, but to no avail. In one lengthy vision, the young seers had looked through the gates of Hell, been informed of another approaching world war followed by the fearful rise of Communism, and given an incomprehensible view of the future that was fearful and confusing.

A photographer snapped a photo of the children that shows their three faces fraught with worry. Lucia looks as though she is about to weep, her pug face contorted with the horror of what she had just seen. It's a poignant photo because it shows the very moment of lost childhood. Life would never be the same for them. Word of the apparitions was spreading fast.

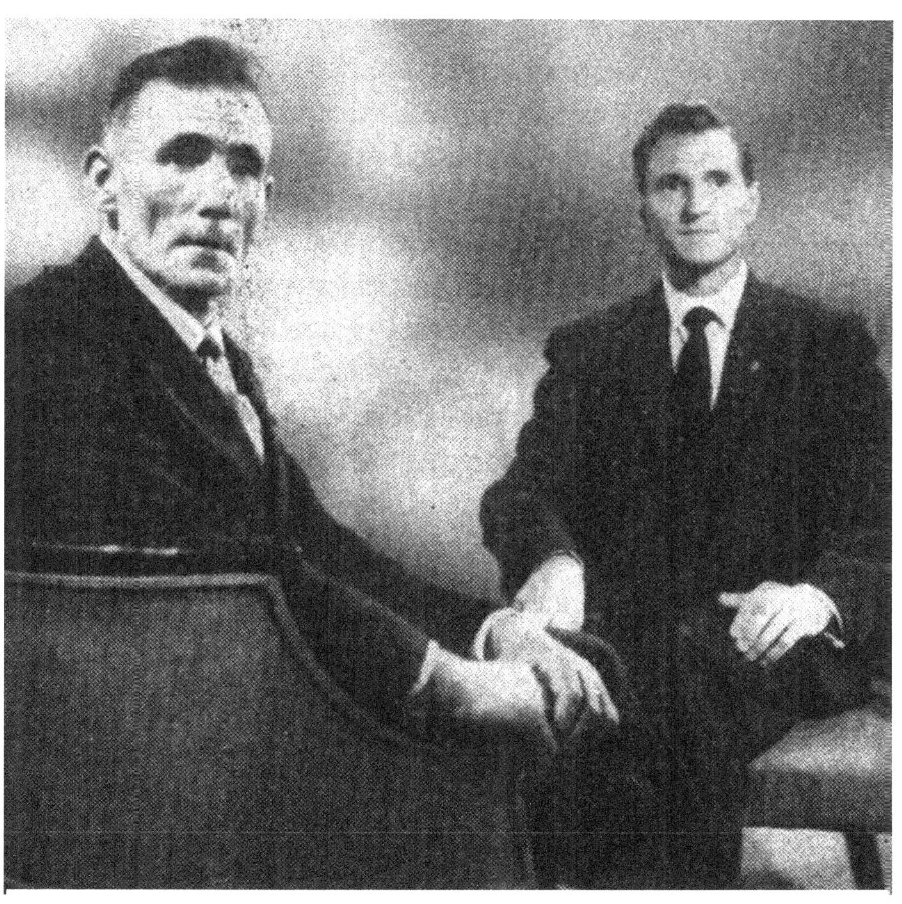

Blue Army Founder John Mathias Haffert in a still from his 1959 television program "Countdown 1960" interviews witness to the Miracle of the Sun Domingos Reis. Reis was one of several Fátima locals that "Mr. Fátima" took back with him to the United States to work on the construction of the Blue Army Shrine in Washington, New Jersey.

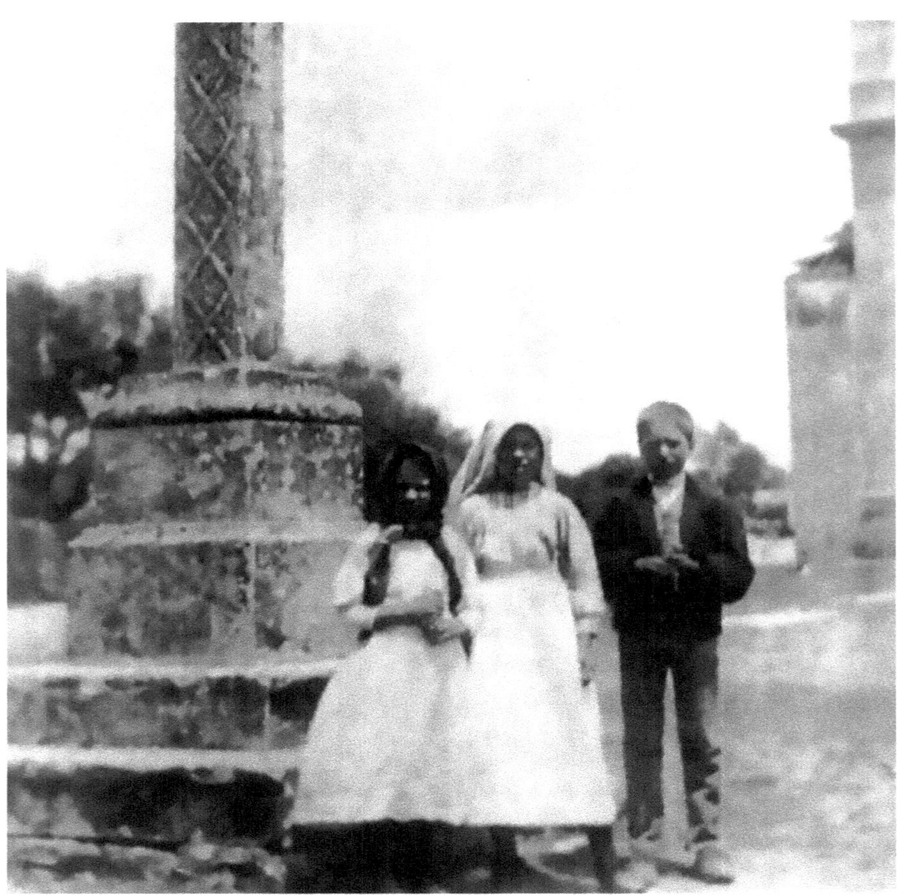

The Fátima Seers photographed between Apparitions in 1917 near the
Mission Cross that used to be located outside the Fátima Parish Church.

5

A Torrent of Faith

What started as a trickle of faithful visitors turned into a torrent as pilgrims came to see for them-selves. With word of the events spreading to other villages, people were now coming to Fátima from as far as Lisbon and Oporto to see the visionary children.

Soon the three seers could not take their sheep out to graze as crowds followed the children everywhere, badgering them with questions and requests of the Virgin Mary. Some of these tourists even approached the young herders, removing strands of hair or pieces of their clothing to take home as relics. Finally neighbors asked that the children be kept at home. The crowds were trampling their crops, causing as much damage as drought or locust infestation. Throngs of thirsty pilgrims drained the local wells of precious rainwater, collected during the winter to see the local inhabitants through the long dry hot summer.

With three more visitations promised by the Lady, Lucia's family contemplated selling their flock at a loss and keep their daughter at home.

Although she agreed that Lucia needed to stay home, she mother was still angry at her daughter for mentioning the event that now intruded on her time. Already verbally abusive to daughter Lucia, the mother now went into daily rages, accusing her child of being possessed by the devil.

And then there were the newspaper articles. Many of them reflected an awe of the events that were taking place in Fátima. But the powerful newspapers that supported the revolutionary government were not in awe of the Apparitions claiming they were frauds perpetuated by the Catholic church. They declared that the Jesuits were staging these events to strengthen the "superstitious beliefs" of ignorant peasants. In political satire cartoons the apparition revealed itself to a local farmer as the skeletal personification of famine.

Perhaps the most vocal enemy of the Apparitions was Artur de Oliveira Santos, the regional administrator of Villa Nova da Ourém and editor of the local republican newspaper. Once a reverent Catholic, Oliveira Santos was a literate tinsmith who had abandoned the faith to embrace local politics at the time of the revolution in 1910. Being one of the few people in the region faithful to the party and the ideals of the new anti-monarchist and anti-clerical Republic, the Government appointed Oliveira Santos representative and head of the Police force.

It was Santos' duty to keep the peace. He therefore saw the repression of these Apparitions to be of the utmost political priority, one that had to be acted on immediately before things got out of control and the Masonic Government in Lisbon intervened.

On August 10, 1917, only three days before the fourth appearance promised by the Virgin Mary, the fathers of the three children were summoned to appear before Santos and the Mayor at the Ourém Town Hall. Santos, who was respected by the local population, considered these Apparitions to be events of mass hysteria and hoped to persuade his fanatical constituents to abandon ideas of restoring Catholicism and the monarchy. Lucia went with her father to the meeting, but Ti Marto decided to leave Jacinta and Francisco at home and come alone. Lucia did not fear an encounter because she knew the administrator well. The males in her family had picked grapes for Santos during harvest, and she had once been hired by his wife to do her household chores while she was under quarentena, a 40-day bed rest following childbirth.

This time, however, the meeting turned immediately ugly.

"Where is the other child?" he barked at Ti Marto the moment he came into the room, not realizing that there were three children involved. Then he turned on Lucia.

"You! You know the secret," he said to the bewildered Lucia. "Come on, tell me what it is!"

Lucia remained silent, and her silence drove Santos into a staged theatrical rage. He hoped that by threatening the child with imprisonment he could scare her into recanting the apparitional encounter. It didn't work. Even the threat of being dropped into a vat of boiling oil like a martyred saint did not change her story.

Lucia remained silent and Santos gave up, telling the bewildered fathers to go home.

The three had to fight their way home through crowds. The newspapers had spread word of the promised apparition and as many as 20,000 pilgrims were now on their way to Fátima to listen to the Virgin's message.

Over the next two days, the homes of the three children were overrun with visitors who peppered the children with questions or requests. Sometimes the pilgrims just wanted to touch the children, and when that happened they were passed around by the spirited crowd like good luck charms or relics, much to the horror of the concerned parents.

Finally, just before the scheduled meeting with the Virgin on August 13, Santos arrived in Fátima in a horse and open carriage driven by one of the town hall's stable workers. He confronted Lucia and the other two children as they were leaving her home and with anger in his voice, demanded that she once again tell him the secrets they had allegedly learned from the virgin's mouth.

When they refused to cooperate, he insisted that they go with him to see Father Ferreira, the parish priest, in the hopes that he could convince the children to tell the truth about the apparitions.

Feeling pressure from Church and state, the parents insisted that the children climb into the Santos' carriage and soon they found themselves at the rectory, being questioned by a very stern Father Ferreira.

"Who teaches you to say the things you talk about?" demanded the priest.

"The Lady I saw at the Cova da Iria!" replied Lucia.

"People who spread lies, like you do, will be judged and go to Hell," said the priest. More and more people are being deceived by people like you."

Lucia stood up to the parish priest.

"If people who tell lies will go to Hell, then I won't go to Hell because I'm telling the truth. I only tell about what I saw and what the Lady told me. And if other people go to see her, they go because they want to. We don't ask them to go with us."

"Is it true that the Lady has given you a secret?" pressed the priest.

"Yes, but I can't tell you what it is. If you really want to know it, I have to ask the Lady whether I can tell you and if she give me permission, I'll tell you what it is."

Unsuccessful in getting the answers he wanted, Santos told the children to get back into his carriage so he could take them to the Cova. Their fathers would have to follow in a separate carriage.

But it soon became apparent to Lucia and the other children that the carriage was not going to the Cova. Rather, admitted Santos said they were first going to stop off at his home in Ourém to visit his wife and children.

Meanwhile at the Cova, the crowd was puzzled by what had happened to the young seers. Many of these people had traveled from distant villages to see the children during the scheduled apparition. When they found the children would not be at the Cova because they had been abducted by Santos, the crowd became unruly. Soon a large group left for Ourém to protest for the release of the seers.

Shouts and threats were heard from the crowd and recorded in the newspapers. Some wanted only to protest, while others threatened to "beat up" the priest and Santos.

But before the crowd could gain momentum, a flash of light and a loud clap of thunder took the crowd from anger to awe.

"They all backed away from the tree," witness Maria Carreira wrote later. "The thunder was followed by a flash of lightning; then we saw a small cloud, very white and delicate. It rested on the tree for a moment and then rose and disappeared.

"When we looked around, we all saw the same thing, which happened again during the following months. Our faces reflected the colors of the rainbow: pink, red and blue. The trees looked as if they had blossoms instead of leaves, as if each leaf had turned into a flower. The earth shone in all colors and so did the clouds; the lanterns on the arch looked as if they were made of pure gold. Our Lady had come, that was certain, although She had not found the children there. As soon as this sign came to an end, everyone went off to Fátima. They protested against the administrator and the priest, and against everyone they believed had had something to do with the abduction of the children including the incredulous parents."

So frightened was Father Ferreira that he posted a letter the next day denying any complicity with the abduction of the children. He did, however, confirm that something supernatural had take place at the appointed time with the mysterious cloud that many had reported seeing on the crown of the tree.

"Thousands of witnesses can testify that the presence of the children was not essential for the Queen of the Heavens to reveal herself," wrote the nervous Priest. "From now on it is not just three children but thousands of people, of every age, from all walks of life and all classes of society, who have seen all these things with their own eyes."

Still, for three days Santos kept the children at his home, pampering them with rare sweets and giving them bright ribbons for their hair.

But their three day stay at the administrator's home involved hours of interrogation, as Santos attempted to get the children to talk about the Apparitions. Each time they refused.

After three days, a frustrated Oliveira Santos was now ready to return them back to Fátima. But before doing so he made one last effort, using reverse psychology.

Santos escorted the children to the Town Hall and showed them an old treasury room with bars on the windows. He told them the securely built room was the town's prison. Here he locked the children, saying "If you won't tell me the secret now you will stay here until you do so or never see your parents again!" "The children were surprised at his actions but maintained steadfast in their stand replying: "You can kill us, but we don't care". "That way we will only get to Heaven quicker," Jacinta shouted defiantly.

The children were locked in the room for hours, alone with their rosaries and an elderly man who had been detained for questioning, probably for criticizing the government in public. The four prayed the rosary, praying for redemption. Still the threats continued.

In desperation, Santos entered the room angrily and declared that he would "boil you all in a cauldron of oil" if they didn't tell him the secrets they had heard during the apparitions.

"Go ahead," Jacinta responded.

Santos was furious.

"You stubborn brat! I am giving you one last chance to reveal your secret. The oil is boiling already!" Jacinta shrugged.

"Good, then take her and throw her into the oil!" he demanded of a guard who grabbed the girl and forced her into another room.

A few minutes later he returned, reporting that Jacinta was "already fried" and that Francisco would be next unless he revealed the secret.

"I can't (talk) sir," said the boy. "I can't tell you!"

The guard was ordered to take Francisco to the "boiling room" where, to his delight, he found no cauldron of oil, just his sister standing in the center of the room, unharmed and patiently waiting for her promised Martyrdom.

A few minutes later, Lucia was promised the same oily fate and then brought into the same room to find her friends still alive.

They waited for more threats from Santos but he had given up. The threats were just psychological torment, a form of torture that Church theologians classify as "dry martyrdom."

By now it was August 15, the Feast of the Assumption of Our Lady, the greatest feast of the Virgin Mary celebrated by the Catholic church. By the time the children were returned to Aljustrel the mass was already underway.

Lucia went home while Jacinta and Francisco went to play in the nearby Valinhos meadow. They were with their brother John when they saw lightening flash in the sky, a signal for them that the Lady was about to appear. Not wanting to leave the site Francisco asked his brother to run home and call Lucia, by now known as heaven's official spokesperson.

As the townspeople were coming home from mass, the Lady appeared to the children above a different tree in the meadow. The appearance of the Lady took the children by surprise.

Because they had not been able to keep the date at the Cova, they feared that the Lady might have lost her trust in them. But they were soon glad to see that that was not the case.

The children reported that The Lady said she had kept her promise to appear at the Cova on the 13th, but "given that man took you to the village, the war which would have ended that day will be prolonged." Had Santos not held the children, said Mary, they would have "seen the Immaculate Heart with the thorns removed, with an arch of flowers overhead and an angel at each side. You would have seen Jesus and Saint Joseph bless the World and the Miracle to take place in October will not be as grandiose!"

The children declared that the world had been deprived of because of Oliveira Santos! It made them understand, what they called, "the world-changing repercussion of just one man's sin."

The Lady added: "I want you to come on the thirteenth to the Cova again and you must continue to pray the Rosary daily. During the last month I will perform a miracle so that everyone can believe."

Then, as she had in the past, the Lady rose above the tree and faded in an easterly direction.

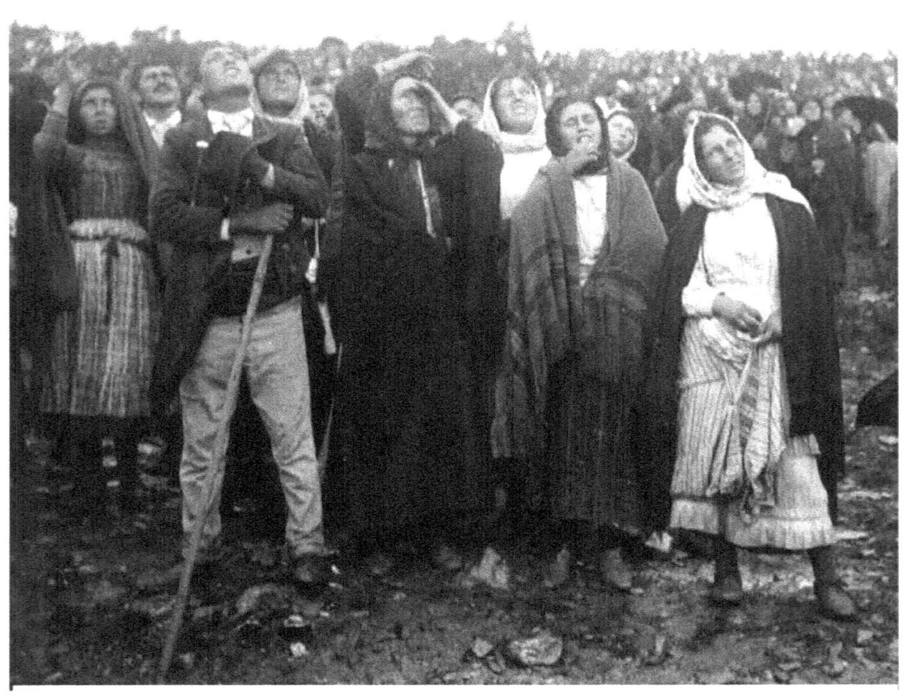

A Crowd of an estimated 70,000 to 100,000 photographed gazing in awe at the prophesied prodigy of the Miracle of the Sun on October 13th, 1917.

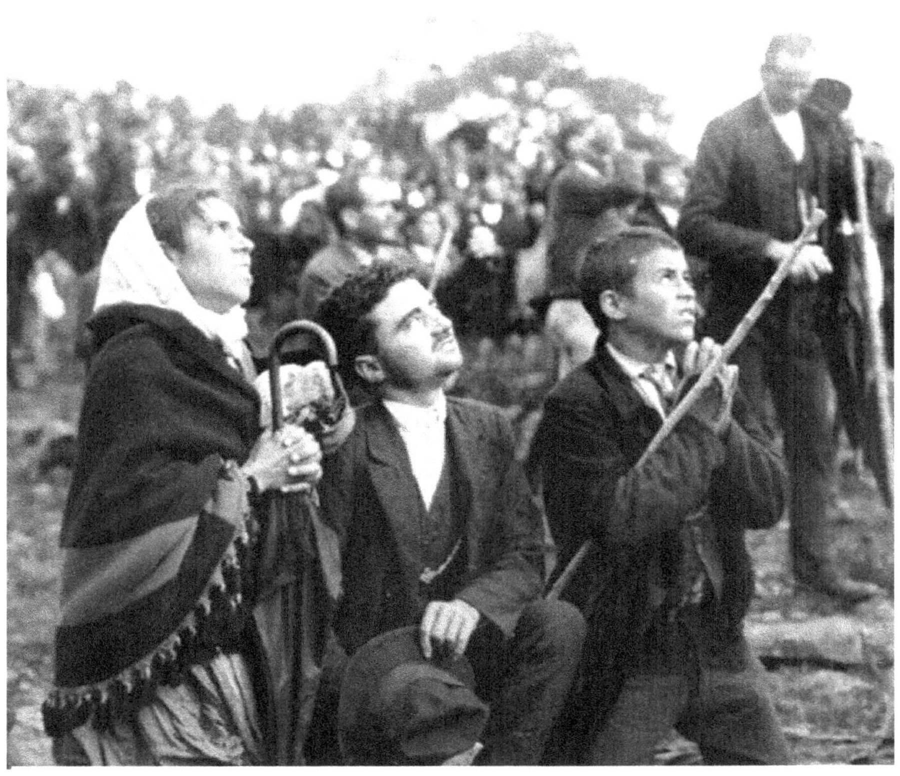

A family (father, mother and son) are photographed kneeling in reverence at the Miracle of the Sun at Fátima, on October 13th, 1917.

6

A Miracle for All

The next Apparition took place September 13. And although it was short and somewhat disappointing, it carried with it a promise from the Lady. She would reveal her identity on October 13, she told the children, and would perform a miracle that would prove the truth of her apparitions to the doubters.

Lucia revealed this information to Canon Professor Dr. Manuel Nunes Formigão, Rector of the Church of the Most Holy Miracle in Santarém. Formigão reported what he saw and heard monthly to the Cardinal Patriarch Archbishop of Lisbon, exiled in the Vatican. He was present at many of the Apparitions, questioning the children before and after and asking Lucia beforehand to ask the Lady certain questions.

Although he witnessed nothing except a slight darkening of the Sun as the girls were having their short encounter with the Lady, he did hear others in the crowd claim they had witnessed heavenly phenomena. Some who had been closer to the tree than the Canon claimed to have seen rose pedals fall and disappear once they hit the ground. Several people claimed to have seen a "shining sphere" gliding from East to West that cast bright reflections on the ground similar to a modern-day disco ball. One of those was a Monsignor João Quaresma, who described a sphere that disappeared, leaving "only a most unusual light."

Several people around Father Quaresma saw the sphere and the light, he said later: "I had the impression that all those around us had seen the same thing, for I heard outbursts of joy from many people. But there were some who were quiet. Near us was a simple and humble woman who wept bitterly, for she had seen nothing at all."

Others reported a cloud of smoke that formed itself around the wooden arch and became larger as it rose into the sky until it disappeared completely at about 30 feet. This took place three times, the witnesses said.

Upon hearing these testimonies, Father Formigão asked the parents of the children if he could perform a detailed interview with each of them separately. The parents agreed, and on September 27, the learned Priest that would come to be known as the "Fourth Witness of Fátima" carried out a series of long interviews with each of the children of which he kept detailed notes, today part of the priceless Formigão Archive. Each described the Lady in the same way. But since she spoke only to Lucia, it was only Lucia who could reveal the words that were spoken during these visionary encounters.

> "How was she dressed?" asked the Canon.
>
> "She wore a white dress that reached down to her feet. Her head was covered by a cloak of the same color and the same length," said Lucia.
>
> "Have you ever asked her who she is?"
>
> "I asked her but she said she would tell us on October thirteenth." "Have you asked her where she comes from?" "Yes, she said she came from heaven."
>
> "When did you ask her this?"
>
> "The second time, on July thirteenth."
>
> Later in the questioning the Canon asked if "Our Dear Lady" had revealed any-thing to her besides the secret that the children would not tell.
>
> "She said she would perform a miracle on October thirteenth so that people will start believing in her appearances."

Word of this October miracle galvanized Fátima and the surrounding area. The first five apparitions had drawn crowds of increasing size and various opinions. But now that the Lady had promised a public miracle, the sixth apparition became an event of significant magnitude. It also became controversial. Newspapers opposed to the Catholic Church ridiculed the notion of a public miracle, declaring the children to be frauds and nothing more than pawns of the Church. Anarchists threatened to bomb the site on the day of the apparition to "put an end to all the nonsense." And members of the Freemasons marched boldly into the Cova a few days before the expected apparition sacrilegiously dressed as Priests and Nuns and parading to the parish church in a mockery of the Catholic faith. Not finding anyone there to mock they then proceeded to the Cova where they chopped down what they thought was the tree of the Apparitions. A group of Parishioners having been forewarned of this spectacle by one of the administrator's men in Ourém left them a subtle insult: a group of asses tied to a tree with the symbol of the republic drawn in the dirt.

The negative comments and events brought fear to the households of Lucia, Jacinta and Francisco. They now saw great danger in their children appearing at the Cova. What if the Lady didn't appear to the children? What if the Lady didn't perform the public miracle as promised? Would the crowd take its anger out on the children? Or what if the government considered the apparitions to be a threat? Could the children be imprisoned, or even worse?

As the date approached, the families became more concerned. Lucia's mother especially saw a dire situation brewing. Two nights before the apparition was to take place, Lucia's mother paced the floor and demanded that her daughter "confess" to having fabricated the events at the Cova.

Lucia's head felt heavy from her mother's demands. She wrote in her memoirs that her mother's fear and anger had once again made her doubt what she had seen. But before she could answer her mother, Jacinta, who was present, spoke bravely into the fray.

"Say that if you want, but we have seen her," said the young girl.

Bolstered by her cousin's comment, Lucia sat upright and addressed her mother.

"I am not afraid that I'll be killed. I am absolutely sure that the Lady will do what she has promised."

+ + +

Events happening outside the house were frightening, too. Rumors of the public Apparition drew droves of people to Fátima. Eyewitness accounts tell of neighboring towns emptying out, their entire populations moving on the rugged roads toward Cova da Iria near Fátima. People on foot, in carts and carriages, riding in cars, converged on the grazing land surrounding the apparition site. Once there they pitched tents or spread blankets and staked claim to a plot of land from which they hoped they would see the miracle.

Estimates put the crowd in the range between 50,000 to 80,000 people, with one college professor estimating the crowd at more than 100,000. The frenzy created a sanitation nightmare, and the sounds and smells that emanated from the pilgrims were alien and unwelcome by the residents of Fátima who saw their crops crushed under foot and their well water reserves depleted.

Then, as dawn broke on the morning of the thirteenth, the slight drizzle turned to a downpour that soaked the mass of visitors to the skin.

As the rain continued, a stiff cold wind blew, creating a wind chill factor.

The desperate pilgrims sought refuge wherever they could. Ti Marto, Jacinta's father, provided a colorful account of the scene that transpired as wet strangers streamed into their tiny house.

"Our house was so full of people we couldn't move," he wrote.

"Outside there was a cloudburst and it was raining so hard that you could hardly see anything. The ground was one big mass of mud. My poor wife was totally upset, for the people in the house climbed on everything, from beds and boxes to tables, and got everything dirty. I tried to soothe her by saying, 'The house is so full that nobody else can get in, so at least it can't get worse.'"

Before noon, the appointed time for the apparition, a woman from the neighboring town of Pombalinho came to Jacinta's home with clothing she had made especially for the children. As the rumble of the crowd could be heard through the walls of Ti Marto's home, the woman nervously helped the children get dressed. Lucia's dress was blue and Jacinta's white, wrote Ti Marto later. On each of the girl's heads, the woman fixed white lace bows so "they looked like angels" as they left the home for their procession to the oak tree.

Francisco who like every mountain shepherd in the district wore a tattered and mended, long, black, woolen hat, was allowed to wear his Sunday hat, on the occasion, only worn to and from Church and placed on the shoulder during Mass, it was known as "The Hat to see God," and on this day it seemed quite appropriate.

On that day, all of the clothing - fancy or not - became soaked from the rain and dirty from the river of mud that ran like a stream past the house. Soon the children were drenched along with all of the people awaiting the Apparition.

As Ti Marto accompanied the children to the Cova he noticed that women were falling to their knees next to the children, some even bowing to kiss the ground as they passed. Others reached out to pull strands of hair or a shirt button to take home as relics.

"Leave them in peace, dear people," Ti Marto recounted later of the event. "They seemed to think that the children were saints."

The further the seers progressed, the thicker the crowd. Soon the three children could barely move, even with Ti Marto behind them begging for the masses to part. Suddenly tall soldier who had come back recently from the front, looked down and saw the children. In one smooth movement, he picked up Jacinta and shouted, "Make way for the children who see our dear Lady." He furrowed his way through the crowd, opening a path for himself, the three seers and a struggling Ti Marto who was bringing up the rear. Ti Marto looked for his wife and couldn't see her. Close to him, though, was Lucia's nervous mother, Maria Rosa.

The crowd was so thick that Jacinta began to cry. A man cleared a spot for the three children to stand comfortably as they awaited the apparition.

A priest who had been praying near the tree all night approached the children and asked them kindly when the Lady was expected to appear.

"At 12 o'clock," said Lucia.

The priest took out a pocket watch and showed it to them. "Look, it's already 12.

Our Dear Lady does not lie."

The children waited. And then waited longer. Nothing appeared. The priest put the watch up to Lucia's face.

"It's long past 12 o'clock," he said. "Don't you see, this is all only an illusion. Go away all of you! Go away!"

When the children refused to move, the priest began pushing Lucia backwards.

Soon tears filled the child's eyes.

"Anyone who wants to go can go, but I'll stay here," she said. "Our Dear Lady said she would come. She came every time before and she will come this time, too." A few moments later, Lucia's eyes fixed on a spot in the eastern sky.

"Jacinta, kneel down, Our Lady is coming! I've seen the flash of light!," said Lucia, turning then to the crowd and shouting, "Please be quiet! Please be quiet! Our Lady is coming."

The crowd fell silent as the children gazed up at the top of the tree. Together the three watched as the lady hovered above the tree top, floating in air, illuminated by an unearthly light.

"What does your Grace want from me?" asked Lucia.

"I wish to tell you that I want a chapel built here in my honor. I am the Lady of the Rosary. Continue to pray the rosary every day. The war is going to end and the soldiers will soon return to their homes."

"I have many things to ask you," said Lucia. "If you would cure some sick people and if you would convert some sinners."

"Some yes, others no," said the Lady. "They must change their lives and then ask forgiveness for their sins. They should stop offending our Lord, for He is already very angry."

"Do you wish anything more?" asked Lucia.

"No, nothing."

"Then I won't ask you for more, either," said Lucia.

With that, the Lady opened her hands and a beam of light came from her palms. She moved upward this time, ascending toward the sky instead of toward the east as she had in apparitions past. The dark clouds parted and the tiny Lady merged with the sunlight streaming down.

"Look there She goes, there she goes! Look at the sun!" shouted Lucia.

Some people claimed to see this apparition as they did for the many apparitions that would amount to the whole of the Apparitions of Fátima. Newspapers and other sources quote many who claimed to see the same apparitions as Lucia. But on this day, the lady had promised a public Apparition, one that all could see. And that is what happened. As the lady left her perch on the tree and disappeared for Lucia into the sky, an event took place that has become known as "The Miracle of the Sun." The newspapers and magazines of the day tell the story in detail:

The newspaper "O Dia," October 17 edition:

"At about one o'clock in the afternoon it stopped raining. The pearl-gray sky cast a strange light on the landscape. The sun seemed to be covered by a veil, so that you could look at it with bare eyes.

"The clouds formed a ring around the sun, which looked like a disk of mother of pearl. Then its color changed to silver and it began to revolve. A cry of surprise went up from the spectators and all the people fell to their knees. The color of the light changed to a lovely blue, as if the sun was shining through the stained-glass window of a cathedral. Slowly the blue color faded and the people, still kneeling with outstretched hands, were bathed in a yellow light. Their faces, their clothes, everything was colored yellow. The people wept and prayed when they saw what they had

come to see. Seconds seemed like hours, the experience was so intense."

The newspaper "O Século":

"A scene right out of the Bible was observed by the astonished crowd, which was standing bareheaded, looking toward the sky. The sun began to trem-ble and went into movements that defied all laws of nature. It seemed to be dancing – that was the expression used by some of the people who described it. Others said that the sun seemed to be trembling, and some swore that it began to rotate like a huge wheel of fire, then came toward the earth as if it was going to scorch it. Many saw the light of the sun changing colors."

The magazine "A Ordem":

"The sun was at one moment enveloped in a red flame, then in yellow and then in deep purple, and it seemed to rotate at an unbelievable speed." A priest, Manuel Pereira da Silva wrote to the vicar of the cathedral, telling him, "the sun seemed to have a clearly defined outline. It rushed down at us and stopped at about the height of the clouds, then started rotating like a ball of fire at a dizzying speed. This lasted for about eight minutes. The atmosphere got dark and all the people seemed to take on a yellow glow. They fell on their knees in the mud."

Abject fear was felt by many who saw the miracle and reported in nearly all of the media accounts. Some claimed the event was accompanied by an increasing heat. Others declared that the sun was whirling and multi-colored.

One of the most detailed accounts of the Miracle of the Sun came from famed poet and playwright Professor Almeida Garrett, of the University of Coimbra, who delivered his account in a Court notarized deposition.

"It must have been about 1:30 pm when, at the spot

where the children were standing, a slender, bluish column of smoke rose to a height of about six feet above their heads and ended about six feet above that. This phenomenon, which I could see clearly, lasted for several seconds. I did not look at my watch and cannot say whether it lasted more or less than a minute. The smoke vanished suddenly, but reappeared later for a second and then a third time. Each time, especially the third time, a clear beam of light went up and disappeared in the gray atmosphere.

"Suddenly I heard cries coming from thousands of people and saw that the crowd had turned away from the oak tree, and were now all looking in the opposite direction, at the sky. The sun, which had been hiding behind dark clouds, broke through and shone brightly. I looked in the same direction and I saw the sun, clearly defined and radiant, but it did not hurt my eyes to look at it."

The professor said that the sun looked like a "shining wheel made of mother of pearl," and that it "did not remain in place, but started rotating at a mad speed," an experience that left spectators feeling that "it was going to scorch us with its fire."

During the solar phenomenon, said Professor Garrett, the color of the atmosphere changed to the color of amethysts, which made the professor think that his retina had been damaged. He turned his back to the sun and still the landscape had the same purple hue. When he turned back around and faced the sun, the atmosphere had cleared.

"Shortly after that I heard a farmer near me call out, 'Look, this woman is completely yellow!' And in fact everything around me, both close and far away, looked as if it was made of old yellow damask. All the people looked as if they had jaundice. I still remember how amused I was to see them looking so unattractive. My hands, too, had the same color." The Miracle of the Sun was observed from more than 25 miles away.

Poet Afonso Lopes Vieira who later composed the famous Fátima Avé sung every day at the Cova since the inauguration of the Fátima Chapel he built for his wife in his home in 1922, wrote that he was "enchanted by a remarkable spectacle in the skies" which he observed from the Veranda of his house. And father Inacio Laurenço Pereira later recalled that school children "were crying and pointing to the sun." He described it as looking like "a ball of snow that was rotating, then suddenly it seemed to fall toward the earth in a zigzag path."

After the solar miracle had ended, the crowd at the Cova discovered another phenomenon. Their clothing – drenched by the torrential rainstorms – were now dry. Many people were now stuck in the mud that suddenly solidified and had to be broken loose. This was proof, many said later, that the sun had truly come closer to earth.

+ + +

Photos from that day are few, but they do show an enormous crowd with most of the spectators turned toward the heavens, their faces frozen in awe as they gaze into the sun. These black and white photos serve as visual testimony to an phenomena that took place in the sky. What we don't have is photos of what happened after the solar miracle. But from eyewitness accounts including those of Sister Lucia, we know that the crowd rushed the young visionaries, touching the children and picking at them, as though touching the seers was the way to capture grace.

Some of the more brazen witnesses unsheathed knives and cut off locks of hair. Lucia's scarf was pulled off and disappeared into the crowd. Hands plucked at the children's clothing, pulling them this way and that. Family members and friends finally stepped in, forming a shield between the children and the spiritually hungry crowd.

The children told the crowd that they had not seen the sun dance. Instead, while the crowd was enveloped in this vision, they were shown Our Lady dressed as the Virgin of Mount Carmel, the Mother of Sorrows. They also claimed to have seen an adolescent Christ and Saint Joseph blessing the crowd.

"What did they look like?", someone shouted. The Virgin appeared in a white robe with a sky-blue cloak along with Joseph and the child Jesus, declared Lucia. Then, after the three of them blessed the world, Jesus appeared alone as the Sacred Heart dressed in red. He blessed the people, too.

"What did the Virgin tell you?" Someone shouted.

"The war will come to an end soon, and you can expect the soldiers to return shortly," declared Lucia.

Jacinta confirmed this interpretation of the words of the Lady.

With this declaration the crowd roared with joy. The people of Portugal were ready for World War I to end, and to hear that the Virgin Mary had proclaimed an end to hostilities on this day was more happiness than they could contain.

Despite the promising words of the Virgin, the war wouldn't end for another 13 months. This long wait led to doubt among the many who had believed the words of the lady as conveyed by Lucia. An unwritten list of questions began to swirl around the Apparitions of Fátima:

- Did the children truly receive information that could foretell the future?
- Were the Apparitions too complex for their young minds to comprehend?
- Was the language chosen by the Lady so obtuse as to be incomprehensible?
- Could they remember exactly what had been told to them by the Lady or only approximately?
- Were the children just a means of conveying symbolic information to church fathers? Or were they intended to be the ciphers of the messages they received?
- And, most important, had the apparitions really taken place?

These and other questions were pondered by many, including the leadership of the Catholic Church, some of whom doubt the authenticity of the apparitions and their messages to this day.

One person who did not doubt the apparitions was John Haffert, the founder of the largest apostolic movement of all time that would come to be known as The Blue Army of Our Lady of Fátima. From the time he read a magazine article in 1935, he saw the apparitions as a solid link to prophecy and divinity. It was the apparitions of Fátima that led Haffert to become the world's number one lay Fátima Apostle and to create an almost surreal world of belief that rivaled even the cryptic messages and surreal images that came from the great surrealist painters themselves, including mind of the great Salvador Dalí. In fact, it was one particular vision from the apparitions in Fátima – The Vision of Hell - that led him to the doorstep of that very man himself.

Oddly enough, it wasn't Haffert's idea to seek out the mysterious surrealist. That idea came from someone else, a stranger with his own mission in mind, a man from Mississippi who saw scaring the Hell out of people as a key to massive recruitment into Catholicism.

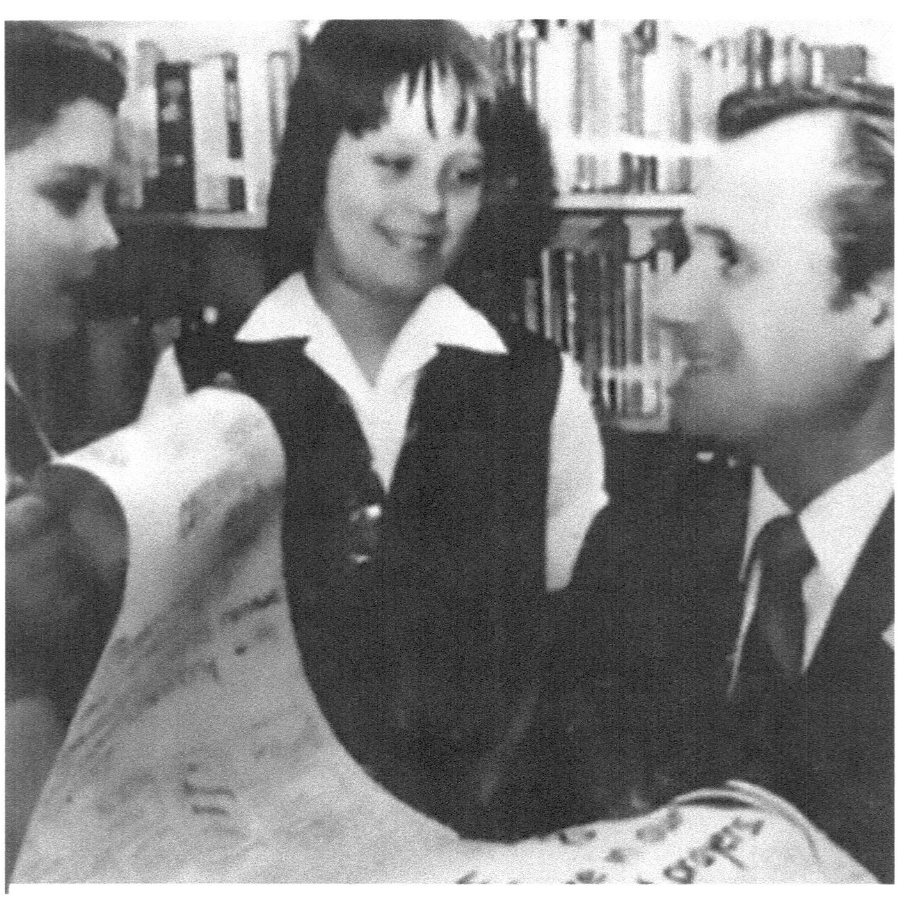

John Haffert photographed in the 1960's with two Blue Army Cadets presenting him with a scroll with thousands of signed petitions offering prayers and sacrifices for the Conversion of Russia.

7

Dear Mr. Haffert

A Seminarian we will call "Brother Michael," since he has asked to remain anonymous, had been working on his master plan for some time. That much is clear from the correspondence. But on this day, as he was about to make his plans public, he thought briefly about the path that had brought him to Jordan Catholic Seminary at Menominee, Michigan where he was studying diligently for the priesthood.

Brother Michael was born in 1924 and raised a strict Methodist in rural Mississippi. Despite his strict upbringing, Brother Michael remained curious about the mystical view of other religions. He was in the Merchant Marine during World War II and stayed in as a Pharmacist Mate until 1958 when he left the merchant marines and the Methodist Church to become a candidate for the priesthood.

His conversion to Catholicism began in 1955 when a Catholic passenger on board his ship told him about the Apparitions of Fátima. The story of the children in Fátima, Portugal who had witnessed six Apparitions of the Virgin Mary over the course of six months both intrigued and touched the young sailor. He wanted to know more.

Several months later he got that chance. His ship docked in Monrovia, Liberia on the West African Coast and Brother Michael went to see a movie. "The Miracle of Fátima" starring Gilbert Roland, happened to be playing and Brother Michael went into the dilapidated theatre. He was deeply touched by what he saw, so much so that he wept through much of the film. "I could not explain this response," he wrote later. "I only knew that I had discovered something wonderfully strange and mysterious and yet very real. I wanted to know even more about this miracle."

On his return to New Orleans, Brother Michael purchased a copy of William Thomas Walsh's book, "Our Lady of Fátima." In that book he read the complete story of the miracle, how the three peasant children – Lucia, Jacinta and Francisco - were greeted by the tiny apparition of the Virgin Mary on May 13, 1917, and how she promised to return to them on the 13th of the month for the next six months with revelations from God that would – or at least should – change the world for the better.

He read of the suffering of the children and how some of their parents – especially Lucia's mother - had doubts that the children were truly communing with the Virgin. He learned of their revelations and how they bravely stood up against the town's elected officials and local Communists to deliver certain messages and to keep others secret.

Brother Michael learned of the Miracle of the Sun that took place during the final Apparition, and imagined a sun that whirled and danced in the sky and even became so hot that the rain-soaked clothing of the crowd dried in minutes.

Brother Michael would later write that the miracle of Fátima taught him two things that led to his conversion. One was the belief that Mary was truly the Mother of Christ. The other was a belief in Hell.

Brother Michael addressed that conversion in a letter he wrote while in the Jordan Seminary.

For several years prior to my conversion I had experienced difficulty accepting the doctrine of Hell. During the first months after my admission to Jordan Seminary this difficulty reached a kind of climax. As a Catholic I could not refuse to face the truth of eternal damnation nor could I minimize its seriousness.

It seemed that I had a clearer more meaningful concept of eternal hopelessness or despair than ever before. I began to sympathize with the damned. I thought that no sin, no matter how serious, could deserve such punishment.

Though I would not admit it even to myself my concept of God during this period of trial was that of a tyrant. I could not reconcile His goodness with the existence of Hell. Yet my reason told me that if God were not good there could be no goodness; everything would have to be bad.

I began to see friends and relatives in Hell. I was concerned about the state of the soul of my own father, who had died about ten years earlier.

I did not want to feel this way about Almighty God. I was convinced that I must face this problem and solve it. I consulted confessors and spiritual directors. They have all the theological answers and explanations, but the difficulty remained. I could not understand why a good and loving Father should allow his children, even the bad ones, to fall to Hell.

Once after a troubled Sunday afternoon I stood before the blessed Sacrament and told Our Lord that I thought He was unjust because he allowed souls to fall into Hell. I do not know why I did this.

I was immediately filled with remorse. I began to realize how much Jesus loves me and the whole human race.

The difficulty remained with me until I learned to flee from thoughts against God. Then gradually I learned to accept Hell as a terrible yet necessary reality that grieves Our Lord far more than it does me.

When I first read of *The Vision of Hell* in Mr. Walsh's book, my only response over and above the normal reaction to so horrible an experience was the conviction that this scene should be painted.

The Vision of Hell Brother Michael was referring to took place July 13, 1917, when Mary opened the earth before the frightened children and took them on a visionary field trip into the bowels of Hell.

Lucia, one of the children who witnessed the Apparitions, described in the most general of terms what the trio had seen when the ground before them seemed to open wide.

"...we were now able to behold a sea of fire. Plunged in the flames were devils and souls that looked like trans-parent embers; other were black or bronze and in human form, these were suspended in flames which seemed to come from the forms themselves – there to remain without weight or equilibrium amid cries of pain and despair which horrified us so that we trembled with fear. The devils could be distinguished from the damned human soul by the terrifying forms of weird and unknown animals in which they were cast."

As the children trembled from what they had just seen, Mary revealed the reason for this visionary revelation. *"You have seen Hell where the souls of poor sinners go... If you do what I tell you, many souls will be saved, there will be peace. The war will end, but if men do not cease offending God, another and more terrible war will break out."*

Having gone through the second World War as a Merchant Marine, Brother Michael found himself deeply moved by the Apparitions and revelations of Fátima. He too felt that men were offending God, and that the Second World War had been a brutal punishment and warning for those offenses. To now find confirmation of those beliefs and to realize that some people deserve Hell made him feel that he had com-mon ground with those had received the mystical messages at Fátima.

Which brought Brother Michael back to his master plan, something others would call his "master plan to produce a masterpiece," because it was his plan to literally turn the vision of Hell that took place at Fátima into a painting that would capture the attention of the world.

With great care as to not disturb his thoughts, Brother Michael quietly removed a piece of unlined paper from his top drawer and placed it before him on the desk. Then after a moment's hesitation, he took a deep breath and began to write a letter to a man named John Haffert.

Subject of letter:

Have an artist paint The Vision of Hell as described by Sister Lucia, the primary seer of the Fátima visions of 1917.

Object of painting: to create a Hell consciousness.

Therefore: It must reach the people. It must attract

attention. People must want to see it. It should be the sort of thing that publications such as Life magazine would publish, also something that would insure as a masterpiece. It must capture the horror of the scene and present it realistically so that anyone, everyone who sees it will experience the same or something of the same fear, dread, horror, that the three children experienced. It must be an authentic record or as near to the actual scene as is possible. Absolute perfection would be a painting that people everywhere would buy prints of to hang on the walls of their homes as a constant reminder of the penalty for sin.

To accomplish we need: Salvador Dalí (sp) as the painter. Because: a picture, any picture by Dalí is news, it attracts attention. I think that the publishers of Life Magazine would publish a print of such a painting and thus carry it to some twelve or fourteen million people.

Dalí recently turned realist. This a perfect trend for our purposes. He is probably the greatest living artist. His works will endure.

If he cannot capture the scene it probably cannot be done. In fact he may be the only artist who can.

It is most desired and perhaps essential that the artist be granted a series of interviews with Sister Lucia. Shades of color, the forms and shapes of bodies in the conflagration, particularly, the forms of the devils, which were, according to sister's description, "animals frightful and unknown," could not be adequately described by mail. To recall these details which are so essential to the overall effect will require almost a miracle of memory and will probably be a very difficult task for Sister Lucy.

But Fátima was a miracle and if Our Blessed Mother wants this project to succeed she will provide another one. But certainly on the natural plane there are many advantages to the interviews as opposed to description by mail which would place an added burden on sister, limit the means of communication to words, eliminate much of the advantage of trial and error, a possible technique where-in the artist could make a number of sketches and try different colors for a particular form until he hit the right one.

Last but not least, the interviews would create a much better impression as to the authenticity of the reproduction. I therefore suggest that we at least try to arrange these interviews.

Please understand that these are just ideas and not conditions and are subject to the approval of your organization. I know almost nothing about art and even less about publicity. But I think that if the painting is to be an effective instrument large numbers of people must see it. The best way to accomplish this is to produce something that they want to see. I think that Dalí is the solution or answer to this problem.

The letter was signed by Brother Michael.

+++

Haffert read Brother Michael's letter a second time. Then he turned to his manual typewriter and with powerful keystrokes began banging out a letter to the future priest.

Mr. Michael,

I agree with you completely on your idea. I have often thought of that Vision of Hell, and its importance to the World.

However, I hold little hope that Sister Lucia could give us a very adequate description, and even less hope that it could be translated onto canvas.

You see, during an interview with her, I asked her about this apparition and she was terrified by the very memory of it. The best she could say was the souls looked as if they were burning from within and from without.

I also recall that when a sculptor was commissioned to do the vision of Our Lady according to Sister Lucia's description, the sculptor worked day in and day out, but Sister Lucia always made changes. Finally in desperation, on the very last day she squeezed the whole face as though desperately trying to change it into what she had seen, and then gave up.

It was impossible to transfer into clay and into physical colors the tremendous light and mystery of what she had seen.

Nevertheless you idea is certainly worth a try. And if anyone in the world could do it, and I think even get the opportunity to interview Lucia on the subject, it would be Mr. Dalí. By all means try, and my suggestion is to write directly to the Bishop of Fátima, and tell him of your desire and purpose.

Wishing you every success, and with every best personal wish, I remain.

Sincerely yours
John M. Haffert

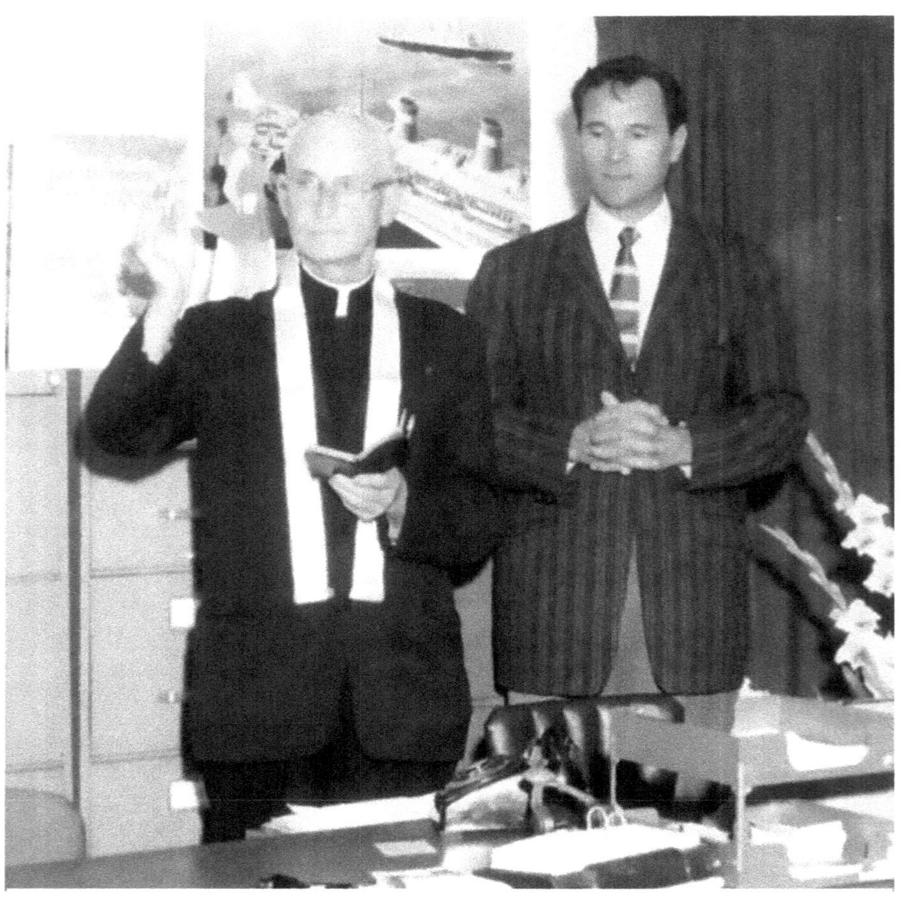

Monsignor Harold Colgan with John Haffert in attendance blesses the new Offices of the Catholic Traveler, Precursor of Fátima Travel, the largest travel agency in the World, responsible for having brought millions of Pilgrims to Fátima.

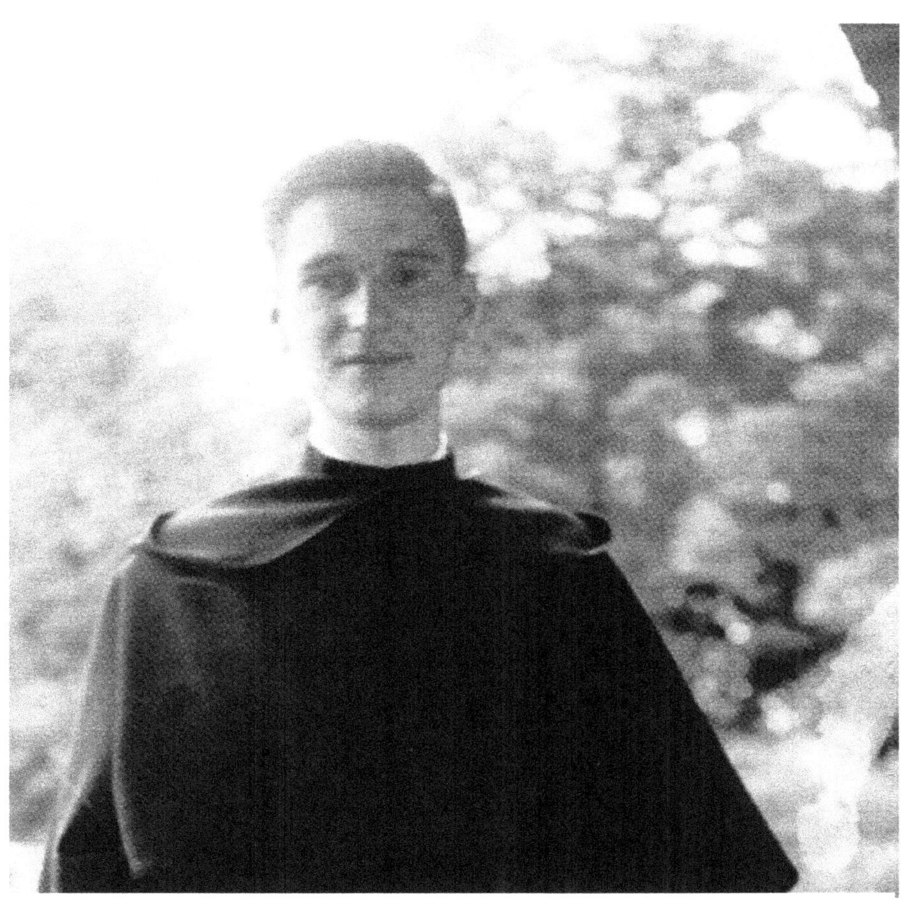

A young John Mathias Haffert, in the Habit of a Carmelite Seminarian during his stay at the Chicago Carmelite Province of the Most Pure Heart of Mary.

8

A Man Devoted

The person to whom Brother Michael was writing this missive was John Mathias Haffert, founder of The World Apostolate of Fátima, also known as The Blue Army. The son of a wealthy publisher of farm trade magazines, Haffert's goal in life was to become a Carmelite priest like his great uncle, Father Anastasius Kreidt, who had been the second American to enter the Carmelite Order in the United States. A driven man, Father Kreidt had taught himself several languages and was an accomplished piano player who always found himself in demand for sermons and funerals. He also published magazines in both English and German and was responsible for building a large Carmelite monastery at Niagara Falls.

If Father Kreidt had a failing, it was that he had too much trust in people. Throughout his life people who discovered he was an easy hit had taken advantage of him in small ways. But despite this failing, he was a trusted man and therefore an excellent fundraiser. Over the course of his life he had been responsible for building one of the largest and most prosperous Carmelite Provinces in the world.

That all came crashing down when he raised money to build his crowning achievement, St. Cyril's College in Chicago. With adequate funds in hand, Father Kreidt began advancing large sums of money to the contractor hired to build the institution. Shortly before the construction was to begin, the contractor absconded with the funds.

Despite serving the church well for many years, Father Kreidt was held responsible and publicly humiliated. A church tribunal decided it was time for Father Kreidt to retire, which is what he did with, as Haffert wrote, "holy resignation." Shortly after being dismissed from his position, Father Kreidt collapsed and died of a heart attack on the doorstep of his sister.

Father Kreidt was a man to be admired. But it was through his failure that Haffert said he learned his greatest lesson, that of the value of humiliation. It was, as Haffert wrote in the hurriedly written autobiography that he penned at the very end of his life, "a lesson that was to have special meaning in my life." At the funeral of his great uncle, Haffert had his first real brush with Catholic mysticism. During the wake, a sweet fragrance began coming from the priest's coffin that increased in intensity to the point that it filled the entire house with, as Haffert's father described it, "an indescribable fragrance, which we felt to be truly supernatural." The undertaker swore that he had put nothing in the coffin.

"Of course, St. Cyril's College was built," and the memory of his great uncle was forgotten, wrote Haffert in his autobiography, "he died in the odor of sanctity, having accepted humiliation as a most precious gift of God after a life in which he had been the object of adulation."

The odor of sanctity was something Haffert was familiar with. From an early age he longed to give his life to the priesthood. Haffert's uncle on his father's side – also named John – followed Father Kreidt into the priesthood, joining the Chicago Carmelite Province of the Most Pure Heart of Mary. Each and every time this Latin scholar and classical musician encountered his nephew he gave him a "principle" to follow. Young John wrote these principles on sheets of paper that he kept in his piano seat at home. It was his uncle who gave him his first communion and it was his uncle who suggested that young John devote his life to the priesthood.

For eight years, Haffert studied the priesthood in the Carmelite formation at the Niagara Falls monastery built by his great uncle. He was guided through a life of prayer and fasting and periods of deep and meditative silence as he reached for God in the way that only the deeply devout can. But he was also young and human and ruled by the teenage hormones that made him painfully aware of the opposite sex. Before entering the monastery, young Haffert had met a girl at a church camp. Nothing sexual had happened between them, said Haffert, but by his own admission he had become infatuated with the young woman. He thought about her constantly while at the monastery. Sometimes he would flagellate himself with a device known as "the Brother's discipline," a cattail whip of knotted rope, that he flung over his shoulder during Friday prayers. More than likely, his prayers revolved around a verse in the bible from Saint Paul, who recommended piety and strongly suggested that a devout person, "Put to death what is earthly in you: fornication, impurity, passion, evil desire, and covetousness, which is idolatry." By performing flagellation and other acts that mortify the flesh, some Catholic sects believe that one can conquer "the insidious demons of softness, pessimism and lukewarm faith that dominate the lives of so many today."

Despite weekly flagellation that were so lengthy that Haffert himself considered them excessive, the young man was not able to tame his thoughts of the young woman.

While in this perplexed state, he met Brother Aloysius, a sort of mystic layman at the monastery whose gentle countenance presided over many of the priests in training. If Haffert ever had doubt about the brother's mystic reputation, it disappeared after their first meeting. Although they had never met, the Brother acted as though he knew Haffert very well. He told the stunned young man that years before they met, God had entrusted him to pray for Haffert *by name*. Before Haffert could express his doubt, the Brother leaned forward and said: "Do you remember when you were faltering in your vocation a few years ago?"

"How did you know?" demanded Haffert, knowing that the Brother was referring to the young girl. "Did God tell you?"

The Brother didn't answer the question.

"I prayed for you by name at each Holy Mass," he said.

Many at the monastery considered Brother Aloysius eccentric. But Haffert, already a devotee of mysticism when he arrived at the monastery, bonded with the Brother. Although there was a rule in the seminary that prevented clerics from talking to lay brothers, John received special permission from the head priests to speak to him. It was almost daily that they spent hours in conversation. Through these conversations they realized that they both had a deep devotion to Saint Mary and her role in Christian spirituality. John had developed his devotion to St. Mary through reading and prayer. Brother Aloysius, on the other hand, had gone one step further. He'd had, he insisted to the young cleric, a visionary encounter with Mary.

"One night, not knowing whether I was awake or dreaming, I saw a very beautiful lady writing in an immense book," Haffert would recall later, writing of the Brother's vision in one of his own books. "The letters as she inscribed them, shone like real gold, gleaming in the brilliant light that radiated from her. When she had finished, I saw that it was my name she had written! And then she turned and smiled at me. That smile was so sweet that it impressed itself indelibly in my heart so that I need but think of it to see it again."

The vision of Mary was then followed by "a series of pictures so real that they woke me, leaving me with a feeling that they were supernatural."

As Haffert stared wide-eyed, the usually secretive brother relayed a series of pictures, or scenes, that could only be described as surreal.

In the first scene, the brother saw himself opening a large wooden crate filled with what appears to be large service items for a banquet. In the second scene, these service items prove to be thousands of damaged images of the Immaculate Conception. With tears in his eyes, Brother Aloysius begins to glue the images back together, rummaging through the respective arms, legs and heads to find the missing body parts. At the end of this scene, the brother is please to find a large and undamaged image of the Sacred Heart.

In the third scene, brother finds himself seated at a large banquet table on the lawn next to a church. As a platter of food was handed down the table, Brother Aloysius noticed a strange piece of food that he had never seen before. When the platter reached him, the brother takes the food and puts it on his plate. A hand reaches from behind him and removes the strange food. With that, the vision ends.

Now as the two men spoke, Brother Aloysius became convinced that the hand that had removed the strange food belonged to Haffert.

"I understood... at the banquet table, where truths about Our Lady are passed down from century to century, this one was saved for general propagation until now, placed before me, and taken by you to be made known to the world."

Searching for another interpretation of the visionary dreams, Haffert and Brother Aloysius wrote a long letter to Haffert's uncle, a Carmelite priest in Middletown, New York. The brother attached his opinion of what the vision meant and together they took the documents to his uncle John.

The two men expected a positive response, so they were surprised when Haffert's favorite uncle told them to gather up all drafts of the letter and any notes along with it and "burn them at once."

The demand for destruction was somehow exciting for Haffert. As he wrote later: "I was enjoying everything that happened because it was as though Butler's Lives of the Saints had suddenly come to life and I was in the midst of them. But brother did not live in feathery idealism as I did, but in an idealism tried and plodding; he lived not so much by enthusiasm as by earnestness... I cannot help admitting that I took the letter to him with a great deal of curiosity, wondering just how he would react to its humiliating message."

If Haffert expected anything less than strict obedience, he didn't say. When Brother read the letter, he turned to Haffert and said: "Will you bring down the papers, Frater?" Haffert responded immediately and the two men spent the next few minutes committing all of their writing on the vision to a blazing furnace.

It was sometime after this event that Haffert discovered just how correct the brother's vision had been. The first indication came with another psychic moment between Haffert and Brother Aloysius. It happened when the two men were in the midst of conversation about St. Grignon de Montfort and his writing about the virgin Mary. A writer and poet whose work influenced many popes, de Montfort wrote more than 20,000 verses of hymns and believed strongly in the notion that, "If we do not risk anything for God we will never do anything great for Him."

On this day, the two men were discussing de Montfort's treatise on True Devotion to the Blessed Virgin. Perhaps they were discussing some of the more controversial portions of this book, like the notion that we belong to Jesus and Mary as their slaves, or the different attributes of true devotion, such as his belief that true devotion "inspires us to seek God alone in his Blessed Mother and not ourselves," and how difficult that might be for mortal man.

There are many ways their conversation could have gone that day, especially a conversation about someone like de Montfort, who has three congregations named after him to this day and whose birthplace and tomb are destinations for more than 25,000 "Montfortian pilgrims" each year. In fact it doesn't matter what they were talking about at the time, because what came out of Haffert's mouth was almost as though the young man had channeled a sentence from Montfort himself.

"Brother, it is for you to find a way to lead men to Jesus through Mary without words."

Haffert was stunned by the sentence he had spoken because it seemed so foreign. But he was also surprised by the look on the Brother's face, which seemed to be one of utter disbelief. The men sat in silence for a moment, speaking only through their posture and the look in their eyes.

Wordlessly, the men parted. Haffert later wrote that he spent the day in a fog, wondering why he said those words and what they meant. Brother, it is for you to find a way to lead men to Jesus through Mary without words. He felt those words had been inspired by the Holy Spirit, but their meaning eluded him. Haffert spent much of that night in prayer.

So too did Brother Aloysius. He prayed for the meaning of the mysterious sentence until, as he told Haffert, a prayer came to him. He wrote down the words of the prayer on a slip of paper and in the morning he knocked on Haffert's door and handed it to him. "What you suggested yesterday could be fulfilled in a Scapular apostolate," declared Brother Aloysius. "(It) would draw men to the Sacred Heart through Mary."

With no further conversation, the Brother walked down the hall and back to his own room. Haffert was disappointed with the prayer Brother Aloysius had given to him. He later wrote that he felt "somewhat confused and disappointed" by the it, mainly because it was merely a well-known morning offering prayer from an organization known as Apostleship of Prayer. Their prayer reads:

> *Eternal Father, I offer You everything I do this day: my work, my prayers, my apostolic efforts; my time with family and friends; my hours of relaxation; my difficulties, problems, distress, which I shall try to bear with patience.*
>
> *Join these, my gifts, to the unique offering which Jesus Christ, Your Son, renews today in the Eucharist.*
>
> *Grant, I pray, that, vivified by the Holy Spirit and united to the Sacred Heart of Jesus and the Immaculate Heart of Mary, my life this day may be of service to you and your children and help consecrate the world to you. Amen.*

Haffert read the prayer several times, searching for the clue to the meaning of the mysterious sentence. Suddenly he saw it! The difference between the prayer Brother Aloysius had given him and the published version of the ancient prayer was an addition made by the Brother telling how one should kiss the scapular to garner favor from the Blessed Virgin Mary.

+++

The way Brother Aloysius interpreted Haffert's puzzling utterance was clearly mystical. A scapular is two rectangular pieces of cloth joined together by a string that allows one piece of cloth to rest on the wearer's back and the other over their chest. Recognized officially by the Roman Catholic Church as a sign of devotion to the Virgin Mary, it is something very special for Carmelites, who believe that by wearing the Brown Scapular, one will be spared the fires of Hell when they die and go immediately instead to heaven.

That such a seemingly insignificant object could carry such significant promise came from the super-natural encounter between Saint Simon Stock and the Blessed Virgin Mary. The 13th century holy man prayed frequently for Mary to give his order a "singular privilege," so it could stand out among other church orders. To this end, the virgin was said to have appeared to St. Simon Stock in 1251, holding a scapular in her hand.

"This is for you and yours a privilege, the one who dies in it will be saved," she is said to have promised the future saint.

The wearing of the Brown Scapular became institutionalized in 1294 when the Carmelite Constitution was amended to make it a "serious fault" to sleep without a scapular. The Brown Scapular was divinely institutionalized by a vision of Mary that Pope John XXII was said to have had on March 3, 1322. According to a hotly contested Papal Bull, Mary would release those who wore the Brown Scapular from Purgatory on the Saturday following their death. Because Mary's intervention was to take place on the Sabbath, or Saturday, this "indulgence" (as a reprieve from purgatory is called) is called "The Sabbatine Privilege."

The wearing of the Brown Scapular became enormously popular among Catholics and not just Carmelites. Much like the rosary, the Brown Scapular was considered the sign of a truly devout Catholic.

But it was also controversial. Some Catholic scholars declared that Saint Simon Stock's vision of Mary never took place. And others insisted that the vision of Pope John XXII never took place and that Carmelite monks fabricated the Papal Bull, blaming the forgery on a monk named Balduinus Leersius.

Several popes have weighed in on the validity of the Papal Bull. Some have confirmed it, others not, and one, Pope Gregory XIII, expressed no opinion about the Bull but declared that the Carmelites could preach its content as long as they did not commission paintings representing the Mother of God descending into Purgatory.

Finally in 1907, the Congregation of Indulgences gave a ruling on the Sabbatine Privilege, approving it and confirming their belief in the power of the Brown Scapular provided that those who wear it, "...have ever observed chastity, have recited the Little office of the Blessed Virgin Mary, or, if they cannot read, have observed the fast days of the Church, and have abstained from flesh meat on Wednesdays and Saturdays (except when Christmas falls on such days), may derive after death -- especially on Saturdays, the day consecrated by the Church to the Blessed Virgin -- through the unceasing intercession of Mary, her pious petitions, her merits and her special protection."

+++

Haffert read the prayer from Brother Aloysius several times. With each reading, his excitement grew.

> *The Brown Scapular is a wordless way to share the message of Mary! He thought. Through the presence of the scapular one would always be in union with the Mother of God! The Scapular was physical yet metaphysical, a perfect bridge to bring people to the feet of the mystical Catholic Church...*

As Haffert thought more about the unexplained words that came out of his mouth and the comments of Brother Aloysius about a Scapular Apostolate, he realized that another epiphanous moment had taken place with his friend. The idea of a Scapular Apostolate was perfect! The notion that he could "draw men to the Sacred Heart through Mary, without words" was perfectly realized by an apostolate that directed both the faithful and new members to wear a subtle yet present object as a constant reminder of the Virgin Mary matched the mysterious words exactly.

For the first time, Haffert saw the direction his life would take after he graduated to the priesthood. He began to study books about Scapular devotion that his great uncle Father Anastasius had brought to the United States from his own studies in Europe. As Haffert later wrote, he became so engrossed in his studies for this special vocation that he wasn't aware of major news events or even of things that happened in the school itself. Snide comments about his lack of worldly awareness from others rolled off his back or went completely unnoticed. Haffert wrote that he was happy in his studious and meditative world. "I had never been, and never expect to be again on this earth, so happy."

Haffert would wear under his shirt until his death a large wool Scapular of the Professed Carmelite Brothers.

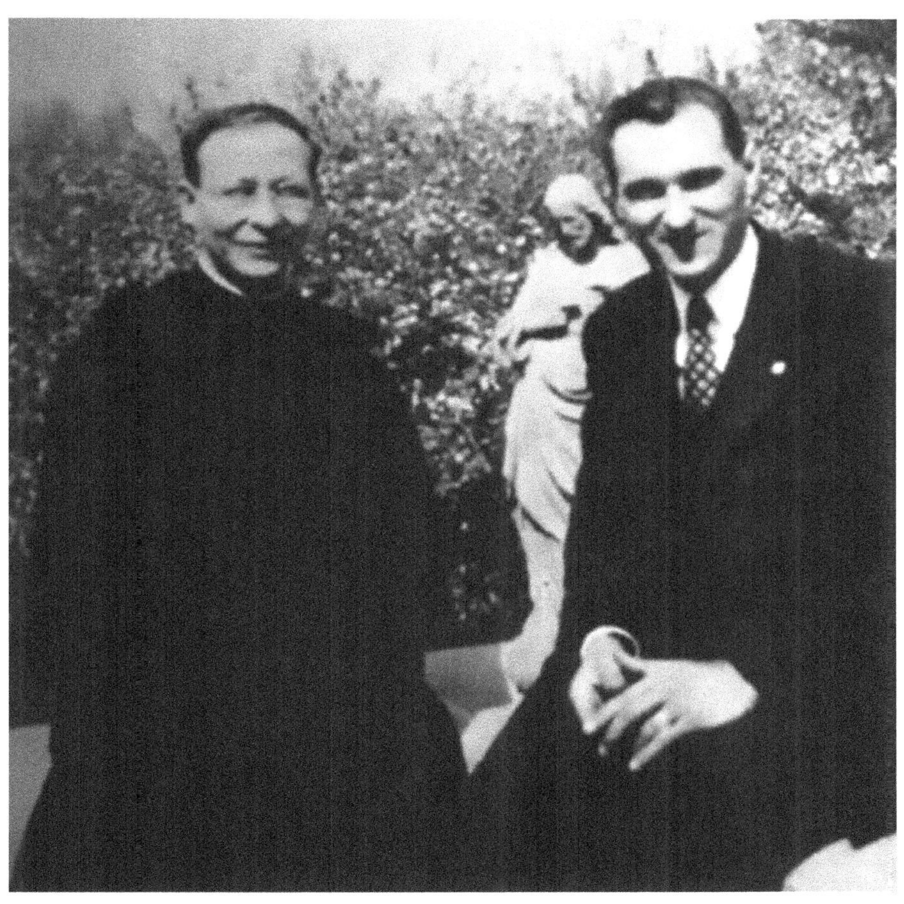

John Haffert and his Spiritual Director, the Mystic Brother Aloysius Scafaldi who was instrumental in directing him to a lay vocation dedicated to the spread of the Messages of Our Lady of Fátima.

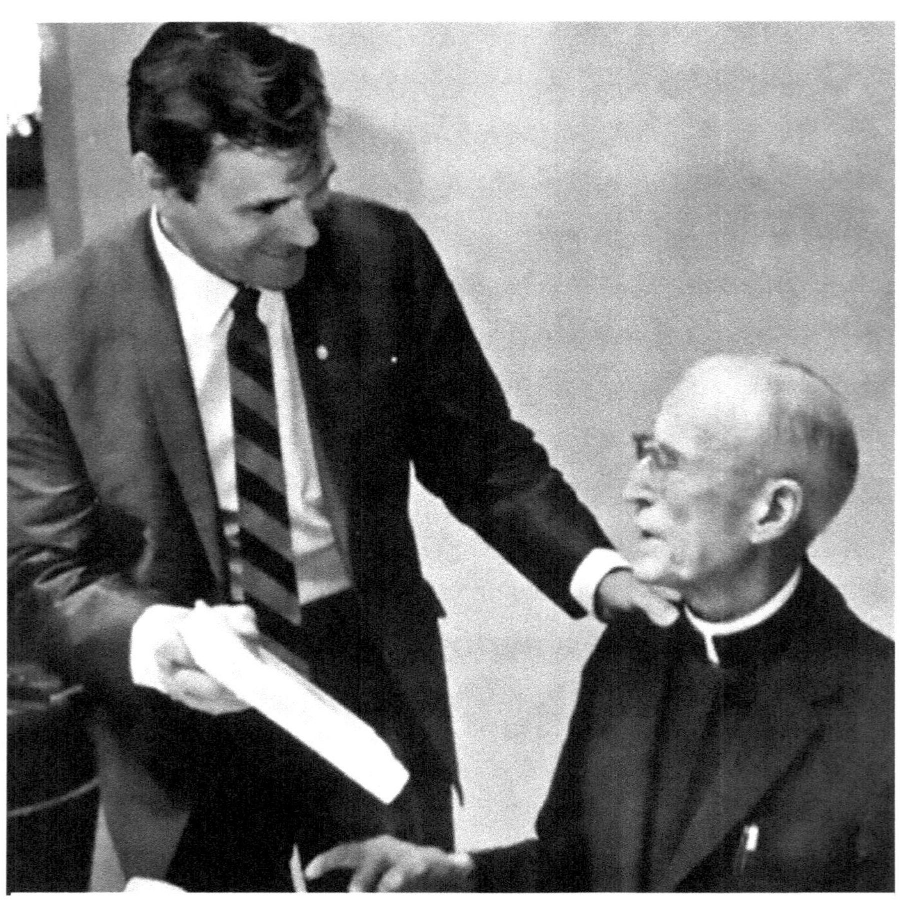

John Haffert presents Monsignor Harold Colgan with a copy of one of his best-selling books on Fátima. Haffert wrote and published at least one book per year from 1946 until 2001.

9

Search for New Devotion

Others at the Carmelite monastery were not as happy with Haffert as he was with himself. Although his saintly great uncle had founded the monastery and his uncle was one of its principle priests, Haffert was not accepted into the priesthood.

In explaining his rejection, Father Matthew O'Neill, the newly appointed Carmelite Provincial, said he felt that Haffert spent too much time in contemplation of spiritual matters and not enough to worldly matters. Hours and days spent in contemplation, and fasting and "grand silences," (as meditation was called) were no longer practical in a world where priests spent so much time teaching and administrating to parish work, the provincial declared.

There was no longer much room for the "overly-contemplative" in the priesthood, declared Father O'Neill. As he told the devastated young Haffert, "we are not going to remain sitting under the broom tree," a painful Biblical reference to religious people who contemplate the spiritual world and ignore the active one.

Haffert was lost. As a man whose goal was the priesthood, being unable to become a man of the cloth left a vacuum in his heart. He had spent eight years studying at the Carmelite monastery in Niagara Falls, the one his great uncle had built and the one where his uncle was a highly regarded priest. Why had he failed to become a priest? And what, John thought in true Carmelite fashion, was God's true intention for his life?

He thought about becoming a secular priest, a knowledgeable layman who performs many of the functions of a priest. When he mentioned this to his uncle John, the veteran priest suggested that he keep himself free to answer the call of God.

Feeling at loose ends and ashamed of his failure to become a priest, Haffert returned to his parent's home in Connecticut where he was greeted by a father with extreme disappointment in his eyes and a mother who could not stop weeping. He recalled the long letters he had written to his parents about the joy he felt in loving God, and now he wondered exactly what that loving God had planned for him. When people ridiculed him by saying that he "must not have been good enough" to be a Carmelite priest, Haffert offered no comment in his own defense, remembering instead his pure devotion and the thought that, yes, God had a plan for him, it just wasn't yet clear yet what that plan was. As he was sometimes fond of saying, "God answers our prayers, he just doesn't always say 'yes.'"

And then, of course, there was the vision of Brother Aloysius. Haffert felt even more guided by it now that he was out of the Carmelite order. He worked hard at interpreting the vision, trying to understand its various elements and what they might mean to him. He had to do this without notes (they had been burned) and without Brother Aloysius, who had been sent to a monastery in the Gaza Strip shortly after Haffert left the Niagara monastery. Relying on memory, Haffert considered the elements of the Brother's surreal dream. He thought about the deeper meaning of the broken images of the Immaculate Conception, each with its missing parts; he wondered why the image of the Sacred Heart would be in perfect condition, and exactly what the nature of the strange food that was passed around the banquet table was and why it had been stolen from Brother's plate by a fast-moving hand. Ever an art fan, Haffert compared it to the kind of imagery that a surrealist painter would pull out of his unconscious mind and put on canvas for others to interpret.

Haffert's conclusion was the same as Brother Aloysius, that the banquet table represented the forum at which the truths about Mary are passed through the centuries and he was now chosen to take a truth – the Brown Scapular – and make it known to the world.

Haffert did not tell his parents about the strange vision of Brother Aloysius, nor did he tell anyone else for that matter. He feared that his parents and others would think he had gone insane if he began to talk about the strange vision of Brother Aloysius and how it was guiding him in this time of need. It wasn't until many years later that Haffert wrote of his deep feelings for the vision in one of his own autobiographical books. "I had a mystical experience that so convinced me of the truth of the Brother's message that nothing, then or since, shook this conviction. But I wondered how it could possibly be carried out."

The answer to that question came from Haffert's uncle John, who suggested that his namesake teach priests. Since his uncle was now the Master of Novices at the Carmelite seminary in Middletown, NY, Haffert approached the Carmelite superior and offered to teach for free. He was still searching for his vocation, he told the superior, and this would give him a chance to continue that search as well as pay back the Carmelite order for the education that it had given him. The superior accepted, and Haffert could soon be found teaching French as well as a new course he developed on Scapular Devotion. Unable to afford an apartment, Haffert later made ends meet by converting his spacious Nash into a flat on wheels, having removed the car seats entirely so that he could lay down a sleeping bag to rest at night.

Haffert expressed a desire to return to the priesthood several times during his tenure in Middletown. But when he did, his uncle and role model suggested that he not even try. Perhaps Uncle John felt that his nephew wasn't made of the stuff of priests. Or perhaps he believed, as Haffert did, that he was being pre-pared to "fulfill the mission of Brother's vision, not in Carmel, but in the world."

That was a retrospective view, written by Haffert shortly before his death, but it may well have been true. The two years spent in the Middletown monastery allowed Haffert to decompress from his rejection by the Carmelites. It also gave him a constant companion in his Uncle John. No matter what Haffert's problem – be it one of doctrine, vocation or feelings of personal failing – Father John was there to act as counselor. "I had a monastic atmosphere," wrote Haffert. "Fr. John guided me, the teaching of Scapularia forced me to spiritual meditation to a considerable extent, and thus I became used to the fact of being a layman, little by little."

Soon, the best part of being in Middletown was the scapular course. For years now Haffert had read about devotion to the scapular. Now, the teaching of this course on Scapular Devotion organized his thoughts. His class notes quickly turned to a book outline. Soon, Haffert was studiously writing a book that he eventually titled Sign of Her Heart, after rejecting his own original title, Mary in Her Scapular Promise.

Haffert sent the book to Archbishop Fulton J. Sheen, the well-known televangelist and inspirational speaker and writer. Sheen wrote an enthusiastic preface to the book, declaring the work a book of devotion that "should bring forth a response which the love that went into its writing deserves."

Although the book was not yet published, Haffert decided to leave the seminary and go on the lecture circuit, stopping first at Immaculata College in Pennsylvania where he discovered to his dismay and horror that only three of the women in the audience of this all-girls school were wearing the Scapular. The same happened at his next stop, Redemptorist Seminary in Esopus, NY, where he discovered that very few in the audience knew anything at all about the Scapular.

Haffert was oddly heartened by this lack of knowledge about the Scapular. What had once been an important devotional item among Catholics seemed to be almost forgotten, even among the faithful. Now his desired vocation as the head of a Scapular Apostolate seemed even more clear and urgent as he realized that church members needed a wakeup call to the power of the Scapular.

When all of this was taking place with Haffert is especially important. It was 1939 and the events that led up to World War II were so overwhelming that even Haffert couldn't ignore them. Hitler had taken Poland and Austria and was clearly amassing forces aimed at taking over Europe. Japan was gobbling up real estate in Asia and planning a secret attack on the United States. For Haffert this meant only one thing: a Scapular had to become a part of every Catholic soldier's uniform. If world leaders could not stave off war and save lives, then it was up to Haffert to use the Scapular to save souls.

With new-found spiritual purpose, Haffert returned home with a business plan for his apostolate. He told his father about his brief speaking tour and the epiphany it gave him about starting a Scapular Society. His first hope would be that The Garden State Publishing Company, his father's business, would publish his recently finished book which he had now switched back to the title of Mary in Her Scapular Promise. He then expressed hope that his father would start a subsidiary to publish other spiritual books, all of which the young Haffert planned to write. Finally, he said, the Scapular community would be bound together by a magazine, called simply The Scapular. Of course, his father would publish that, too.

The senior Haffert immediately rejected his son's plan. He was a hardened businessman and didn't entertain such business ideas without doing his own due diligence. Plus he had other problems. His daughter

Betty wanted to become a Carmelite nun. It was a fate worse than prison, he told his son. "The walls of a cloister seem almost like the walls of death," he declared. "They are so isolating."

Haffert could detect bitterness in his father's voice and with good reason. He had been a devout Catholic all of his life, but between his son being rejected for the priesthood and his daughter being accepted as a nun, the elder Haffert may have felt that he had sacrificed enough with little in return.

Haffert was painfully aware that his refusal into the priesthood was a major disappointment for his parents. To have a son in the priesthood was a dream for his father, a dream that the young Haffert could see had crumbled in his father's face. Friends of the family who knew of Haffert's rejection seemed at time callous about the family's feelings. It was common for people to say that something must be wrong with the young Haffert because the Carmelites refused to make him a priest. Haffert could see his father age before his eyes when things like that were said.

And now here he was, asking for more from his father. Haffert backed off and let fate take over. Within a few days his father's attitude changed completely. Yes, he would start a book imprint to publish his son's book and other Catholic works, including The Scapular magazine. Why the sudden change of attitude?

Haffert later wrote in his autobiography that his father became somewhat embarrassed when his son asked that question. According to young Haffert, his father told him that his life had been a "muddle of odds and ends" until Haffert and his sister were born. "When the lives of you and your sister suddenly appeared in the muddle like magic keys, and the odds and ends formed a radiant mosaic of the Blessed Virgin."

It seems like a very unlikely comment on his father's part and indicates that either the senior Haffert was extremely devout, or that the young Haffert had rewoven his life around the Virgin Mary, even to the point of re-framing memory. It is impossible to tell which is true, although declarations of Mary's divinity arise frequently in conversation of others, as reported by Haffert.

Whatever the case, Haffert immediately readied his book for publication.

Self-publication is fraught with difficulty, even when your father owns the publishing house. But Haffert's luck was finally with him. Buttressed by the a perceived need for the hope that Catholic mysticism would provide during a period of pending war, a preface from Bishop

Sheen, and a general rise in the popularity of Catholicism, Mary in Her Scapular Promise rode the wave of other successful Catholic books of this era. Within a matter of weeks, Haffert's book became a Catholic bestseller, selling more than 100,000 copies and making a small fortune for the Haffert family which owned the Scapular Press.

Haffert, who was not one to rest on his laurels, toured relentlessly, giving lectures in churches all over the East Coast. He was a handsome man, with a bright smile, fit physique and a posture that most men had to go to boot camp to attain. His relaxed bearing and confident smile were enough to freeze the attention of a church congregation. Years later, when Haffert interviewed then Senator John F. Kennedy for a television show, it was remarked by many that the two looked like they belonged to the same family. But it was Haffert's eloquence as a speaker that engaged the attention of those who heard him. And it was the entire package that made him popular with the women.

When it was announced that John Haffert would be speaking at church, more women than men were sure to be in attendance. Part of that was likely the subject matter. The mystical power of Mary, "Mother of God," was always a subject that garnered a lot of female attention. But to hear such a message from a looker like Haffert was a double-draw for a female audience.

Such was the case at the convent of the Third Order Carmelites in Philadelphia. It was there, sur-rounded by an audience of nuns and lay people that Haffert noticed an attractive woman who was being both attentive and flirtatious. Before he could ask the priest in attendance about her, she approached him and asked to speak to him. She was a widow, and a wealthy one at that. She told Haffert that she had been looking for a cause in her life and after hearing him speak with such grand conviction, she was sure that she wanted to devote her life and money to reviving the Brown Scapular to an elevated place of devotion.

Haffert was thrilled, and not just with the fact that someone had offered to spend a fortune on his heart's project. He had given up on the possibility of becoming a priest. Only weeks before meeting the wealthy widow, Haffert had prayed with a Bishop over the very question of whether he should marry. After sincere conversation and deep prayer, the Bishop announced that Haffert would better serve the church if he were to "remain in the world," and not be bound by the insular responsibilities of the priesthood. It is impossible to say if the church saw in Haffert an entrepreneur who could not be happy attending to the narrow concerns of the priesthood, or a man who would have difficulty with his vows of celibacy. Whatever the case, the Bishop suggested that Haffert think hard about marriage, "a holy state to which I should be open."

And now this… a wealthy widow. Was she a gift from God, perhaps? Within a few weeks, as he wrote later, "I had come to know this young lady well. She was a daily communicant, very devoted to Our Lady, well educated, tall, smartly dressed, attractive. And after that short time, she seemed to be in love with me." Haffert too was in love with her. Within six weeks of meeting, the two had set a wedding date for October 7, 1940, the Feast of Our Lady of the Rosary. Then by Haffert's standards, his future wife made a critical mistake. She decided to spend a small portion of her large fortune on a Cadillac. Haffert was beside himself. The thought of spending such a large sum of money on a car was not in keeping with his way of thinking. He tried gently to convince the widow to purchase a lesser-priced vehicle. When that failed, Haffert erupted in anger. Still the widow wouldn't budge. She wanted a Cadillac, apparently more than she wanted Haffert.

"She thought it queer that I should object to, of all things, a new Cadillac," wrote Haffert. Within days of the argument, the wedding date was canceled, and the couple broke up.

Haffert was both heart-broken and heartened. He felt this woman had been somewhat of a God sent, someone sent to show him a new path. Yet even though the break-up was traumatic, his interlude with the lovely widow had shown him other possibilities in life besides the priesthood. He marveled at how much his life had changed. In only the past few months he had gone from being a failed priest and an unpaid teacher at a seminary to being a bestselling author and respected lecturer, one who had the looks and charisma to attract the attention of a wealthy and sophisticated woman. Now he prayed nightly to find a woman he could marry, one who shared his values and deep belief in the power of the Virgin Mary and the mystical Brown Scapular.

The Scapular Press was doing extremely well. Sign of Her Heart had climbed to number one among spiritual books and Haffert had just completed a memoir, The Brother and I, about his relationship at the Carmelite monastery with Brother Aloysius. In this book he spoke freely of the Brother's vision of the banquet with the unknown food, and how this vision had guided him to become an apostle of the Scapular and its message. He was no longer concerned about what anyone thought of this vision and his interpretation of its surreal elements. It was the vision after all that had guided him to write his bestseller and to start the Scapular Press. And now he was convinced that it could lead him to even grander things.

In addition to his own books, the Scapular Press published and handled other works. He acquired the rights to reprint The Mystical City of God, an autobiography of the Virgin Mary alleged to have been revealed by the Virgin herself to the 17th century nun, Maria of Agreda. Haffert also bought up copies of The Glories of Mary by Saint Alphonsus from The Redemptrix press and sold them through the Scapular Press. By early 1941, the Scapular Press was bringing in enormous amounts of money, more than anyone but Haffert could ever dream.

There were benefits to being a rising church figure besides money. Haffert was considered so valuable to the efforts of the church, that the Very Reverend Gabriel Pausback went to Haffert's draft board and obtained an exemption from military service, testifying that "his service is as valuable as that of a priest." Haffert continued to follow the vision of Brother Aloysius, remarking frequently about its uncanny accuracy. Now convinced that he was destined to start a Scapular Apostolate, he wrote a letter to the Prior General of the Carmelite Order, asking to be named "President of an American Scapular Society" with "the power to appoint officers in the Confraternity in America who might become apostles for Our Lady in their own locale."

Before Haffert could send the letter, he received one from Reverend Gabriel Pausback, the Assistant General of the Carmelite Order in New York City, asking Haffert to preside over a Scapular Society that his order wanted to start. It was April of 1941, eight months before the Japanese sneak attack on Pearl Harbor. It was clear, said the Reverend, that America was going to be swept into at least one war – Europe or Asia – before long and he wanted to make sure that as many soldiers as possible went into combat with the mystical protection of the Scapular beneath their uniforms.

Haffert was delighted. He opened an office in New York City near 28th Street and First Avenue and immediately plotted his next moves. Ever the writer and publisher, Haffert decided to start the magazine he had pressured his father to publish. He called the magazine The Scapular. Its goal: to communicate with growing membership of the society, called "the Scapular militia."

Starting a pattern that he would follow later when he founded The Blue Army, a future apostolic organization, Haffert didn't charge for subscriptions to the magazine. Rather, he relied upon donations and as a result received far more money than he would by asking members to pay a specific subscription price. Leaning on the need to protect our men in uniform, the membership grew rapidly to 7,000 "active militia" in just a few months. After the start of World War II, the membership soared to more than 300,000 members, including units of Scapular Militia in nearly every large city across the country. The magazine was publishing a whopping 163,000 copies per month. As Haffert's father would say to him years later, "I think if you were a hobo kicked off a freight train, you would land in a gold mine."

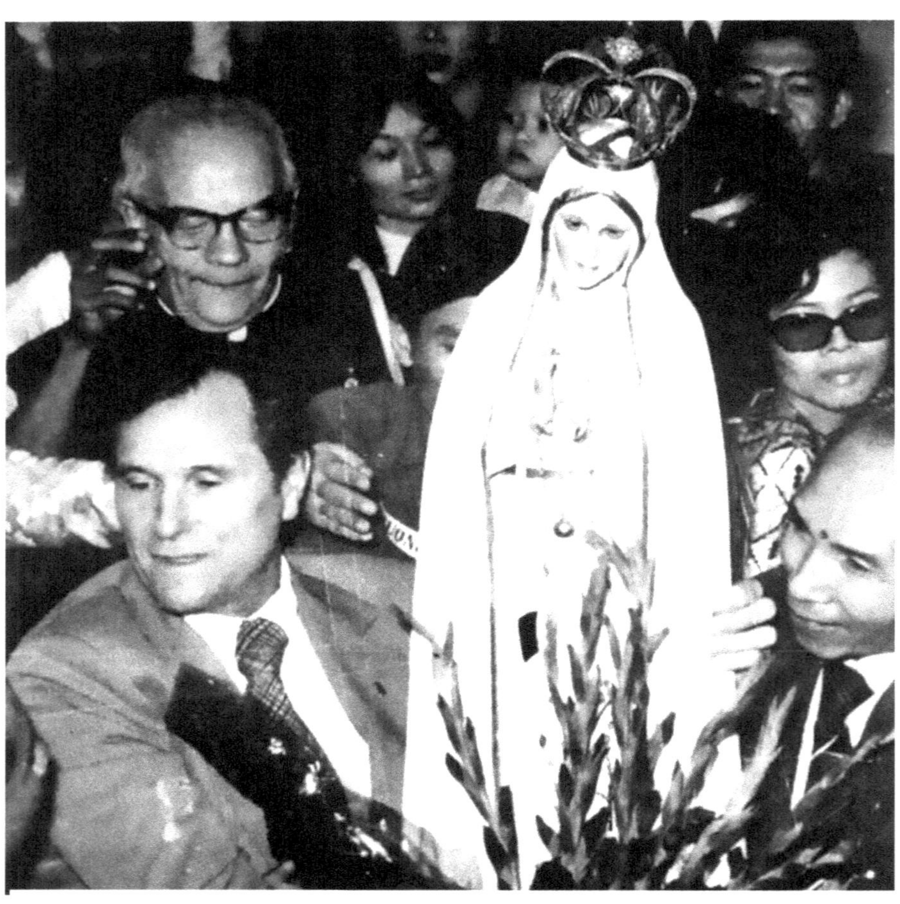

John Haffert carries his Miraculous Pilgrim Virgin Image through a crowd of devotees during one of Her Visits. The image carved by the Michelangelo of Portugal, Master Sculptor José Ferreira Thedim in 1947 has travelled all over the World. In October of 1972 She shed human tears during a Rosary Rally in New Orleans.

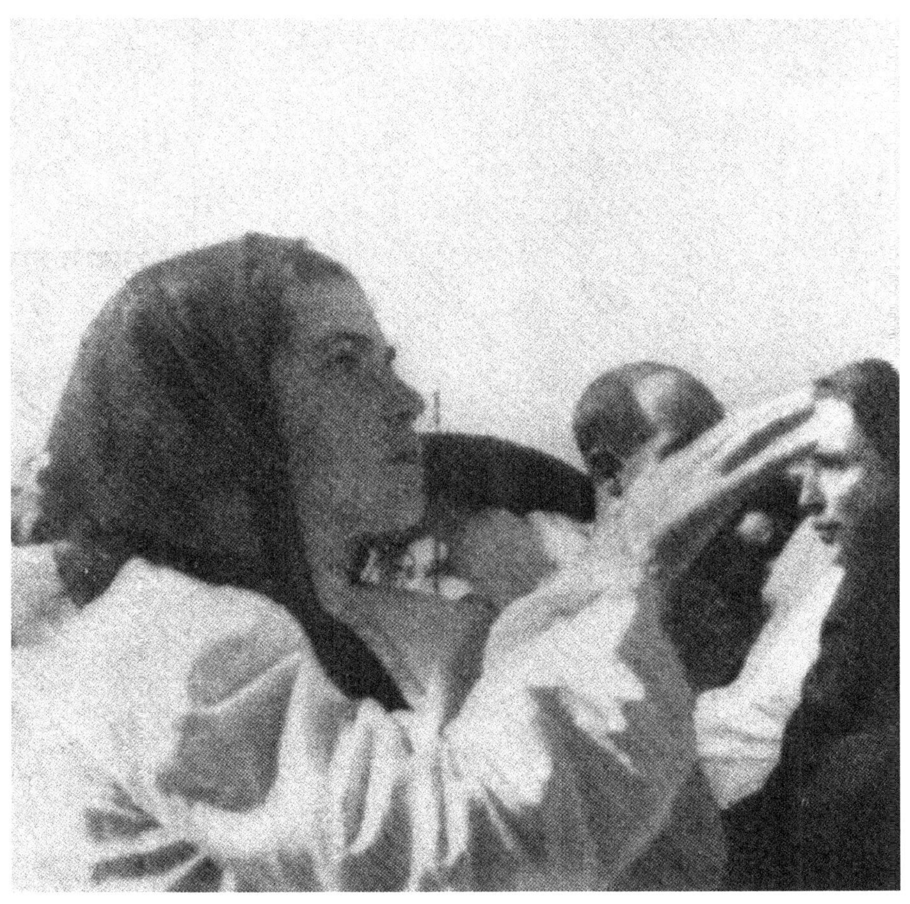

During his first visit to Fátima on May 13th, 1946, John Haffert witnessed and photographed the spontaneous miraculous cure of Arminda de Jesus Campos. Arminda had been paralyzed from the waist down and was dying. She was seen to be pulled to her feet by an invisible Apparition with whom she engaged in conversation. An instant celebrity, Arminda was invited by Sister Lucia to visit her and after becoming a nun, travelled to Rome for a private audience with Pope Pius XII. During the Audience the Pope he asked her what she would reply if God asked her to become paralyzed once again? Arminda replied: "His will be done in me!" With that she tripped on the hem of her habit and fell down the stairs of the Papal Apartments, and broke her spine. Once again a paraplegic, John Haffert rediscovered Arminda at the Fátima Shrine 50 years after the Miracle and afterwards, sponsored her stay in Fátima until her death, having confirmed at the time that the Miracle he had witnessed in 1946 was a sign he had requested from Heaven for his decision to dedicate the rest of his life to the Message of Fátima. Arminda his considered the spirit Godmother of the Blue Army and Oureana Foundation.

10

Mr. Fátima

Haffert couldn't have agreed more, especially given the circumstances of the meeting of his wife-to-be, Anne Kraushaar.

A friend of Haffert's sister-in-law, Kraushaar had been invited to a party thrown by Haffert's brother at a lakeside cabin in the Pennsylvania woods. Unbeknownst to Haffert, his brother Horace invited the pert blonde just for him. Before long they were in deep conversation about Haffert's Scapular Society and his intense devotion to the Virgin Mary.

Anne owned a children's clothing store in downtown Philadelphia and was not looking for a boyfriend or husband. But when she first saw Haffert as he was throwing a log into the campfire, she saw the man she wanted to marry. A year later, the two were married at the Carmelite monastery by his Uncle John.

As World War II raged, the success of the Scapular Society continued to grow. Thousands of members came on board, largely because of the promise of the scapular itself: those who die wearing a Scapular will be saved from Hell. By signing up for the society, parents were sending this celestial rabbits foot to their soldiers in the field. By the end of the war, there were more people wearing Brown Scapulars than at any time in history, even the Middle Ages. Catholics had signed more than a million pledges to the Scapular Apostolate by the end of 1946.

Haffert could have rested on his laurels for years to come. He had started a religious society from scratch and turned it into an influential and wealthy organization with worldwide reach. His book publishing company was doing well and there was no end in sight to the number of subjects that he wanted to cover in his own writing.

But Haffert was a man of action who couldn't resist pressing ahead – sometimes without adequate forethought – on ideas of his own germination.

One such idea came along in 1946 with the 100th anniversary of the consecration of the United States to the Immaculate Conception. Despite the obscurity of the event, Haffert was still able to convince the Mutual Broadcasting Network to cover it by promising a proclamation from Cardinal Spellman of New York. The cardinal was delighted at the notion, promptly notifying Haffert that he would write an appropriate statement.

Haffert beamed when he heard the prelate's response. Such coverage was a coupe for Haffert and put him firmly on the Cardinal's radar screen. But the position turned into a target, however, when the network canceled the broadcast at the last minute. Cardinal Spellman blamed the cancellation on Haffert, who had not told him when the network first threatened to cancel the coverage. The Cardinal was very well connected, he told Haffert, certainly with a touch of irony. Maybe he could have convinced those in charge at the network to change their minds. Instead Haffert had waited until it was too late, and as a result had squandered an opportunity, at least in the eyes of the cardinal.

The rebuke was devastating for Haffert, but not enough to stop the ambitious publisher and author from pursuing other successful and profitable projects. One of those projects was to travel to Fátima, Portugal where he would begin research on a biography of Dom Nuno Alavares Pereira, a scapular devotee from the 14th century and the George Washington of Portugal.

The year was 1946 and this was the first time Haffert had been to Portugal. His first stop was Fátima. He wanted to visit the site of the apparitions and meet friends and family of the seers. Two of the children – Jacinto and Francisco - were dead, lost to Spanish flu which swept the world in 1918, only a year after the Apparitions. But Lucia was still living, now a cloistered nun living in Coimbra. Although she rarely accepted visitors and then usually spoke through an intermediary that she whispered to, Haffert was hoping that his charisma and good luck would get him an audience with the silent witness.

Things worked out for Haffert better than he planned. He visited

Ourém Castle near Fátima and fell in love with the magical fortress. So much in love that he began to purchase valuable historic property, including relics of Nuno, his patron and protector. Eventually, Haffert would buy much of the land and housing on the perimeter of the stupendous castle, much of which is still held in a foundation he founded for that purpose.

Haffert told many people over the years that he became Portuguese on that first visit, in part because of its beauty and history, and in part because of a supernatural event that took place on this first trip. It was May 13, 1946, the anniversary of the first vision of Fátima, and what Haffert witnessed that day would change the course of his life. From that day foreword he would be a man entirely dedicated to the Blessed Virgin Mary but under the banner of Her Fátima Message.

Haffert went to the tiny chapel built on the spot of the apparitions and stood where a group of sick people had assembled in wheelchairs and stretchers. Suddenly he noticed, as many people did, a young Portuguese woman named Arminda De Jesus Campos as she became deeply engaged in a conversation with an invisible being she claimed to see standing behind the Cardinal.

According to Arminda's account, this apparition was a shining figure clothed in white that beckoned her to: "Get up and walk." But Arminda was incapable of walking. Her organs were shutting down due to a degenerative disease and she had been unable to walk for several years. She was protesting loudly that walking was impossible for her to do.

Haffert turned on his movie camera and began to film Arminda when she was forcibly pulled to her feet by an invisible hand that grabbed her by her coat, precisely at the chest.

At that moment probes and tubes were pulled right out of her limbs and an open fissure in her abdomen closed up!

Doctors and nurses in attendance were dumbfounded. And so was Haffert. He knew the miracle had taken place as a supernatural healing for Arminda, who was now on her feet and looking puzzled, but he felt it had happened for his benefit as well. Haffert had carried a certain amount of skepticism for the apparitions at Fátima, but now his doubt disappeared.

Arminda was indeed cured and became an instant international Catholic celebrity. That year and for years following, she was on the cover of popular Catholic magazines like Stella and was even invited to visit the sole surviving Fátima Seer Sister Lucia, the sole surviving Fátima seer. But the miracle witnessed by John Haffert made him want to live and breathe everything Fátima and to dedicate his life's mission to the message of Our Lady: the devotion of the First Saturdays, the praying of the rosary and the wearing of the scapular.

Emboldened by the witnessing of the miracle, Haffert decided to visit Bishop D. José Alves Correia da Silva of the restored Diocese of Leiria who ruled over the cult of Fátima. He was a man who had been tortured by the anti-clerical government in 1910 and who was now confined to a wheelchair.

As if by chance on the day he visited the Bishop, the Prelate had just received a visit from the Marquesa de Cadaval, Olga Cadaval. A direct descendant of Saint Nuno she had given D. José a major relic of the Carmelite hero, who happened to be Haffert's Patron Saint.

The coincidence was seen as a divine sign for both men and sparked a friendship that would endure until the Bishop's death.

Olga Cadaval, it should be said, was not only an aristocrat but also a volunteer with the sick at the Fátima Shrine and eventually became Portugal's greatest Patron of the Arts. She was the first person of influence to support and promote contemporary art in Portugal and had personally helped and welcomed into her home in Lisbon, artists like Pablo Picasso and later Salvador Dalí. Her legacy today lives on in Portugal's Olga Cadaval Cultural Centre.

Olga had another important volunteer job. She was Sister Lucia's personal, (albeit unofficial) secretary and interpreter, having been later authorized by Pope Pius XII to meet with the seer after she entered the Cloistered Carmelite Order in Coimbra, whenever necessary and without impediments of any nature, provided she reported back to the Pope after every visit.

With a handwritten letter from the Bishop saying "You are to receive this person as if he were the Bishop himself," Haffert strode with confidence into the convent.

Haffert expected to find a person who was both confident and at peace. What he found was quite the opposite. He presented the card to the Prioress who ushered him into a private room where he waited for the seer.

A sister wearing an apron came into the room, bowed with a smile and began sweeping and scrubbing the floor with a brush and pail. When she finished she left. Shortly the same sister returned without the apron and presented herself as Sister Lucia. Haffert was perplexed. What was the

Seer of Fátima doing scrubbing floors?

The answer, said Lucia, was that the Prioress, out of jealousy, had submitted Lucia to the humiliation of cleaning the room before receiving her guests and in the presence of her very guests. Out of humble obedience Lucia complied without complaining.

Haffert was amazed. He expected to find a nun who was as radiant as the Apparitions she had seen. Instead he found a taciturn woman who was unhappy at how little she had been used to spread the message of Fátima. She had been in the Convent now for 25 years and in many ways felt as though she was the church's parrot.

Not being in a cloistered Order but rather a religious congregation of teaching sisters, Lucia was made responsible for chores. She longed for the contemplative life and the cloister and asked Pope Pius XII in a letter and through Olga Cadaval for permission to join the Carmelites. The Pope instead gave her a sabbatical. A one-year vacation to return to Portugal and visit Fátima and then decide if indeed she wanted to become a contemplative nun.

Haffert felt sorry for the nun but tried to stick to business. "Have you written what you remember of the apparitions?" he asked.

Lucia confirmed she had already written for the bishop everything she had experienced in 1917, including the three-part secret of The Vision of Hell. Now she wanted peace and quiet. She wanted to return home to Portugal and find protection behind the walls of a Cloistered Carmelite Convent.

Contrary to what is commonly believed, the Pope, the Bishop of Leiria and all of the high ranking local and Vatican Officials wanted the exact opposite. They wanted her in a secular institution where she would be readily accessible for consultation much like a highly valued original copy of a precious manuscript.

Lucia told Haffert that she felt trapped. She related how on Sundays when she could go for a walk with the nuns across the bridge that separated the border between Spain and Portugal, they would be met halfway by pilgrims and curiosity seekers who would inquire if the Seer of Fátima, Sister Lucia, was at the Convent?

Calmly Sister Lucia would reply: "I can tell you for certain she is not there!" The sad crowd would then head back to Portugal not knowing that they had actually met the Fátima Seer. Lucia would smile and continue on her walk not having to be pestered by her fans. The World was falling apart around her, she told Haffert, as no one had heeded the requests for the Pope to Consecrate Russia in order to prevent the spread of Atheist Communism.

For years, said Lucia, Olga Cadaval and other visiting nobles from Portugal had informed the Bishop of Leiria and the Pope that Lucia was being mistreated by her Spanish Superiors at the Convent, who per-haps didn't believe she had actually seen the Apparitions she was known for.

But she'd had more Apparitions and Visions since joining the Dorothean's, she told Haffert. One time she had seen the child Jesus in her room at the Convent in Pontevedra, Spain, and spoke to him for fifteen minutes. When she told the other nuns of the Apparition they acted as though she were subconsciously imagining things in order to get back the public attention she had enjoyed as a child Seer.

The same thing happened with a second Apparition of the child Jesus, she told Haffert. She was given the odorous job of carrying waste from the Convent cesspool to the sewer in the street when a child approached and watched her sadly. Jokingly she told the little boy to go to the church and see if a few Hail Marys would earn him some play time with the Child Jesus. Suddenly, she told Haffert, she realized that the little boy was the Child Jesus.

"What is being done to promote the devotion to the Immaculate Heart of my Mother in the World?" the little boy asked.

She promised to talk to the Mother Superior, but when she did it was clear that the jealous nun didn't believe the Apparition had ever taken place.

Haffert summed up his meeting with Sister Lucia in his own words, saying: "Lucia had felt complete-ly helpless, in the restrictive capacity of a Dorothean nun, to propagate the Message of Fátima. One by one, the prophecies were coming true." But Sister Lucia was trapped in a convent.

+ + +

But while he was in Portugal, Haffert came up with an idea that he later deemed as being "a fatal error." Pope Pius XII declared the image of Our Lady at Fátima "Queen of the World." This thrilled Haffert, who proposed to the Bishop of Leiria that they should have a sculpture create two traveling images known as Pilgrim Virgins to bring the message of Fátima to every country of the world. The bishop thought this was a wonderful idea, and Haffert wasted no time. He paid for the Sculptor José Ferreira Thedim, known as the Michelangelo of Portugal, twice as much as his usual fee to carve two twin images of Our Lady. Thedim was thrilled, and carved both images on his knees to show his devotion to the Lady and the project.

Haffert's idea was that each image would be blessed and crowned at Fátima by the Bishop and then crowned by the Pope and every leader of every country it visited so in this way Mary could truly be inter-nationally acclaimed as Queen. One image would be owned by the Fátima Shrine and the other personally by Haffert.

The sculpture would be photographed at each of its stops, showing that the word of God, through the presence of His mother, was everywhere. At each place these images received physical homage as Queen from the locals. In many countries the image received gold bejeweled crowns, scepters, halos, rosaries, robes, and other priceless gifts. And at each place She visited, regardless of race, color or creed, she was heralded Queen of that Country. The passage of the image in Spain and France opened borders for the first time that had been closed for many decades and one of the great highlights of the Pilgrim Virgin's travels was the Consecration of Spain to the Immaculate Heart pronounced by Generalissimo Francisco Franco before the image on his knees in the great Plaza in Madrid.

Haffert and Bishop da Silva's ultimate plan was that one of the two twin international Pilgrim Virgin images would visit all of the Countries of the East and the other all of the Countries of the West. Eventually when they had both covered all of the countries on the globe, they would both meet in Red Square in Moscow for the triumph of the Immaculate Heart of Mary over Communism.

Such an act was highly illegal in the Soviet Union, leading to possible imprisonment or worse for the person transporting such a religious icon. Haffert prepared for such an event. Naming devotee Robert Nesnick a "Fátima Secret Agent," Haffert helped him plan his journey to Moscow. Unbeknownst to Haffert, Nesnick took with him cyanide tablets in case the plan turned sour and the Fátima Secret Agent was captured.

The Pilgrim Virgin plan was in place. Unfortunately for Haffert, he forgot to request the permission of Cardinal Spellman. For a man so firmly in the Cardinal's cross hairs, this was a critical error. He claimed to the end of his life that he didn't think that he needed the consent of Cardinal Spellman to bring in the images. "It was the purpose of the Pilgrim Virgin to go to any diocese to which it was invited," he wrote of his venture. In retrospect, though, conferring with the "US Vatican," as Cardinal

Spellman's office was only half-jokingly referred to, should have been foremost in Haffert's mind.

As Cardinal Spellman seethed, Haffert took the images to Canada, where Archbishop Vachon warmly greeted him at the airport. The motorcade of local politicians and religious officials was "miles long," according to an account written by Haffert, and the faithful who gathered at the Cathedral in Ottawa numbered in the thousands. It was there that Archbishop Vachon consecrated his diocese and then all of Canada to Her as "Queen of the World."

Hearing of the success of the Pilgrim Virgin in Canada, Bishop O'Hara invited Haffert and the image to come to Buffalo, New York, where traffic jams were the resulted from the crowds who came to see the Queen.

Bishop O'Hara was thrilled. At a Bishop's meeting in Washington, DC, O'Hara told his fellow prelates about the public reaction to the image. He even offered to accompany Haffert and the Pilgrim Virgin to any diocese in the United States that wanted to display the charismatic image.

Many of the Bishops were impressed with O'Hara's message. They knew that the faith of the followers required constant renewal. Given the attendance records they had heard so far, it seemed likely that the faith of a large number of Catholics would be strengthened by such a show of camaraderie.

Cardinal Spellman didn't agree. Processing the image of the Blessed Virgin Mary was inappropriate, he declared. He felt that local homage to the "Queen of the World" should be less a circus and more of a solemn dignified royal and aristocratic affair.

After all, Cardinal Francis Spellman was old school and wore the full trappings of a Church Prince with Pride. In matters of US Catholic affairs he was the infallible Mini Pope! If anyone should welcome and accompany the Queen of Heaven it should be he!

Cardinal Spellman's strong opinion on the public display of the Pilgrim Virgin did not resonate with all of the Bishops. Bishop Waters of Raleigh, North Carolina asked Haffert to send him the sculpture so he could display Her for veneration and homage. And when he was finished, the Pilgrim Virgin was passed along to Bishops all across the country until, as Haffert wrote, "(T)he wave of devotion swept through all America until almost EVERY BISHOP finally had received the image and laid his crosier and miter at Our Lady's feet."

Haffert was so delighted with the Pilgrim Virgin's acclamation process that he was completely blind-sided by what came next. Disturbed that he was being ignored by a layman, Cardinal Spellman wrote a letter to the Carmelite provincial suggesting that Haffert as the leader of the movement, be replaced by a priest.

On a Friday afternoon, Haffert was summoned by a nervous and red-faced priest from Spellman's office who told him he was no longer the head of the Scapular Apostolate. The priest kept it short. As Haffert sat stunned, he was told that Cardinal Spellman had made the request to replace him. The "why" of his decision was not made clear, but Haffert couldn't help but see that his relationship with the Cardinal had not been good.

Haffert was escorted from the offices. When he told his wife what had happened, she could hardly believe it. No explanation had been given to him, other than the Cardinal's desire to have a priest in Haffert's position. So when he told his wife why he thought he had been fired, she didn't believe him. She doubted that so powerful a Cardinal could be so petty as to replace her husband in the hardships of this volunteer duty to escort his own image. For years after the replacement, Anne didn't fully believe that her husband had been removed for such a small transgression. She like many Catholic women believed Spellman to be a Saint and so if he chose to replace Haffert, something else must have caused that. The painful event drove a wedge between Haffert and his wife that festered for years to come.

If his replacement didn't seem real on Friday, it truly sunk in on Monday when he returned to gather his personal belongings. When he went into the offices, an embarrassed priest refused to let him enter his own private office. Instead the priest had gathered the files and effects that were his and promised to deliver them to his apartment later in the week. Within minutes, John Haffert, was out on the street. He was now, officially, the "ex" President of the Scapular Apostolate.

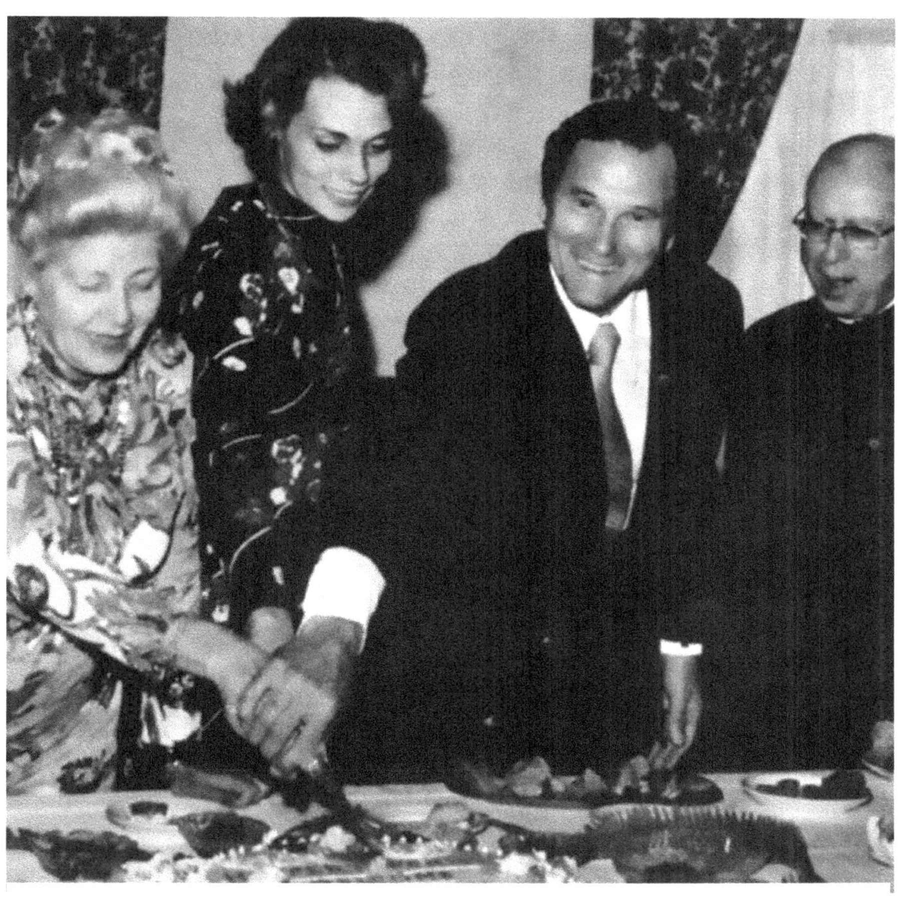

John Haffert with his first wife Anne and daughter Betty host the Bishop of Leiria - Fátima D. João Pereira Venâncio during a family party held at their home in New Jersey.

11

The Calling

Being fired was devastating. Not only had it left him with no direction in life, it also left him with no means of financial support to take care of his wife and their newly adopted daughter, Elizabeth. Afraid of financial ruin, the Hafferts had been forced to put their Long Island home on the market. Haffert felt as though he would have to take up a new career, perhaps working as an ad salesman for his father's magazines. The thought of moving to a profession so far from his heart's calling was so distressing that Haffert feared he would soon have a nervous breakdown.

He wrote all of this to Brother Aloysius, expecting mountains of sympathy. Instead, the Brother insisted that God had his reasons for giving such a strenuous trial to Haffert. "Your greatest work lies ahead," wrote the Brother.

Believing that no good could come of this personal tragedy, Haffert was almost offended by the Brother's positive response. Plus, there were other problems brewing on the near horizon. The Hafferts were living in central New Jersey now, on a 127-acre farm that Haffert purchased before his wife had a chance to inspect the property. She was distraught at what she saw. A 200-year-old stone house was the main living quarters. All four bedrooms of the farmhouse could have fit into the living area of their home on the Long Island Sound. Next to it was a garage with a room above it that Haffert planned to use as an oratory, a place for private prayer. Across the open field was a large barn for the animals that would become the heart of the farm that Haffert was planning.

A place like this was Anne's personal nightmare. On her first visit she looked out the window of the ancient house and saw a dirt road that was close to the front door and was the source of clouds of dust every time a car passed. There were few neighbors, and a far distance to walk to their front door if she even chose to go. Anne was a city girl who'd had a life of city sounds, smells and activity. A farm in Washington, New Jersey was not some place she wanted to live. Add to that the fact that the firing of her husband by a powerful Cardinal traumatized Anne to such a degree that she never got over it, and you have a recipe for domestic disaster.

Haffert was aware of his wife's discontent, but largely ignored it. He was happy on the farm and soon purchased 63 cows and several horses. He began writing another book, this one with the bold title, Russia Will Be Converted. He also began to dissect his life, searching for moments in the past that could lead him in future endeavors.

And with that, the idea of an apostolate for Fátima began to bore into Haffert. He saw it as a powerful area of Catholic mysticism that was being ignored, one that combined visions, miracles and even the Brown Scapular. With an apostolate that focused on the Apparitions of Fátima, Haffert would have everything he'd had in the Brown Scapular apostolate and more, including a contemporary story, an attractive geographic location, and miracles witnessed by tens of thousands of people. For a Catholic layman like Haffert, Fátima was an apostolate dream.

But still he was gun shy. Cardinal Spellman had shut him down once. Would he allow Haffert a second chance with another apostolate? Haffert had no idea and was not interested in seeking an audience with Spellman to find out.

Still the idea of starting a Fátima apostolate was very much on Haffert's mind.

But there were other things on his mind, too. There was the secret Pilgrim Virgin, the image he had snuck out of Fátima and returned to his New Jersey home. Eventually Haffert hoped to sneak the image into Russia. For now, however, he planned to enthrone the effigy in the oratory he had built over his garage.

Acclaiming and enthroning the Pilgrim Virgin involved more than just putting her on a pedestal. The Pilgrim Virgin image had been around the world, acknowledged by presidents, prime ministers, dictators and royalty. The magnificent image had been lucky to make such a journey safely, and because of that Haffert felt the Pilgrim Virgin was infused with mystical power. To treat her with the respect she deserved, Haffert went in search of a priest who could enthrone the image with a prayer ceremony, while at the same time keeping her presence in New Jersey a secret from church officials. He found just such a priest in Monsignor Colgan, a longtime priest in Plainfield, New Jersey.

Haffert had met Msgr. Colgan on his first trip to Portugal. When he returned to New Jersey, Haffert had gone to Colgan's parish to speak and found himself impressed by the devotion he found there, not only Colgan's but the entire congregation.

The hall where he spoke was filled with the faithful. Almost everyone was wearing blue, a sign that they had joined the March of Pledges, a promise made to follow the message of Our Lady of Fátima, that Haffert was speaking about that night. Haffert had great expertise in the pledge. At his meeting with Sister Lucia, the two had written the pledge so that others could understand what it was she expected of believers. Colgan was one such believer and promoted devotion to her as a means of receiving guidance. He told those who had taken the pledge to wear something blue that night as "a sign of our pledge to be The Blue Army of Our Lady."

Haffert remembered Colgan and decided to call him to enthrone the Pilgrim Virgin and bless the oratory.

Colgan arrived, accompanied by two nuns and a parishioner who was festooned in blue ribbons as a sign of her devotion.

Before leaving that night, the parishioner, whose name was Marie Hart, suggested that Haffert work with Colgan. She most likely meant that Haffert help the Monsignor in his bid to get more Catholics involved in the March of Pledges. Haffert saw it a different way. He saw Colgan as someone who could help him start and operate an apostolate devoted to the message of Fátima.

Colgan was looking for just such an opportunity. Several months before meeting Haffert, the priest had a massive heart attack. He was given only six months to live by his doctors and prescribed complete bed rest.

While lying in bed, Colgan prayed for recovery. He bargained with God, telling him that he would spend the rest of his life spreading devotion to Our Lady of Fátima if he could walk out of the hospital a well man. A week later he discharged himself from the hospital and walked to the church where he delivered Christmas Mass to the children in his parish.

He began to promote devotion through the pledge that Haffert and

Sister Lucia had written together. As he promoted the pledge, he encouraged his parishioners to wear the color blue Mary was reported to have worn in the Fátima Apparitions. By wearing something blue, he declared, the parishioners would "stand up and be counted on our Lady's side in the struggle with the powers of evil."

In Msgr Colgan, Haffert saw a man with enough dignity and devotion to help lead an apostolate for Fátima. Haffert had no doubts in Msgr Colgan's abilities as a priest and his loyalty to Our Lady. His doubts were in himself. Could he really start a new apostolate without it being taken from him by Cardinal Spellman?

A few days after his meeting with Msgr. Colgan, Haffert got his answer. In a "confluence of truly extraordinary happenings," Haffert was in New York City for the first time since being fired by the Cardinal. He was walking past a restaurant when he happened to see Father Daniel Lord sitting alone at a window table.

Father Lord was the founder and director of a lay society called the Queen's Work in St. Louis, MO. He was a good friend of Haffert's and had wanted the layman to come to work for him after he was released by Cardinal Spellman. Before Haffert could decide, the offer was withdrawn by Father Lord out of concern that the offer may look like a challenge to the Cardinal's authority.

Haffert held no grudge. In fact, he saw this chance meeting as a sign from God. Surely Father Lord would know if it was God's Will that he start an apostolate dedicated to the message of Fátima.

Haffert stormed happily into the restaurant and sat down with the surprised priest. Both agreed that for them to be in town on the same day, and to be at the same street corner at the same time in the largest city in America was truly providence. There must be a reason, said the priest. There is, declared Haffert.

"What would you think if I were to team up with Father Harold Colgan to promote the message of Fátima," asked Haffert.

Father Lord lit up. "There would be an explosion for our Lady," he declared.

Haffert was so enthused that when he returned home he told his wife Anne that he was starting the apostolate as soon as possible. She was delighted for the first time since moving to New Jersey. She missed the days of the Scapular Apostolate and wanted her husband to start another such lay operation. She never truly believed that Cardinal Spellman had fired her husband for such a petty infraction as touring the Pilgrim Image without his express permission. She felt there had been other issues that were not told to her by her husband. This doubt in Haffert caused tension in their marriage. Now she enthusiastically backed her husband, hoping that he could indeed return to the lay priesthood with no interference from the pow-erful Cardinal.

Haffert immediately wrote to Bishop Griffin of Trenton, NJ, for permission to start a publishing house to promote the message of Fátima. Impressed with Haffert's work in the Scapular Apostolate, the bishop gave him the necessary permission.

With permission in hand, Haffert went to Msgr Colgan, who agreed to join as the co-director of the new apostolate, one they would call The World Apostolate of Fátima, or "The Blue Army" a reference to Msgr Colgan's request to those who had signed the March of Pledges to wear something blue. "We will be The Blue Army of our Lady against the Red Armies of atheism," he declared.

With his wife's blessing, Haffert committed all of their savings to start a new publishing company. Called the Ave Maria Institute (AMI), the new press was dedicated to publishing apostolate books as well as a magazine called *Soul*. In addition, he asked the Carmelites to return the Scapular Press to him, along with the rights to all of its books and its mailing list. They did so, and with that, Haffert was back in business.

+++

The first issue of *Soul* was published in January 1950 and went out to only about 800 people. Haffert's marketing genius was clear from the very beginning. In the first issue he wrote that neither Msgr Colgan nor the parish he worked for contributed money to The Blue Army. All of the finances for the organization, he pointed out, had come from the Haffert's personally.

There was no subscription price for *Soul*. Subscribers paid what they wanted, even if it was nothing at all. At its peak, the magazine had more than 240,000 subscribers. And those who signed The Blue Army

Pledge (formerly the March of Pledges) contained in the magazine were never solicited for money, but their names and addresses were buried in the ground at Fátima under the large tree, near the place where the Apparitions had taken place. Over the years, say apostolate officials, the names of more than 25 million people were buried on the grounds before they quit counting.

The success of *Soul* was at the center of The Blue Army. Without it, there would have been no way to build and link the membership. And Haffert knew it. He approached the magazine very methodically, tailoring each issue to six questions:

1/ Does this issue persuade readers to make the PLEDGE, keep it, and get other to make it?

2/ Does it explain the URGENCY of this commitment?

3/ Does it elicit SUPPORT?

4/ Does it increase RESPECT for The Blue Army as the official World Apostolate of Fátima?

5/ Does it include articles on the SCAPULAR, THE ROSARY, and THE FIRST SATURDAYS?

6/ Is there a THEME (a special message) in this particular issue?

Haffert saw the magazine as his opportunity to reach thousands of interested people, six times per year. Before long, though, he was reaching tens of thousands of interested people and then hundreds of thousands. At its peak, *Soul* was mailed to 243,000 people, each a contributor of money and goodwill to the organization.

From its beginning in 1950 in the oratory room above Haffert's garage, The Blue Army grew to become one of the wealthiest and most influential apostolates in the Catholic world. Not only did they build a huge church and rectory on the 140 acres in Washington, NJ, they also built a World Center for The Blue Army at Fátima that included a 300-room hotel. To get people there, Haffert started the Fátima Travel Agency, and eventually purchased two Boeing 707 to offer less expensive flights. He opened offices in a number of locations worldwide. He wrote at least one book a year. Yet he was always on the prowl for another way in which to promote The Blue Army.

In many ways that was why he liked the idea of having Salvador Dalí paint The Vision of Hell. It was 1959 now, and Haffert faced a marketing dilemma. Baby Boomers – people born after the war – were coming of age and few of them were interested in church activities over such modern culture distractions as music and art. That was when Brother Michael's letter about Salvador Dalí came to mind.

A Dalí painting of any of the Apparitions of Fátima would bring an entirely different group of people to Fátima and The Blue Army. A painting by Dalí would bring the attention of a wealthier and more refined audience to the apostolate. He was, after all, the most prolific and reproduced artist in the world.

If his paintings were in most every public art gallery in the world, his lithographs and prints were made available through mail order to all most every household in North America. When Dalí declared in his impenetrable Spanish accent that he was the best-known artist in the world, he was probably correct. Fine art marketers of all kind, including tissue companies, had made sure of that. It was not uncommon for a household in the sixties to receive as many as two or three solicitations for Dalí artwork. Dalí had his wife Gala to thank for that. She was both the dream and nightmare of the master artist. She worked him hard – some say relentlessly – to produce volumes of works of all types and quality so she could sell it to the many different markets that had demand for her husband's genius.

She was among the first of the post-war art marketers to realize that fine art for the masses was a viable way to make a mint. If everyone wanted to own a masterpiece by her husband, Gala was ripe for providing it, even if it were one of ten thousand. For Gala, the art was in making money, and there was nothing her famous husband liked more than lots of it. As a result, Gala was free to practice her art, too. And as a result, Salvador Dalí had become among the richest and most famous artists to ply a brush.

A Dalí painting of *The Vision of Hell* would not go unnoticed. Haffert felt it would be a major event in the art world.

He had been following Brother Michael's progress through the religious bureaucracy and was impressed with the young man's drive. Brother Michael wrote eloquently of his plans to the Bishop of Leria in

Portugal, the bishop in charge of Fátima. He also wrote to the Cardinal in Bologna, Italy, considered one of the cardinals most interested in promulgating the message of Fátima. He sent copies of his letters to Haffert.

The purpose of the letters was to enlist the help of these powerful clergymen in gaining Sister Lucia's cooperation. Brother Michael explained that he had personal money in the amount of "eight and nine thousand dollars" that he wanted to use to commission "a great painter, preferably Salvador Dahli" (sp) to paint *The Vision of Hell* seen by the three children. It was his hope that Dalí would be able to interview Sister Lucia, who was the only survivor of the three visionary children, to recreate the vision through her description. He knew sister Lucia did not want to talk about the horror she saw in that vision, but he felt it was her duty to do so. As he told Bishop Venâncio:

> (*The Vision of Hell*) *could not have been soley for the benefit of the children. Their death and the salvation of their souls had been foretold. Surely it was given because God recognized a great need.*
>
> *Knowing that souls can be saved by a fear of damnation, and seeing that eternal punishment has ceased to be a reality to millions, He gave this vision that men might come to know of the existence of Hell and have a vivid mental picture of the penalty for sin. No doubt such an image in the minds of many could be a great deterrent to evil and is therefore infinitely worthwhile.*
>
> *Actually, the fact that God, in his infinite wisdom, granted this vision is a clear indication of its value. God, who cannot be wrong, who cannot make a mistake, gave it for the salvation of souls. But if it is to be fruitful the people must know about it, they must see it, it must be presented to them in the most vivid possible medium.*

To Cardinal Lercaro, Brother Michael wrote:

> *But this, like the other great gift of Fátima, is conditional. All of us know that unless men demonstrate the necessary faith and devotion and make the necessary sacrifices,*

Russia will not be converted. Unless a few men have enough faith in the wisdom of God to see and recognize the fact that He who cannot make a a mistake, who can do no wrong, gave this vision for a purpose, the salvation of souls, and unless someone is willing to act on this faith and present the gift to the people, it will be wasted and the souls that our Lord intended to save may be lost.

Brother Michael acknowledged that he had discussed the idea with many, including Haffert, yet none thought she would cooperate. He requested of both clergymen that they ask Sister Lucia to grant Dalí interviews about what she saw when the earth cracked open before her.

Sister has given herself completely to God and has done extraordinary penances for sinners. Surely she will not refuse to cooperate with what may well be God's plain for saving many. Surely if she realizes that out Holy Mother gave this vision for souls, that it must be presented to the people to be of any value, and that a realistic reproduction on canvas of what she saw is the logical way of presenting it, she will willingly give her cooperation and assistance.

Brother Michael ended his letter to the cardinal with a bold statement about the project's importance. "I hope this letter meets with your Eminence's approval. I believe that if this project is completed God's will shall be done and mankind will receive a grand blessing."

The letters were sent to the two clergymen on September 25, 1960. On October 25, Cardinal Lercaro responded.

I am convinced that there are many people today who do not deny Hell but who put it way back in their minds; as a result, the idea of Hell does not have any effect on their moral and spiritual lives.

Your project looks to me like a useful instrument for reminding men of a truth that is at once certain and potent.

But I doubt that it would be easy to arrange direct collaboration with the surviving prophet, Sister Lucia.

However, I think that a good artist might glean from Lucia's published pronouncements the elements necessary for a work of art that would be capable of inspiring the soul of men.

**Asking the Lord's blessings on you and your work,
I remain, devotedly, Yours in Christ,
Giacomo Cardinal Lercaro, Archbishop**

Although Brother Michael was disappointed to receive no promise of help from the Cardinal, he accepted the possibility that the artist could work from her public descriptions. Maybe Dalí could even go to Portugal and seek inspiration himself from the site of the Apparitions, Brother Michael suggested. Whatever the case, nothing would stop the production of this painting. As he wrote in a letter to Haffert.

"Regardless of the cooperation that sister gives us we will go on with the painting," he wrote. "If she refuses to give any assistance the artist can fill-in where the description is incomplete. However I still think that the more authentic the reproduction is, the more effective the painting will be."

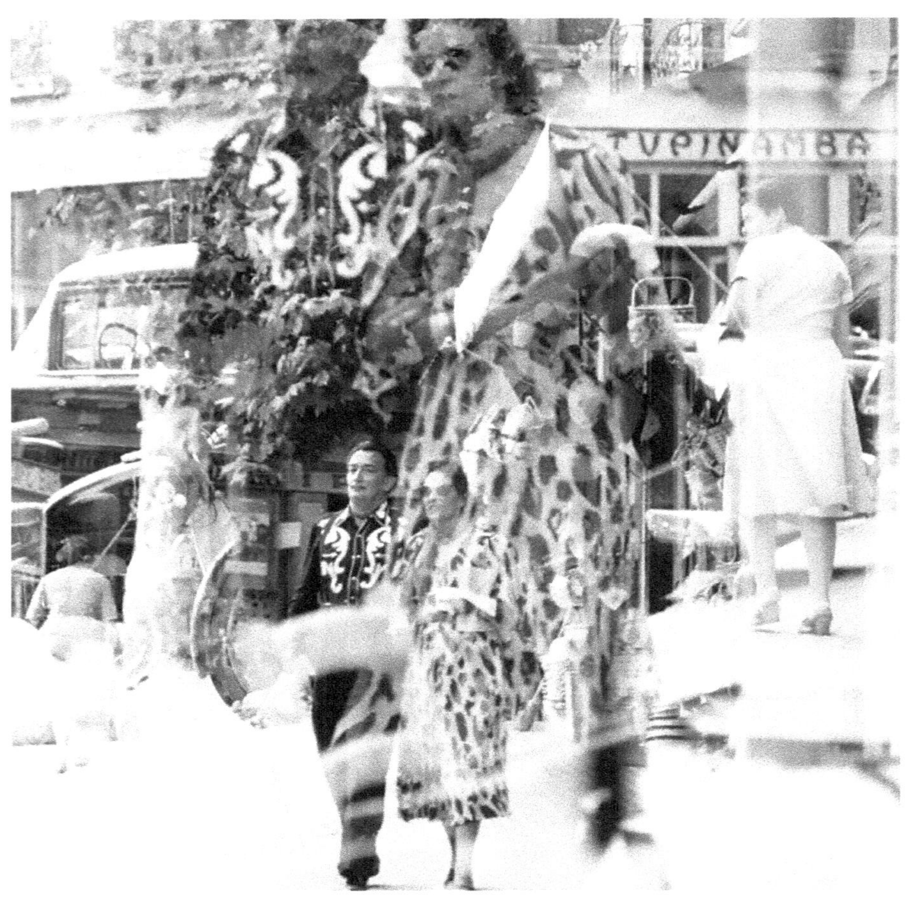

Salvador Dalí and his wife Gala photographed by Robert Descharnes casting their reflection in a department store window.

12

Dear Mr. Dalí

The letter was carefully translated into Spanish and mailed via regular post to the two places Dalí would most likely be found: his home in Port Lligat, Spain, and his American residence at the St. Regis Hotel in New York City, where it was handed to him by the gloved hand of a bell hop as he sat in the lobby reading a newspaper. The man with claim to being the greatest artist in the world looked at the envelope carefully. The return address was something called "Jordan Seminary" in someplace called "Menominee, Michigan." Dalí did not know anyone from Menominee nor had he ever heard of it.

He asked the bellman for a letter opener and then slit it open with the stiff silver blade. With his thumb and forefinger he freed the letter inside and began to read.

Dear Mr. Dahli (sp):

As you may know, in 1917 Mary the Virgin mother of Our Lord and Savior Jesus Christ appeared six times to three shepherd children near Fátima, Portugal. During the third apparition the children were privileged to witness a scene of Hell.

There is only one surviving member of this trio, Lucia dos

Santos. She is now a member of a religious community of the Order of Discalced Carmelites. Sister Lucia's description of the scene has been widely publicized. The following is a translation taken from a popular book on the apparitions, <u>Our Lady of Fátima</u> by William Thomas Walsh, published by the Macmillan Company, New York, 1954:

"As the Lady spoke the last words she opened her lovely hands as before, and poured down from them the revealing and penetrating radiance that had warmed the hearts of the children on the previous occasions. But this time it seemed to pass into the earth, disclosing beneath – and these are Lucian's words, written in 1941 – "a sea of fire; and plunged into this fire the demons and the souls, as if they were red-hot coals, transparent and black or bronze-colored, with human forms, which floated about in the conflagration, borne by the flames which issued from it with clouds of smoke, falling on all ideas as sparks fall in great conflagrations – without weight or equilibrium, among shrieks and groans of sorrow and despair which horrify and cause to shudder with fear. The devils were distinguished by horrible and loathsome forms of animals frightful and unknown, but transparent like black coals that had turned red hot."

The purpose of this letter is to acquaint you with a project that I have been developing for nearly two years. I want to commission you to paint this scene approximately as described above. I say approximately because one or two minor discrepancies between this and other accounts must be discussed with Mr. Walsh. However, these changes are minor and you may consider these as almost the exact description that we want painted.

Several prominent churchmen approve of the project, among them are His Eminence Cardinal Lercaro, Archbishop of Bologna, Italy, and is Excellency the most Reverend Don João Venâncio, Bishop of Leiria, Portugal, the diocese in which Fátima is located. I also have the full support of The Blue Army of Our Lady of Fátima, an organization of some fifty million Catholics dedicated to prayer, Holy communion and other good works in keeping with conditions that Our Land gave at Fátima for the conversion of Russia. This painting may indeed be considered a Blue Army project as it will be turned over to that organization when completed.

Our purpose is simple. We believe this vision was a great gift from God to mankind. Knowing that Hell has ceased to be reality to millions we believe that God gave this vision that man might know that Hell does exist and that he might have a vivid image of the penalty for sin.

Naturally the published description must be followed exactly by the artist as far as it goes. I had hoped to arrange for interviews between the artist and Sister Lucia so that he could obtain information for essential details not included in her description. Apparently this will be impossible. There is a possibility that the artist may be permitted to submit sketches for criticism and questionnaires for information. I am trying to arrange this limited participation through The Blue Army. If her cooperation cannot be obtained the artist will be requested to fill in the description with details of his own invention.

The decision as to whether or not the figures of the Blessed Virgin and the three children should be included on the canvas will be left to the judgment of the artist. We want the most effective scene for the indicated purpose. If these figures would in any way detract from this effectiveness they should not be included. If the artist feels that they will add to the effectiveness they should by all means be included but not as a predominant part of the overall scene...

...It is said that this vision of Hell lasted only an instant and if it had continued the children would have died of fright. We know that the scene cannot be perfectly re-produced on canvas. We hope that a great painter may be able to capture much of its frightening quality so that the painting will inspire the souls of many. We hope that copies may

*eventually be placed in public places and private homes as
a constant reminder of the penalty for sin.*

In his direct fashion, Brother Michael asked whether Dalí would: take the commission, or "if you cannot say definitely, whether or not you are interested. I also need to know how much your fee will be for this commission."

The letter was signed, "Brother Michael, Jordan Seminary, Menominee, Michigan."

Holding his head high, Dalí handed the letter to his wife Gala. She was his agent, business partner and prime motivator. If Dalí's creative energies were inexhaustible, then so too were Gala's business energies. She was the prime reason that his detractors knew him as "Salvador Dollars." Through her prodigious efforts, Dalí had become the most reproduced artist in the world. By 1947 he was already being paid as much as $2500 for ads, $5000 for book illustrations and $600 to produce magazine covers. A list of his commercial accounts included Gunther's furs, Ford motor vehicles, Wrigley's chewing gum, Gruen watch-es, Schiaparelli perfume, Abbott Labs and the Container Corporation of America, Walt Disney and even a dream sequence in the Alfred Hitchcock film, Spellbound.

But there were other deeper reasons that Dalí considered Gala to be a goddess, a woman who "drove the forces of death out of me," and who, as he said so eloquently, "brought me back to light through the love she gave me." Gala had a fanatical believe in Dalí and never ceased to provide his every need, from ego stroking and business to being a good sounding board. Many people compared their relationship to that of the Duke and Duchess of Windsor because he was so deeply in her thrall. Dalí rarely made a decision without first consulting Gala.

Gala read the letter and the two discussed the painting. Religion, science and their elements of mysticism were occupying Dalí's mind and work these days. Shortly before receiving the letter from Brother Michael, he had read the Nobel Prize winning work of Francis Crick and James Watson, the discoverers of the DNA double helix. The two scientists even visited Dalí at the St. Regis where Crick was quick to make his point that their discovery proved there was no God. Dalí was vocal in his disagreement. No, he said, "It is real proof of the existence of God." Dalí believed that the world was held together by a mysterious and universal glue of religion, physics and genes.

The notion of painting *The Vision of Hell* held a lot of interest for Dalí. For one thing he knew next to nothing about the details of the Apparitions. Were they real? Did others beside the children witness the Apparitions? What secrets did Sister Lucia hold that she had not yet told? And most important was the information for the actual painting: What did Hell look like? Sister Lucia knew the answer to these questions and others that Dalí had not even anticipated. For a man so obsessed with the nature of death as Dalí was, the chance to create such a painting offered more opportunity than just the money it would bring.

Since no figure was mentioned in the letter from Brother Michael, Dalí and Gala mulled it over and came up with $15,000, an amount equal to more than $120,000 in 2016 dollars. A lot of money to be sure, but Gala felt certain that a large religious organization of devotees could gather such a sum from the faithful. They had no idea that the only money currently available was the $10,750 from personal savings that Brother Michael had committed, but that probably would have made no difference to Gala, who knew the worth of a Dalí painting.

Gala contacted Brother Michael at the seminary and they agreed to meet at the St. Regis Hotel on December 18, 1960. An excited Brother Michael sent the letter to Haffert at his home in New Jersey.

Haffert's recent thoughts had been of Brother Michael and the "Dalí project" (as he now called it) since discussing it with his friend Olga Cadaval, at a party she hosted for Umberto II of Savoy, the last king of Italy. Cadaval knew art and was thrilled at the idea that Salvador Dalí might be interested in painting The Vision of Hell of her friend Sister Lucia.

Within a few months of his conversation with Cadaval, Haffert received Brother Michael's letter of invitation from Gala. An attached note from Brother Michael asked if Haffert would like to come with him as the representative of The Blue Army. Haffert, who was a smooth and tactful negotiator, accepted the offer immediately.

He made plans to meet the young seminarian in New York City.

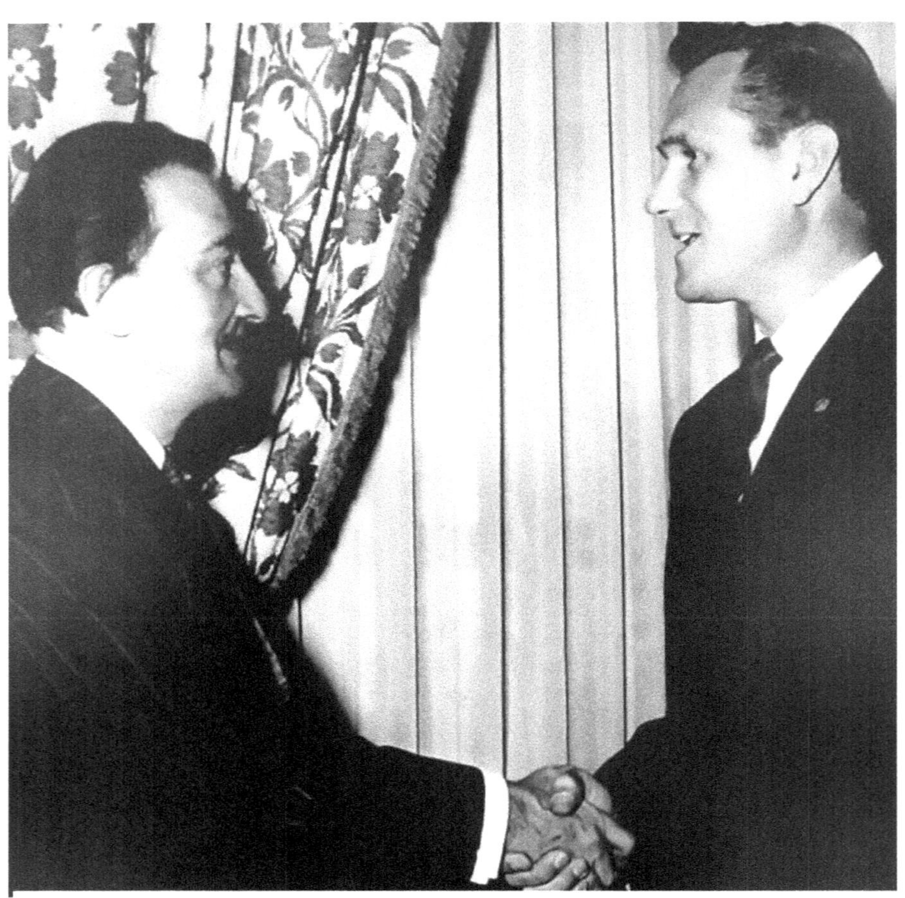

Recently discovered, never-before published, photograph of John Haffert shaking hands with Salvador Dalí during their first meeting at the Saint Regis Hotel in New York in 1960 to discuss the Commission of *The Vision of Hell at Fátima* painting.

13

Meeting Dalí

The St. Regis Hotel was the perfect New York haunt for the Dalí's. Elegant and slightly baroque, Dalí loved the hotel's crystal light fixtures and the soft light that emanated from them because he thought it made him look younger. Gala liked the hotel for other reasons. With its comfortable ambiance and convenient midtown location, the Dalí's were able to lure rich women into their studio where they convinced them to pay as much as $25,000 to have a genuine Dalí portrait. Most of the customers were happy with the results. Included in his gallery of commissioned portraits were Lady Mountbatten, Mrs. Charles Swift of Chicago, Helena Rubinstein, Dorothy Spreckles of sugar company fame and others all loved the regal, somewhat detached portraits that were presented to them after making their final payment for a sitting.

Others were less than happy – and sometimes even appalled – at what showed up on canvas. Art collector Charles Dale thought the painting Dalí did of him looked more like his poodle than him, and socialite Ann Woodward turned her back on the drawing Dalí did of her. It looks moody and depressing, she said, and showed far too much cleavage for her young son to see. Another, Marie-Therese Nichols, thought she looked elderly and overweight and decided to donate it to charity. When Dalí found out, he confronted her in a midtown restaurant and said loudly, "Somebody so stupid as to give away a Dalí has to be a cuckold!" Dalí encountered her again at a dinner party and swore, to her horror, that he had purchased the portrait and was sticking pins in it. "I have magic," he told the horrified woman. "And do you know where I'm going to stick pins? Into your eyes."

+ + +

Brother Michael and Haffert breezed into the St. Regis Hotel a few minutes before their appointed time. Even though they were both wearing suits, the two were a study in contrasts. Brother Michael had the nervous look of someone totally out of his league. Haffert, on the other hand, had the smooth posture and easy smile of a man who had been through many first meetings with important people. The two made small talk until Haffert saw a smallish, slim woman with black hair step out of an elevator. He recognized her immediately and walked toward her with an outstretched hand and a beaming smile. They shook hands, made small talk for a moment, and then took the elevator to the royal suite, which the Dalí's occupied several months each year.

It was in the royal suite that Dalí stood from the couch he was sitting on and presented himself, shaking hands with both men before returning to the couch. Haffert found him nothing like his public persona. Rather than the flamboyant creature he expected, Haffert found Dalí to be as "subdued as a businessman. Brother Michael, his nervousness unabated, began telling the Dalís about the philosophy that drove his dream.

"During the two years I've worked on this project I formulated a kind of motto," he told Dalí. "'Try for the best and settle for less.' That we would be able to settle for the best was kind of a wild dream that I didn't think would come true. Your acceptance of this commission was no less than the complete realization of this dream."

Dalí accepted the compliment with a nod.

Brother Michael's glee at meeting quickly melted when Gala began talking terms. Haffert who was a shrewd businessperson on par with Gala, suggested they discuss the particulars of the painting and the price over a drink at the hotel's intimate oak bar. It was there that Gala got down to business.

Both Brother Michael and Haffert expected a bid from the crafty Russian that would be well within the $10,000 that Brother Michael was donating to the project. So it came as a jolt when Gala insisted on a $30,000 fee to produce the painting.

Despite receiving a glare from Gala that could pierce a bank vault, Brother Michael began to argue for a lower price. Before he could get far, though, Haffert placed a confident hand on the young seminarian's shoulder and accepted the bid with a confident smile.

"$30,000 will be fine," he said looking Gala in the eyes.

With the business of art behind them, the mood changed. Drinks were ordered and the Dalís warmed up to their newest customers.

Haffert explained the goal of The Blue Army to the curious Dalí. He knew that the Spanish artist had some difficulty understanding English so he enunciated carefully before resorting to Spanish. Haffert's fluency in seven languages including Latin had already marveled a pope as it now fascinated Dalí.

Haffert said that The Blue Army had been founded as a means of spreading the Message of Fátima, much of which involved the defeat of Communism, the true barrier to world peace. God had sent His own mother to bring the message of warning and hope for the world. And if the world does not heed this message, said Haffert, then the sinners will get the full brunt of Hell as described by the three child seers of Fátima. The world risked nuclear annihilation according to what people believed was the content of the third secret of Fátima and that was surely why the Vatican earlier that year had announced it would not be officially revealed in 1960.

"It's up to you to present this Vision truthfully and vividly," said Haffert. "You are being chosen to be Our Lady's Artist. A visual interpreter for God!"

With Dalí's rapt attention, Haffert then read a version of The Vision of Hell, a very powerful account as told to him by Sister Lucia herself and published in her Memoirs: As the Lady Spoke.

"She opened her lovely hands and light radiated from them as though passing through the Earth disclosing a sea of fire, plunged into which were demons and souls, like red-hot coals transparent and black or bronze-colored, with human forms which floated about in the conflagration, borne by the flames which issued from it with clouds of smoke falling on all sides as sparks fell in great conflagrations without weight or equilibrium, among shrieks and groans of sorrow and despair which horrified us and caused us to shudder with fear. The devils were distinguished by horrible and loathsome forms of animals, frightful and unknown, but transparent like black coals that had turned red hot. During this vision we heard the Blessed Mother say, 'You see Hell, where the souls of poor sinners go. So many souls are lost because there is no one to pray and make sacrifices for them.'"

A glint in Dalí's eye told Haffert that the artist liked what he had just heard. He was hooked.

Now Haffert had only to work on the painting's price.

Surrounded by sounds of glasses clinking and the gaze of curious onlookers, Dalí ordered escargot so as to present "Mr. Fátima" with his innovative idea on what Hell should look like. When the escargot arrived, Dalí began prying at it with the slim, long escargot forks and said: "You know Señor Haffert, Dante and the old Masters have always depicted the devils in Hell with pitchforks prying at soul. But we shall use escargot forks instead!"

"Snail forks?" Haffert asked. "Why snail forks?"

"The soul of a sinner is like a snail." Dalí explained. "It curls and cowls up in the shell and the only way to retrieve it is by using an escargot fork!"

Haffert had no objection. It sounded unique and logical and of course surreal! But one of the main concerns he had was how Dalí was going to depict Our Lady, the Mother of God. He asked him this question after they had finished the meal and Dalí quickly replied. "She will be modeled after Gala. I always use Gala as the model for the Blessed Virgin!"

That thought terrified Haffert, who knew of Gala's reputation of having a stable of boyfriends. He thought to mention the rumors about Gala but decided to keep silent so as not to insult the Master. And besides, he was still interested in the price of the painting. As always, Haffert wanted the most he could get for his money.

"For the money we've discussed, how large a canvas will we receive?" asked Haffert.

Dalí stroked his mustache a moment and slowly lifted up one of his ornate walking sticks. "$30, 000 for the size of my cane," he said. "Or $15, 000 for a painting half its size!"

Haffert pushed. He would pay $15,000 for the painting, but he expected one the size of Dalí's cane.

Dalí nodded an affirmative and before long Haffert was drawing up a contract on a St. Regis Hotel napkin.

The two signed the napkin and the deal was done.

Dalí requested to meet Sister Lucia, or to go to Fátima, or both.

Such a meeting, said Dalí, would help make the supernatural connections he needed to accomplish his assignment.

"I need to know everything about the Apparitions of Fátima," he declared, his eyes wide and fixed on Haffert, who would later declare that Dalí looked like Rasputin the Russian mystic.

Haffert promised he would do what he could to bring the artist and the seer together for an informative meeting. Perhaps he could even get Sister Lucia herself to accompany Dalí to Fátima, he suggested optimistically.

The artist shrugged.

"From the moment I was presented with this idea I knew this was a painting I wanted to do," he said as Haffert stood up to leave.

"Good," said Haffert. "Because it's your duty now to remind the World of the penalty for sin." Haffert had a smile on his face as he boarded the elevator that dropped to the lobby. Brother Michael would later admit he was stunned by the amount that the painting would cost. So too was Haffert. But the veteran fund raiser didn't show it. He knew that God would provide as he had in the past. After all, hadn't he been in this position many times before and hadn't a benefactor always come through?

Haffert also felt that he had landed a public relations coup. Although Dalí had committed hundreds of paintings to canvas, he had accomplished only five religious paintings to date. One of those was the symmetrical masterpiece, The Crucifixion, which is a low-angle view of Christ being crucified on a hovering cube-shaped cross as Mary Magdalene, played by Gala, looks on in a sad yet adoring manner. Another was the Last Supper, a postmodern version of da Vinci's classic that has the apostles and Christ dining under a glass dome through which they are being observed by God.

At the time this painting was hung, it was the most reproduced painting in the National Art Gallery in Washington. Haffert most likely held hope that *The Vision of Hell* would join those other religious paintings as being paramount among his work and would therefore draw great attention to The Blue Army.

"When completed, the new painting will be exhibited around the world, and ultimately will be hung at the International Centre of The Blue Army in Fátima... where there are hundreds of thousands of visitors a year," wrote Haffert in *Soul* magazine.

When the elevator opened, Brother Michael was sitting on a couch waiting for Haffert. When he heard that the deal had been consummated, he shook Haffert's hand in gratitude. The two men walked across the lobby and onto 55th Street. There was a smile on Haffert's face and a lilt in his step that was contagious. As the two men sprang down the street, Brother Michael broke into a wide grin. His dream was becoming a reality.

When Haffert returned home, he drafted a check for $5,000 Dollars for the first installment, and had it delivered to Dalí at the St. Regis Hotel. In the sealed envelope was a handwritten note written on Blue Army stationary. It read:

J.M.J. (Jesus, Mary, Joseph)

Dear Mr. Dalí,

Herewith please find enclosed the down payment for the $15, 000 Dollar painting of The Vision of Hell at Fátima which I would appreciate you painting the size of your cane.

Warm Regards
John Haffert

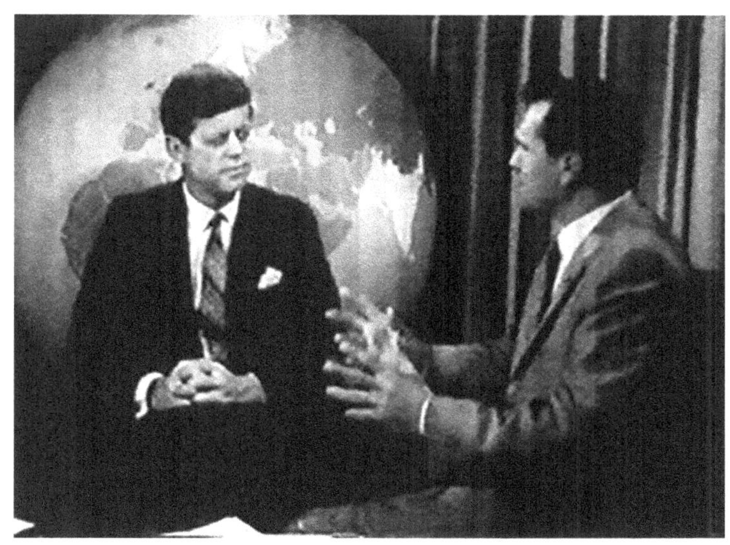

A still from the film of John Haffert interviewing John F. Kennedy in 1959, for the TV Program "Countdown 1960"

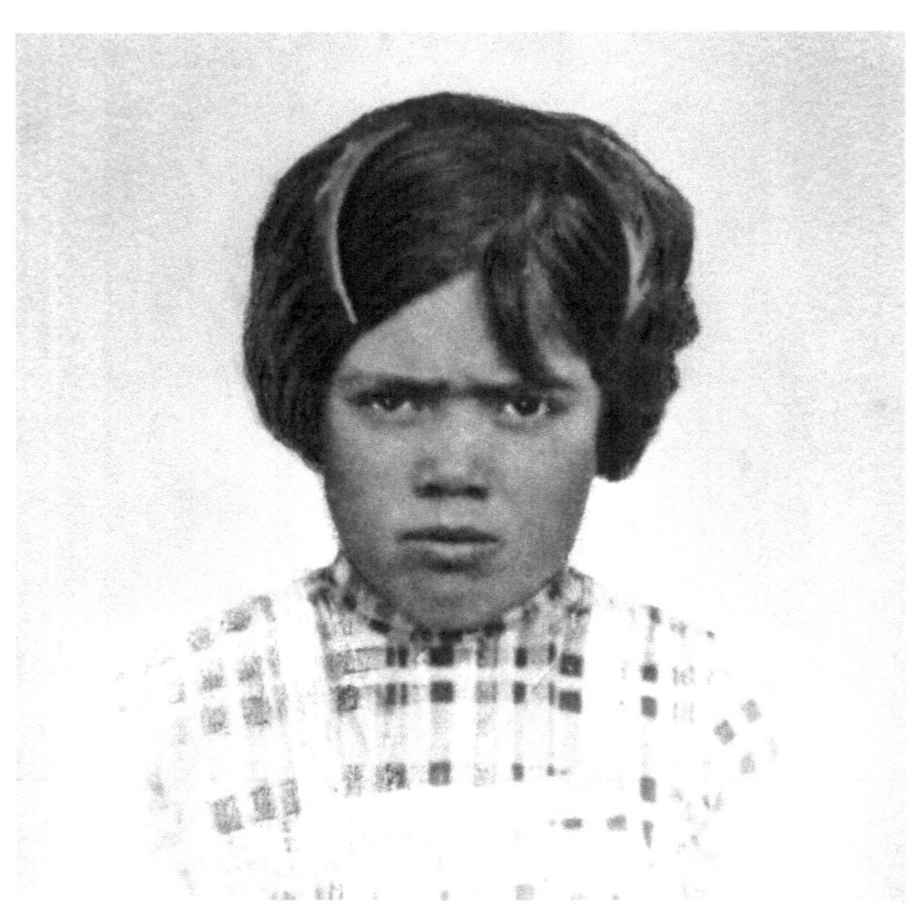

Rare photograph of the young Fátima Seer Sister Lucia shortly before moving
to the Dorothean Sister's Boarding school in Vilar, near Oporto.

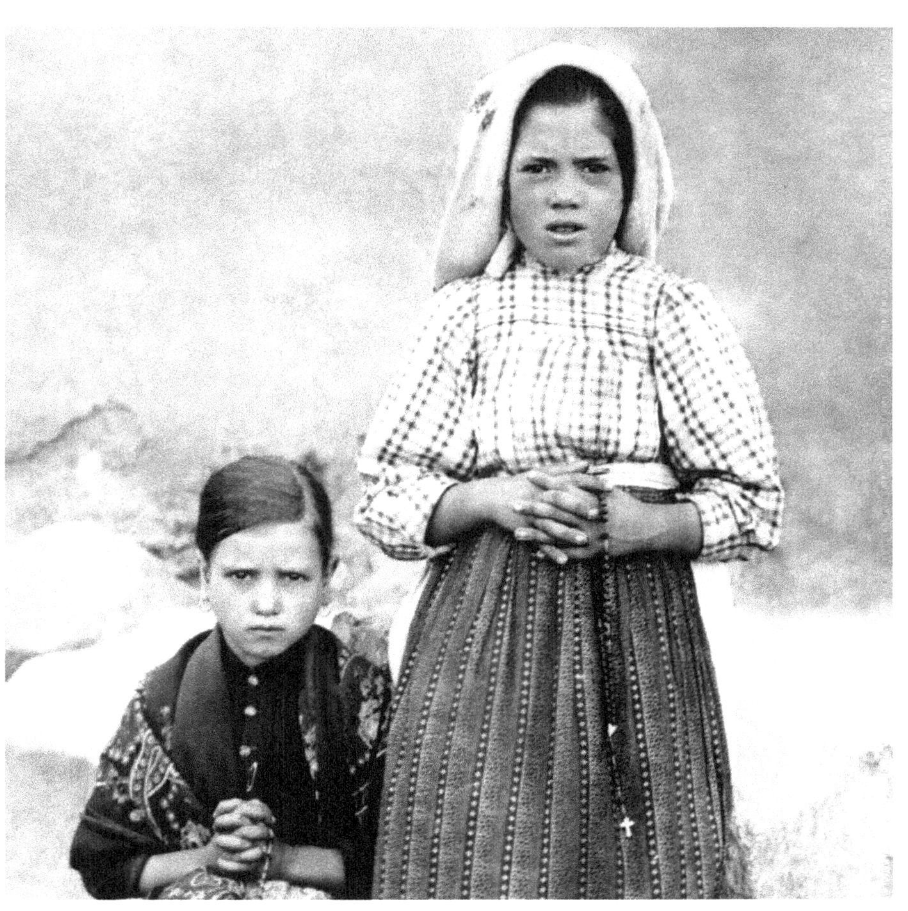

Heaven's Spokesperson Lucia dos Santos with her cousin Jacinta Marto photographed in September of 1917.

14

The Cloistered Sister

With the size of the painting settled, Haffert began to wonder how he would get the great Salvador Dalí and Sister Lucia together in the same room to discuss what she had seen when the earth opened and Hell became visible to her visionary mind. Haffert knew firsthand that such a meeting would not be easy, perhaps impossible since she had freely entered the cloistered life in a Carmelite Monastery in Coimbra, Portugal. He himself had met with Sister Lucia twice starting in 1946 when the two of them composed a document saying that the scapular was an important symbol of devotion to the Virgin Mary – one as important as the rosary - and should be worn by all who consider themselves to be faithful followers.

But when Haffert met the seer face to face she was still considered a secular religious nun. That changed in 1949 when she decided to become a cloistered nun. Since his own sister was a Carmelite nun, Haffert knew that no one except cardinals as princes of the Roman Catholic Church could enter a cloister. Close family members, chaplains and the local bishops of the dioceses of Coimbra and Leiria could also meet Lucia but in a speaking parlor separated by a thick iron grill that resembled a prison and impeded a full vision of the nun.

Olga Cadaval, Bishop João Venâncio and Canon José Galamba de Oliveira were among that handful of few people that could still visit with the Seer in the parlor. Sometimes, unbeknownst to the Vatican but with the permission of the local prioress, they took along with them friends and relatives. Since it was rare, it became a treat for Lucia who liked to see new faces and the guest who would get to meet the sole surviving seer of Fátima.

Hundreds of recorded Vatican authorized official visits took place during the 50 years that Sister Lucia lived in the cloistered community of Saint Teresa in Coimbra. But many more unauthorized persons visited the seer having been snuck in by family or local officials during private visits held on the occasion of major holidays or the seer's birthday or anniversary.

But the general public had not seen or heard the seer of Fátima in over ten years. Fátima conspiracy theorists claimed she had been taken up to heaven, imprisoned by the Vatican so as not to reveal the third secret, or substituted by an imposter.

When Haffert met Sister Lucia for the second time in 1952, he had gone to the Carmel with Canon Galamba of Fátima. Since no photographs were allowed of cloistered sisters under the rigorous pre-Vatican II rules, Haffert later had a sketch made of the seer published in *Soul* Magazine. Because of this sketch, which he also reproduced in some of his books, Vatican officials discovered Haffert had been unofficially snuck in by someone and communicated to the local authorities that because of his imprudence, he was not to be taken back there again.

During that meeting Lucia revealed serious frustrations that were occupying more of her life. Lucia felt she was unable to properly communicate the message of Fátima. After all she had been unable to convince the Pope to Consecrate Russia to the Immaculate Heart of Mary in 1929 and World War II had resulted, or so she believed. As a result of this failure Communism had spread and the world was now locked in a Cold War.

"Lucia felt completely helpless, in the restrictive capacity of a (cloistered) nun, to propagate the message of Fátima," Haffert later wrote in a memoir. "One by one, the prophecies were coming true. The second World war had come... Russia had become a 'super power' and was disseminating militant atheism 'throughout the entire World.' The nuclear bomb had been developed and already the atheists were bran-dishing it in the face of a terrified World, threatening the annihilation of entire nations, which Our Lady had warned of in Her message was not heeded."

Lucia was so frustrated at the fading of the Fátima Message that she had considered leaving the Dorothean Convent and starting her own Apostolate, one just like The Blue Army, she told Haffert.

Haffert knew the truth in what Lucia had said. Her life since the last Apparition at Fátima during the Miracle of the Sun on October 13th, 1917, had been anything but pleasant. Believers and non-believers alike, who had become so vehement in their pursuit of her that she was afraid to come out of the house, had threatened her life and the lives of her family. Finally the local bishop told her to keep silent about the apparitions and the three secrets they held and concentrate on getting an education at a private religious faculty.

She was fine with that, especially given the fact she needed to learn to read and write in order to accurately transmit the Message of Fátima.

The children were greatly stressed by events following the apparitions in 1917. School became difficult, as did their home life. In the months after the Miracle of the Sun, Jacinta had three more apparitions, but out of respect to her frightened mother, chose to tell them only to closest members of her family.

To her mother's horror, Lucia told her mother of one such vision predicting a "war to come" in which many people would die and "so many priests will be killed." Lucia's mother became angry. World War I had just ended, she reminded her daughter. What kind of vision is it that reveals the past? It was two decades later that Lucia revealed the vision to others outside the family, saying it had been predictive of World War II all along.

Lucia's mother had good reason to be distressed. The government had sent members of the Republican National Guard on horseback to prevent pilgrims from visiting the site. Despite their commanding presence, the pilgrims streamed by, ignoring orders to leave the premise. Soon local officials blamed Lucia for the civil disobedience.

Even the believers represented a certain amount of stress for Lucia and her mother. They would observe the young girl's every move, watching her and her cousins like "curious animals" whenever they could. People pursued the young girl all day, asking questions that she couldn't or wouldn't answer. And it didn't stop at night, when strangers would knock on the door of the family's modest home and ask to speak to Lucia for just a few minutes, that would turn to hours until Lucia's mother or father had to insist that the visitors leave.

Within months, Lucia's mother became so ill that all of the children gathered around her bed to receive her last blessing and to kiss her dying hand. When Lucia got to the bedside, her mother put a limp hand around her neck and sighed.

"My poor daughter, what will become of you without a mother? I die with you crossed in my heart." The woman began to weep so hard that

Lucia's oldest sister pulled her from the bedside and forbid her from returning to the sick room.

As Lucia sat at the kitchen table, her two oldest sisters came in presented a solution.

"Lucia, if it is true you saw our Lady, go now to Cova da Iria, and beg Her to cure our mother. Promise Her whatever you want and we will do it and then we will believe."

Lucia snuck out to the Cova and prayed to the lady, promising that she would pray the rosary for nine straight days with her sisters if her mother was made well again. When she returned home, her mother was out of bed and feeling well. A few days later, after praying the rosary, Lucia's mother said to her daughter, "It is strange that our Lady healed me and yet somehow I still don't believe. I don't know why this is."

+++

It was during this time – December 1918 – that both Jacinta and Francisco became seriously ill with Spanish flu, which was rampant throughout Europe. Within four months, little Francisco was dead, taken by an inflammation of the lungs. The day before he passed away, Lucia was allowed a short visit. As she recalled later in one of her memoirs, the young man wasn't frightened of death. Rather, he looked at Lucia and said, "I'm going to Heaven. There I will pray a great deal to our Lord and our Lady to take you there very soon, too."

Jacinta lingered longer. According to Lucia's memoirs, her little friend had a number of visions while in her sickbed, including one in which the Lady told her she would die in Lisbon. And so it came to pass that a doctor from Lisbon visited the region and insisted that Jacinta be moved to his hospital where a special surgery could help the noted seer regain her health. With no argument, the girl was transferred to Lisbon.

"The farewell cut me to the quick," wrote Lucia in her first memoir. "She hugged my neck for a long time and said crying, 'We shall never meet again. Pray for me a lot until I go to heaven, and afterwards I will pray a lot for you. Never tell anybody the secret even if they kill you."

From Lisbon, Jacinta corresponded with Lucia, telling her friend that the Lady had appeared to her many times, even revealing to her the exact day and hour of her death, which proved to be February 20, 1920 at

10:30 p.m.

Lucia felt terribly alone when she heard of Jacinta's death. There were times after the passing of her cousin that Lucia would go into her aunt's house and call out the name of her best friend. Jacinta's parents understood Lucia's grief. They stopped her before she got to Jacinta's room and reminded her that her cous-in was no longer there anymore. When the coffin containing Jacinta's remains arrived from Lisbon, it was a moment of stark reality for the surviving seer, who spent hours in the graveyard at Vila Nova de Ourém, sitting by the grave of her young friends, Jacinta and Francisco.

The deaths came as no surprise to Lucia. She wrote in her fourth memoir that the Lady had told her during the second Apparition that her friends would be taken soon, but that she would remain on earth for some time.

> *"Jesus wishes to make use of you to have me acknowledged and loved," Lucia recounted in her fourth memoir. "He wishes to establish in the world the devotion of my Immaculate Heart."*

> *Lucia says she expressed concern about being left alone, but the Lady gave her solace. "No daughter. Do you suffer a great deal? Don't be discouraged. I will never forsake you. My Immaculate Heart will be your refuge and the road that will lead you to God."*

Lucia remembered these words. But now, visiting the graves of her only true friends left her with a growing sadness. She became increasingly depressed and wondered what the Lady meant when she promised refuge from loneliness.

That refuge came in the form of Don Jose Alves Correira da Silva, a newly appointed bishop of Leiria. The bishop's first act when he took office was to launch an investigation into the Apparitions of Fátima. He arranged for Lucia and her mother to go to Lisbon where Assunção Avelar, a pious benefactor, had agreed to pay for Lucia's schooling at a convent in Spain.

Before leaving for the convent, Lucia and her mother were brought to the bishop's residence at Leiria where he sternly lectured the two on the need for secrecy. The government was looking for Lucia, he said. It would be best if she simple disappeared.

"You should tell no one where you are going," the bishop said to Lucia.

"No sir, I won't," she said.

"You should not talk about the apparitions at Fátima anymore," he continued.

"No sir," she said.

In many ways, it was as though the young visionary had been placed in the witness protection program. Was this too much protection? Probably not. Shortly after Lucia left Fátima, Freemasons attacked the Cova again, this time placing four bombs in the chapel that blew the roof entirely off the structure. A fifth bomb attached to the tree where the vision had taken place did not go off, leading believers to declare that another miracle had taken place.

The "Fátima cult" that had sprung up around the site was now the focus of government intervention. More soldiers had been called in to discourage pilgrims and the mayor of Fátima declared that processions to the Cova had to be approved by his office. "Keep me informed personally about every incident of a superstitious nature that occurs in connection with the so-called Miracle of Fátima," he demanded.

So upsetting was the political climate in Fátima, that members of the Catholic Church removed the image of the Lady from what was left of the chapel and brought it out only on feast days.

This did not bother Lucia, who later wrote, "I was rather disappointed when I saw it. To start with, she looks too happy, as if free of care. When I saw Our Lady, she looked sad and full of pity. But in any case, it is impossible to make a image which can be even remotely as beautiful as she is."

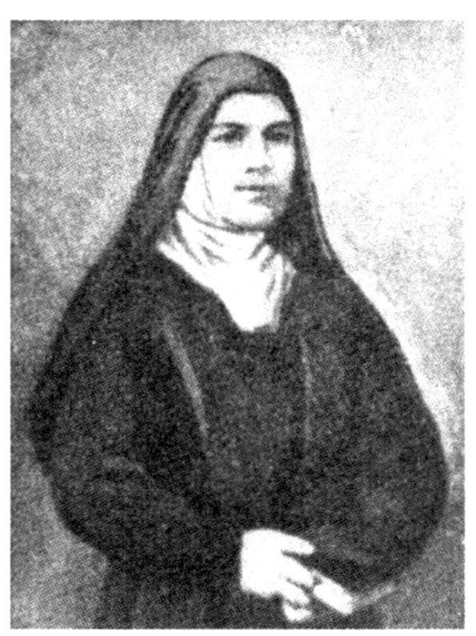

Sketch of Sister Lucia by artist James Ramsey Hunt of Soul Magazine depicted as John Haffert saw her on October 18, 1952

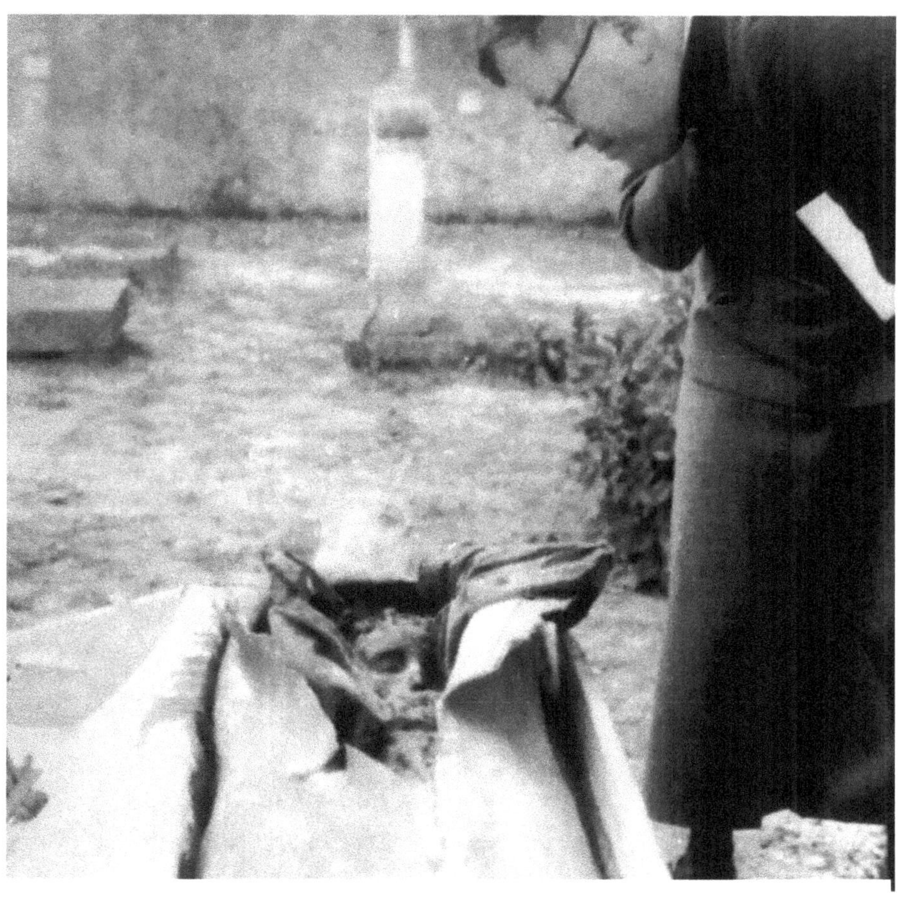

Canon Luis Fischer examines the incorrupt body of Jacinta Marto during the exhumation in 1936. This was the photo sent to Sister Lucia by the Bishop of Leiria.

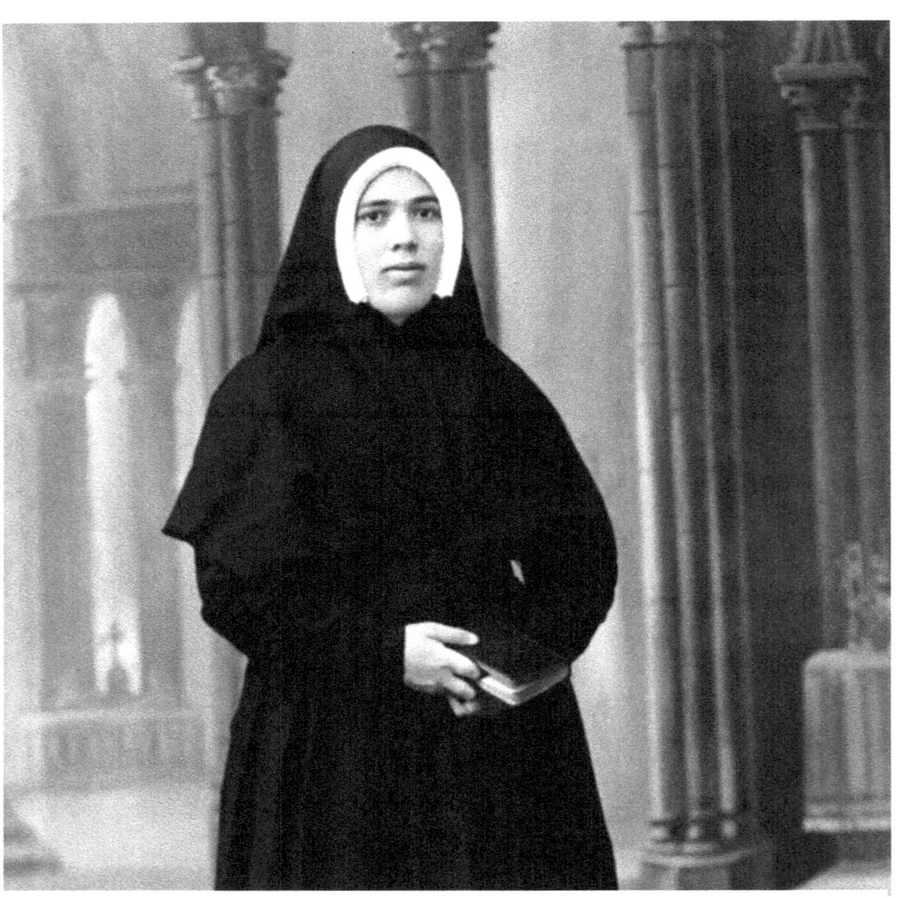

A young Sister Lucia poses in the habit of a Dorothean nun following her Profession at the Convent of the teaching Order in Pontevedra, Spain.

15

Keeping Her Secrets

On June 17, 1921, Lucia entered the front door of the school of Asilo de Vilar. A nun who had been appointed by the bishop to care for her introduced her to the mother superior, Mother Maria das Dores Magalhães, a stern woman with searing eyes that looked the troubled country girl over completely.

"She is a wild animal," she said. "But we'll tame her."

Lucia's new name was "Maria das Dores," from somewhere in Lisbon.

"You will never talk to anybody about the events at Fátima," said the mother superior.

"Yes mother," replied the newly christened Maria.

"You will ask no questions and give no answers."

"Yes, Mother."

"You will not go for walks with any of the other girls, and you will not tell them why, even if they ask you. Do you understand?"

"Yes Mother."

And so it was for the next three years, Lucia lived incognito and practically in silence, giving no one a clue as to who she was. She was allowed to write to her mother rarely, and letters from her mother were opened and censored of all news about Fátima. After a year, she received permission to write an essay about the happenings at Fátima, which was held by the mother superior.

It wasn't until she graduated from Asilo de Vilar in October 1925 and joined the order of the Sisters of Saint Dorothy in Tui, Spain, that she realized Fátima was still a very hot topic in the church. The Bishop of Leiria had completed an investigation of Fátima and had written a pastoral letter on May 3, 1922, in which he found nothing immoral or contrary to the faith with the Apparitions.

"We ask ourselves, how can this girl (Lucia), now fourteen years old, have the kind of influence on people that explains the stream of pilgrims to Fátima? How can her personal appearance attract such crowds? It is unlikely that something like this would happen, since we are dealing with a child who had only the simplest upbringing and no education whatsoever."

Other miracles were reported at Fátima, including healings and a bizarre incident on May 13, 1924 in which a rain of flower pedals fell on a crowd of more than 200,000 people.

Perhaps it was the warm welcome that her new order gave her or the discovery that Fátima had been legitimized, but Sister Lucia began having visions again. The first one happened on December 10, 1925. Lucia had just completed dinner and returned to her cell to pray the rosary when the Lady presented herself. She was standing on a cloud next to the child Jesus, waiting patiently for Lucia to notice her. Lucia later recalled how she lost her breath upon seeing her visionary friend again.

"Tell the world that I promise to be there, at the moment of death, with all those who, on the first Saturdays of five months in a row, confess and receive Holy Communion. They must recite five decades of the Rosary and keep me company for fifteen minutes while meditating on the mysteries of the Rosary."

After delivering the message, the apparition disappeared.

At the behest of the mother superior and the priest to whom she confessed, Lucia wrote down an account in a report.

Then, on February 15, 1926, Lucia had another vision, this one in the convent's garden where she had gone to empty trash. There she saw a small boy standing alone. When she asked who he was, he replied, "Have you told the world what the Heavenly Mother asked you to?"

She reported the vision to her Mother Superior, declaring that the boy was the child Jesus she had seen with the Lady.

On June 13, 1929, Sister Lucia had another vision of the Lady, this one at the chapel of Saint Dorothy. As she stretched out on the floor and prayed before the altar, the "entire chapel was filled with a supernatural light, and above the altar there appeared a cross of light that reached up to the ceiling."

The vision was elaborate, like *The Vision of Hell* and the third secret. The torso of a man hovered above the cross with a dove of light on his chest. Under that, another man – probably Jesus – was nailed to the cross. Beneath that was a large chalice and host. Blood was running across the host from the wounds of the man on the cross and dripping into the chalice. The Lady stood under the right arm of the cross and the words Grace and mercy formed under left arm of the cross.

"I realized I had been shown the mystery of the Holy Trinity and I received an inner understanding about it I cannot reveal," Lucia wrote later. The Lady spoke to Lucia.

"The moment has come where God wants the pope to dedicate Russia to Me, promising to save it this way. Sacrifice yourself for this, and pray." Lucia translated this vision in a letter to her confessor.

"If I am not mistaken," she wrote. "God promises to put an end to the persecution in Russia if the pope will perform a solemn and public act that will consecrate Russia to the devotion of Mary, and if all the bishops of the world will do the same."

In the context of the time, such a vision seems logical. Joseph Stalin ruled Russia with an iron fist and a true hatred of organized religion. When he took over after Vladimir Lenin's death in 1924, Stalin launched the "Union of Militant Atheists," a radical group who destroyed churches and icons at will. The Catholic Church was horrified by events in Russia and mystified at what to do to stop them.

Through the Bishop of Leiria, Sister Lucia was allowed to write of the vision to Pope Pius XI. On March 19, 1930, the pope did celebrate a "mass of penitence, reconciliation and atonement" for crimes committed against Jesus, but it was unclear to Lucia and the Bishop as to whether this ceremony was carried out as a result of her letter.

It was only two months later, on the May 13th anniversary of the Fátima Apparitions, that Bishop Silva wrote a pastoral letter that ratified the apparitions. The bishop digested the events of the Apparitions in a letter of about 2,000 words, recounting the facts as he gathered them about the children, their home life, the physical environment in which the apparitions took place, and the miracle of the sun, about which he wrote was "simply marvelous and caused the greatest impression on those who had the happiness to witness it."

It was only two months later, on the May 13th anniversary of the Fátima Apparitions, that Bishop Da Silva wrote a Pastoral Letter that ratified the Apparitions. The Bishop digested the events of 1917 in a letter of about 2,000 words, recounting the facts as he gathered them about the children, their home life, the physical environment in which the Apparitions took place, and the Miracle of the Sun, about which he wrote was "simply marvelous and caused the greatest impression on those who had the happiness to witness it." The Miracle of the Sun the Bishop believed was the greatest Miracle ever worked since the Resurrection of Jesus!"

He asked his fellow bishops to "permit... the cult of Our Lady of Fátima," by declaring the Apparitions "worthy of credence," which they did.

Now just one nagging problem remained: no one except Lucia knew the secrets that were told to her by the Lady of Fátima.

+++

Sister Lucia had never told anyone the secrets given to her by the Lady on that July day in 1917. Contrary to the verbose tendencies of most who would be blessed with such a revelation, Sister Lucia found her silence to be anything but enforced. Rather than aching to tell the three secrets of the Lady, Sister Lucia found her silence – which she says was ordered by God - to be a blessing.

"Where could I have hidden myself to avoid answering endless questions which would have been asked if this matter had been disclosed?"

she asked Bishop Leiria in one of her long missives to him. As she wrote, "Keeping silent has been a great grace for me."

No, she wrote, God had ordered her to remain silent until certain events took place. One of those, the rise of Russia as a Godless force in the world, was taking place at a quickening pace. Another, "a night illuminated by an unknown light," as she would later write, took place January 25, 1938. On that night, the sky over much of Europe turned blood red and was so bright that people believed a massive fire had broken out just over the horizon. The light was visible in Greece, Italy, Spain, Portugal and some of North Africa. Scientists declared it to be an expanded version of the aurora borealis, but many in Europe saw it as a supernatural sign of the coming conflagration that would be World War II. Hitler who saw the celestial spectacle in his Bavarian home overlooking the snowcapped mounts saw the phenomena turn the snow blood red and declared this was the sign that the Nazi regime was to conquer the World in a blood bath.

Sister Lucia, who tied the event into the visions almost three years after it took place, said it was another sign that the time had come to let the world know about the secrets. But still the Church asked her to remain publicly silent over the 1917 Apparitions and the subsequent Apparitions and Visions she had had.

Then in September 1935, an envelope arrived for Lucia that had been delivered from the Bishop's office. Inside was the photo of a dead girl, one that would have been horrifying to anyone who did not know the whole story as Lucia did. But the Dorothean nun knew the whole story and knew who she was looking at and what the photo meant and it brought her great delight.

The dead girl who lay in the coffin was Jacinta. She had been in a coffin sealed in lead and laid on a shelf in a sealed above ground marble mausoleum for 20 years. Bodies kept in such mausoleums take a minimum of 200 years to decompose, so the body was only partially decomposed and perfectly recognizable by Sister Lucia as that of her cousin Jacinta.

As she looked intently at the photo of Jacinta's mortal remains, she was certainly greeted by a rush of memory that went back those 20 years, to 1917, when the two girls and Francisco had their visions. The images and information contained in these Apparitions swam through Sister Lucia's mind. The mummified face in the photo went backward in time until Sister Lucia saw the youthful body of her friend as the two walked the verdant grazing fields.

After hours of gazing at the photos of her friend in the coffin taken by the Baron of Alvaiázere, Sister Lucia picked up a pen and wrote to D. José Alves Correia da Silva, the Bishop of Leiria. He had sent the photos to Sister Lucia of the exhumation. This meant that the young girl's body was being moved from the private burial chamber of the Barons to an above ground tomb placed directly over the grave of Francisco in the Fátima Cemetery, because the Apparitions had been approved and the children would someday be declared Saints and afterwards the Baron or his descendants might not be willing to give up such an important and saintly relic.

Part of the translation process called for the positive identification of the remains and so this had to be carried out by the Church appointed Notary Canon Luis Fischer and by the child's parents and relatives and the Baron and his wife.

That was when they found the remains so perfect that they considered them "incorrupt." The Bishop had ordered photos taken of event and considered her lack of decomposition a miracle.

After hours of reminiscing over the photos of the late Jacinta, Sister Lucia assembled her thoughts and wrote a note to the Bishop.

"I am truly grateful for the photographs," she wrote. "I just cannot tell you how much I appreciate them. Especially the one of Jacinta, I wanted to remove those clothes that were covering her so as to see her completely, even in the photo. I was anxious to uncover the rest of the body, without taking into account that it was a photograph. I was half in the clouds, such was my joy at seeing again my closest childhood friend."

I have hopes that Our Lord, for the glory of the Most Holy Virgin, will grant her the crown of sanctity. She was a child only in years. As for the rest, she knew how to practice virtue and to show God and the Most Holy Virgin her love, through the practice of sacrifice. It is to her companionship that I owe, in part, the conservation of my innocence. It is admirable how she understood the spirit of prayer and sacrifice that the Most Holy Virgin recommended to us. How often, in the midst of the most animated game, she would say, "Let us not eat in. Let's give it to some poor person for the conversion of some sinner,' etc. For these and for innumerable others, I hold her in high esteem as a saint.

When the Bishop received this missive he realized a very serious gap had been left in the research into the Apparitions of Fátima. Although all of the press on the events had been archived, witnesses inter-viewed, and Sister Lucia cross-examined in a court of law, there was no memoir by the sister herself. This was a major gap that had to be remedied, thought the Bishop of Leiria.

With great purpose, he wrote to Sister Lucia ordering her to write everything she could remember about Jacinta's life.

Sister Lucia responded humbly.

"Very well then. I need no more than this: obedience and abandonment to God who works within me. I am truly no more than a poor and miserable instrument which He desires to use, and in a little while, like a painter who casts his now useless brush into the fire so that it may be reduced to ashes, the Divine Artist will Himself reduce His now useless instrument to the ashes of the tomb, until that great day of the eternal Alleluias. And I ardently desire that day, for the tomb does not annihilate everything, and the happiness of eternal and infinite love begins – now!"

She took the photo back to her cell and admired it further. A smile certainly passed over her face as she remembered the childhood fun they'd had before the visionary encounters with the Lady forced them into a peculiar sort of adulthood. Alone with the photo, Sister Lucia most certainly felt the pressure of eternity on her back and the weight of responsibility on her shoulders. After all, she and she alone was left to recount the message of our Lady of Fátima, and to share with the world the three secrets that she had kept inside of her and never let out. These were secrets with the power to change the world, or so she thought. Yet she kept them to herself because she felt she had been told to remain silent by God and also because she feared telling accounts of the secrets that might vary with each telling. She wrote of this fear to Bishop Silva, using the first secret, The Vision of Hell, as the best example.

"What about the revelation of Hell? I can't even find the exact words to explain its reality. What I saw is nothing, it only give a vague idea of it. What would have happened if I had said one thing this time and another that time trying in vain to explain myself? I might have caused such a confusion of ideas as, perhaps, to hinder God's work... Ordinarily God causes an interior and exact discernment of their meaning to accompany His revelations. But I don't dare speak about this for fear of being led by my imagination, which, in my opinion, can very easily happen."

On that day in November 1935, after having two months with the photo of Jacinta in her coffin to inspire memory, Sister Lucia began writing the first of four memoirs. Her goal was to recount all that she could of her friends Jacinta and Francisco and of the visionary events that took place over the course of six months at the Cova in her hometown of Fátima.

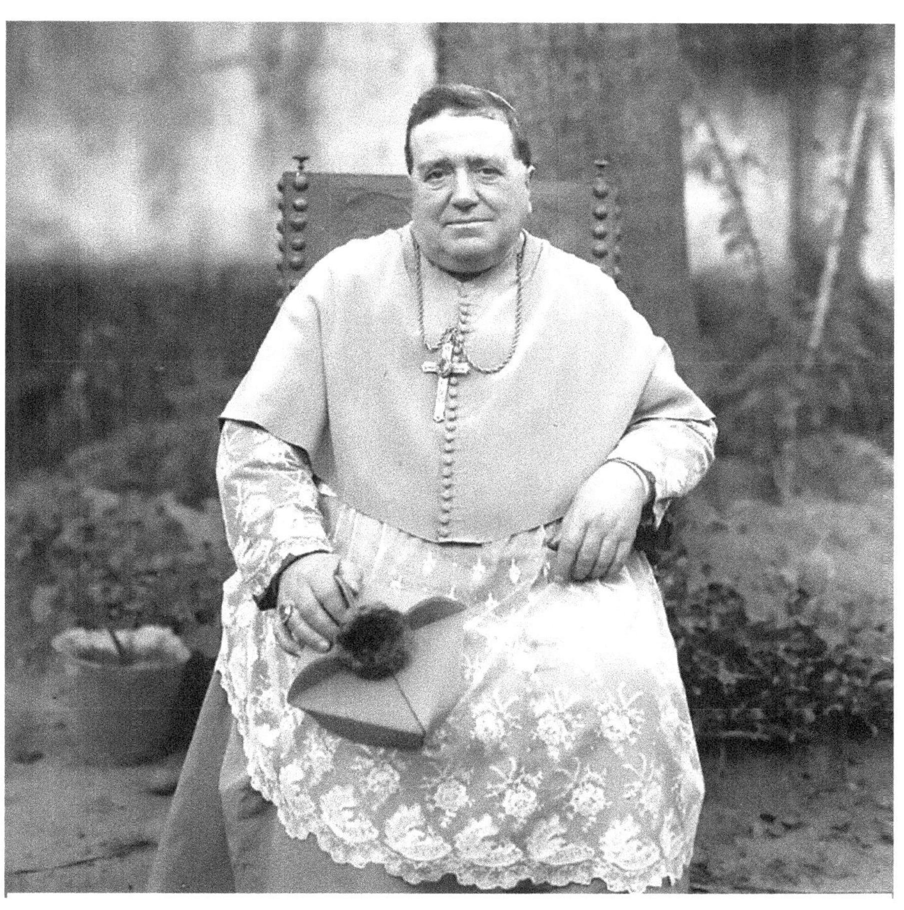

D. José Alves Correia da Silva, First Bishop of the restored Diocese of Leiria and First Guardian of Sister Lucia's manuscript of the Third Secret of July 13th, 1917.

16

Visions Revealed

Over the course of the next six years, Sister Lucia produced three memoirs about her experience with the Lady of Fátima. The first of these, completed Christmas day, 1935, was a hagiography of her beloved cousin and friend, Jacinta. Inspired by the photos of Jacinta's mummified remains, the memoir tells the story of Jacinta's devotion to the Catholic church and the Virgin Mary. Although it reveals plenty about her fellow seer, it does not mention any of the secrets revealed by the Lady.

Convinced that the events of Fátima had to be studied more deeply, Bishop Silva ordered Sister Lucia to write another memoir. She did so between November 7 and 21, beginning this missive with a promise that this would not be a comprehensive document. "(W)hen the repugnance of, or the love for, my secret will make me want to leave some things still hidden, it will be my norm and my guide."

The following memoir must have been a frustrating read for Bishop Silva. It contained a fair amount of information about Sister Lucia's poor relationship with her mother as well as more stories about Jacinta and Francisco. Yet despite containing a detailed accounting of the questioning that went on at the hands of local officials in their effort to attain the secrets, the memoir mentions almost nothing about the secrets themselves.

Still Bishop Silva was not satisfied. In a letter to Sister Lucia, the bishop ordered the seer to reveal the secrets and record everything else she could remember relating to Jacinta for the new edition of a book being published.

The abruptness of the order took Sister Lucia by surprise, a surprise that clearly showed in a letter she wrote to a friend.

> *"This order struck me in the center of my soul as a ray of light, telling me that the moment has arrived to reveal the first two parts of the secret... But the repugnance of manifesting it makes me uncertain. The notes are written out but I am unsure if I will hand them over or if rather I will throw them into the stove. I don't know what I will do, not what is better or more perfect. I do not doubt that the revelation of Hell and of the mercies of the Immaculate Heart of Mary is going to do great good to souls, just like the virtue that it drove Jacinta to practice. But will I also be able, at this time to keep quiet on this and speak only of things of less importance? I dread the questions that will be asked me about Hell."*

Yet despite this dread of revelation, Sister Lucia turned to her notes and finally, five days after receiving the demand letter from Bishop Silva – and one month after Salvador Dalí's celebrated arrival in the United States – wrote down for the first time two secrets revealed by the Lady of Fátima on July 13, 1917.

The First Secret: The Vision of Hell

> *Our Lady showed us a great sea of fire which seemed to be under the earth. Plunged in this fire were demons and souls in human form, like transparent burning embers, all blackened or burnished bronze, floating about in the conflagration, now raised into the air by the flames that issued from within themselves together with great clouds of smoke, now falling back on every side like sparks in a huge fire, without weight or equilibrium, and amid shrieks and groans of pain and despair, which horrified us and made us tremble with fear. The demons could be distinguished by*

their terrifying and repulsive likeness to frightful and unknown animals, all black and transparent. This vision last-ed but an instant. How can we ever be grateful enough to our kind heavenly Mother, who had already prepared us by promising, in the first apparition, to take us to heaven. Otherwise, I think we would have died of fear and terror.

The horror of the vision had a similar effect on Sister Lucia, too. And Jacinta, for that matter. In her third memoir, Sister Lucia writes in detail about Jacinta's reaction to the Hell shown to them by the Lady.

"The Vision of Hell frightened her so much that she did all the penances and mortifications she could to prevent some souls from going here," wrote Sister Lucia. "There are people, even devout ones, who sometimes are afraid to speak about Hell to children lest they frighten them, but God did not hesitate to show it to three children, one of who was only six years old. He knew she would be horrified to the point – I would say – of shriveling with fear. Frequently she sat, meditating, on the ground or on some stone, and began to exclaim, "Hell! Hell! How sorry I am for the souls that are going to Hell! And people burn there alive, like wood in fire!"

With that, wrote Sister Lucia, she would kneel, join her hands, and say the prayer taught to them by the Lady: "O my Jesus, pardon us, save us from the fire of Hell, draw all souls to Heaven, especially those in most need!"

The Second Secret: Mary's Immaculate Heart

You have seen Hell where the souls of poor sinners go. To save them, God wishes to establish in the world devotion to my Immaculate Heart. If what I say to you is done, many souls will be saved and there will be peace. The war is going to end: but if people do not cease offending God, a worse one will break out during the Pontificate of Pius XI. When you see a night illumined by an unknown light, know that this is the great sign given you by God that he is about to punish the world for its crimes, by means of war, famine, and persecutions of the Church and of the Holy Father. To prevent this, I shall come to ask for the consecration of Russia to my Immaculate Heart, and the Communion of reparation on the First Saturdays. If my requests are heeded, Russia will be converted, and there will be peace; if not, she will spread her errors throughout the world, causing wars and persecutions of the Church. The good will be martyred; the Holy Father will have much to suffer; various nations will be annihilated. In the end, my Immaculate Heart will triumph. The Holy Father will consecrate Russia to me, and she shall be converted, and a period of peace will be granted to the world.

It is fair to note that the second secret is controversial, not so much for what it says but when it was written. This secret predicts a horrifying World War II as well as the rise of a Godless Russian empire.

However, when it was written, the European war had already started. This has led some to believe that the second secret of Fátima is an example of a post-dated prophecy.

+++

These three memoirs revealed two of the three secrets of Fátima. A fourth memoir that revealed the third secret was written in 1944 but not released until January 2000.

The only secret that concerned Haffert was The Vision of Hell, and how he could get Sister Lucia to relate in person its details to Salvador Dalí.

J. M. J.

A terceira parte do segredo
revelado a 13 de julho de 1917
na Cova de Iria - Fátima.

Escrevo em acto de obediên-
cia a vós Deus meu, que mo
mandais por meio de sua
Exc.ª Rev.ma o Senhor Bispo
de Leiria e da Vossa e mi-
nha Santíssima Mãe.
Depois das duas partes

The opening part of the manuscript of the *Third Secret of Fátima* written by
Sister Lucia in her own hand.

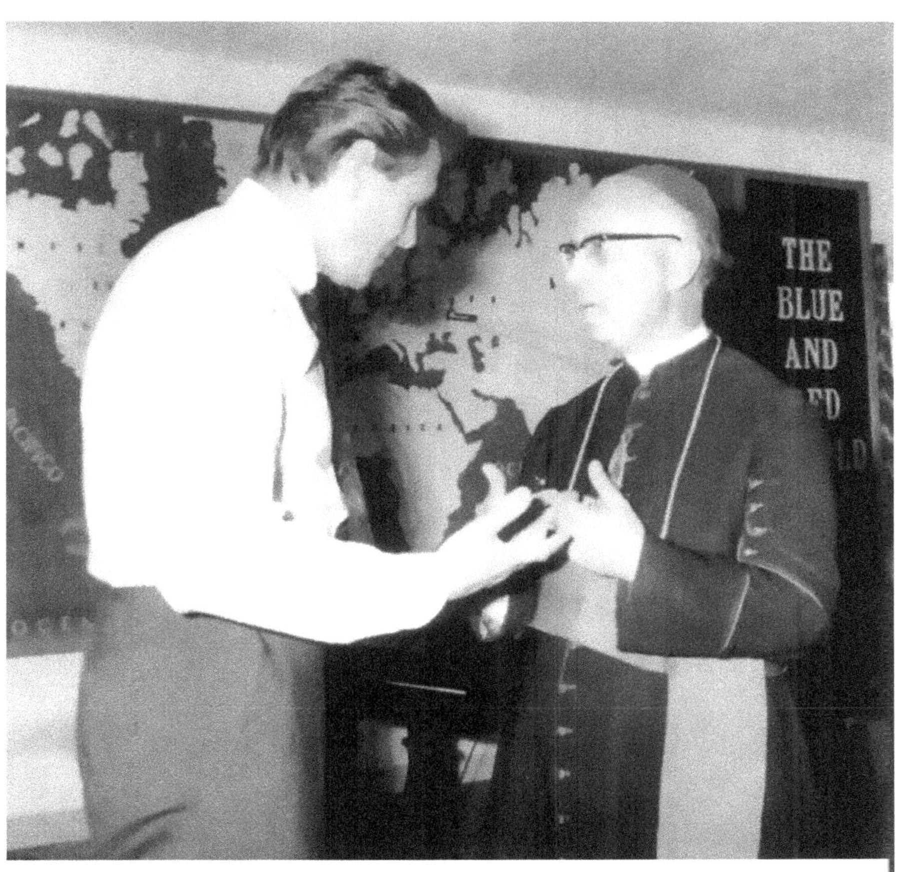

Blue Army Lay Director John Haffert and World Apostolate of Fátima President Bishop D. João Pereira Venâncio photographed during a heated discussion. The Bishop of Leiria had asked John Haffert to stay away from Salvador Dalí because he believed his reputation would ruin the Blue Army's credibility. After the reception of the painting by Monsignor Colgan the Prelate warned Haffert not to reproduce it but rather destroy it or hide it from public view. John Haffert eventually took the Saintly Bishop's advice and hid it under the bed of one of the Handmaids of Mary Immaculate where it remained for 30 years.

17

A Brick Wall

John Haffert was a dapper and well-spoken man who was accustomed to getting his way. And with his good friend the Bishop of Fátima D. José Alves Correia da Silva that had pretty much been the case. But things changed drastically for Haffert after Bishop da Silva died in December of 1957. From the moment he tried to get Sister Lucia to talk to Dalí, he ran head-on into a brick wall.

First, he asked the new Bishop of Leiria his friend D. João Venãncio and Cardinal Lercaro of Bologna, Italy for their help. Both refused however to get involved and contact the seer on Haffert's behalf. Times were changing rapidly. Even Olga Cadaval could not help. Pope Pius XII was dead and with his passing Cadaval stopped entering the cloister to meet with the Fátima Seer as she figured this was a privilege given her by the deceased Pope that she no longer had. She too now only saw Lucia only on special occasions and through the thick iron grill of the parlor.

The new Pope, John XXIII, had just read the Third Secret of Fátima in the company of his Secretary Father Loris Capovilla and to put an end to speculation over the public disclosure of the document in 1960, had the Vatican announce that it would not be revealed.

Haffert who had prepared the Catholic World for the revelation with his TV talk show Countdown 1960. Now he had egg all over his face. Haffert had also burnt himself and those who had secretly snuck him in for the last visit with Lucia by publishing an artist's depiction of the seer as she looked during that meeting. Now even the Bishop of Leira refused to get involved. Venâncio himself was heavily criticized in the Vatican for having attempted to read the content of the envelope of the Third Secret by holding it up to a candle.

Venâncio gave Haffert the excuse that it would be too stressful for the sister to talk about The Vision of Hell. In fact, said the bishop, he had literally seen her quake at the mere mention of Hell. Plus, what if she provided additional description that was not already in her official Memoir? Wouldn't that make people think that she was manufacturing details and stir trouble in the Vatican with the new Pope?

The powerful Italian Cardinal also refused to arrange a meeting of these two very different Visionaries. "Too different actually", he said. He had seen some of Dalí's paintings and considered his work to be profane. Melting clocks and Jesus on a modern cubist cross was one thing, but he had seen paintings of women with penises and men with vaginas. There was even one painting where a woman's anus was being violated by a giant finger! In fact, there may have been more than one such painting that portrayed that act! Didn't The Blue Army and Haffert have something better to do with such a large sum of cash than have Dalí paint *The Vision of Hell*? What about giving the money to the poor?

As he had done at times in the past, Haffert ignored the opinions of the Church Hierarchy and continued to probe for a way to get Dalí to Sister Lucia. On a trip to Fátima, Haffert went out of his way to study a means of getting Dalí to see Sister Lucia. Haffert sent a message to Sister Lucia through a niece named Maria do Fetal, requesting that she obtain permission for Dalí to meet with her regarding *The Vision of Hell*. Previously she had given personal instructions to the Master Sculptor who carved the Pilgrim Virgin images and also to the Amelia Carvalheira who sculpted the image of the Angel of Portugal and of Peace. She had helped and Italian artist hired by John Haffert to depict the Mighty Vision of the Holy Trinity she had witnessed in 1929 at Tuy. Sister Lucia also modeled for the colossal marble statute of the Immaculate Heart of Mary carved for the Fátima Basilica facade. But now she refused to ask permission of the Vatican to meet with Dalí and relive the horrors of The Vision of Hell.

When Haffert returned to the US he told Brother Michael that he didn't think Sister Lucia would meet Dalí but that he would at least try to get him to Fátima and then hope for the best. He also doubted if Lucia could give an adequate description even if she wanted to of Hell.

"You see, during an interview with her a few years back, I asked her about this Apparition, and she was terrified by the memory of it," wrote Haffert. "The best she could say was that the souls looked as if they were burning from within and from without."

Brother Michael was concerned that the lack of face time with Lucia would spell the end of the project. A first-person description of the Vision was not only a requirement to the project, but Lucia's duty to mankind, thought Brother Michael. Prior to her death, Jacinta had pleaded with Lucia to speak freely of The Vision of Hell so all people would know the torment that were the wages of sin. Didn't that make it her duty to tell what she had seen?

Brother Michael put his opinions on paper and sent them to Cardinal Lercaro, who had obviously calmed down by now. To Brother Michael's pleasant surprise, the Cardinal responded a few months later. Yes, said the Cardinal, he felt that the project had some merit, especially for "reminding men of a truth that is certain and potent." But no, he would not use his considerable influence to force Lucia to request a meeting of the Pope for Dalí. Rather, the artist would have to rely upon the descriptions of Hell that Sister Lucia had already committed to paper.

Although Brother Michael appeared to have given up on the idea of a face-to-face meeting with Sister Lucia, he nonetheless wrote her a letter asking for her prayers for the project.

Dear Sister,

You may be pleased to know that the great Spanish painter Salvador Dalí has accepted a commission from The Blue Army of our Lady of Fátima to paint The Vision of Hell that you witnessed in 1917 and so vividly described in your memoirs.

Mr. Dalí will not require your collaboration but will reproduce the scene from your description using his own imagination to fill in the details.

The project is obviously strongly favored by Our Blessed Mother. Without Her help we could not possibly have succeeded. Mr. Dalí was most enthusiastic and agreed to do the painting for a much smaller fee than he would normally receive for a work of this kind.

When completed, the painting will be exhibited by The Blue Army throughout the World and will eventually be hung in the International Center of The Blue Army at Fátima.

The project has the approval of His Eminence Cardinal Lercaro, Archbishop of Bologna, Italy and His Excellency Bishop João Venâncio, Bishop of Leiria, Portugal.

Sister, please pray often for the success of this endeavor and please request the prayers of the individual members of your community for its success.

Some of our group is praying privately each day to Jacinta and Francisco for their inter-cession on behalf of the painting.

It is our firm belief that the Vision was given to you for all of mankind. It is our most fervent prayer that this reproduction of it will be an effective instrument for the salvation of many souls.

Please join us in this prayer.
Very truly yours,
Brother Michael

Sister Lucia never responded to this letter. She received sacks of mail every day but only replied to letters from cardinals, bishops and other prominent Catholic figures. She was simply not allowed to speak about Fátima anymore without permission from the Pope or the Sacred Congregation for the Doctrine of the Faith.

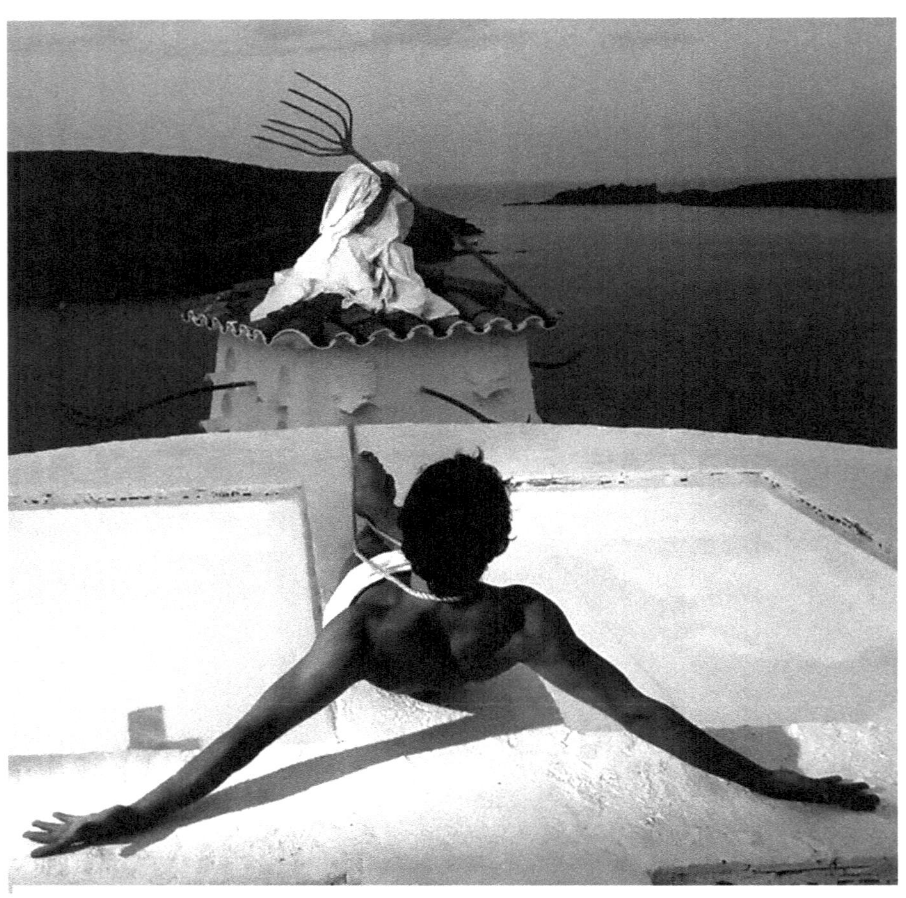

A Photographic Study of the Crucifix of Saint John of the Cross as composed by Salvador Dalí and captured by the lens of Robert Descharnes.

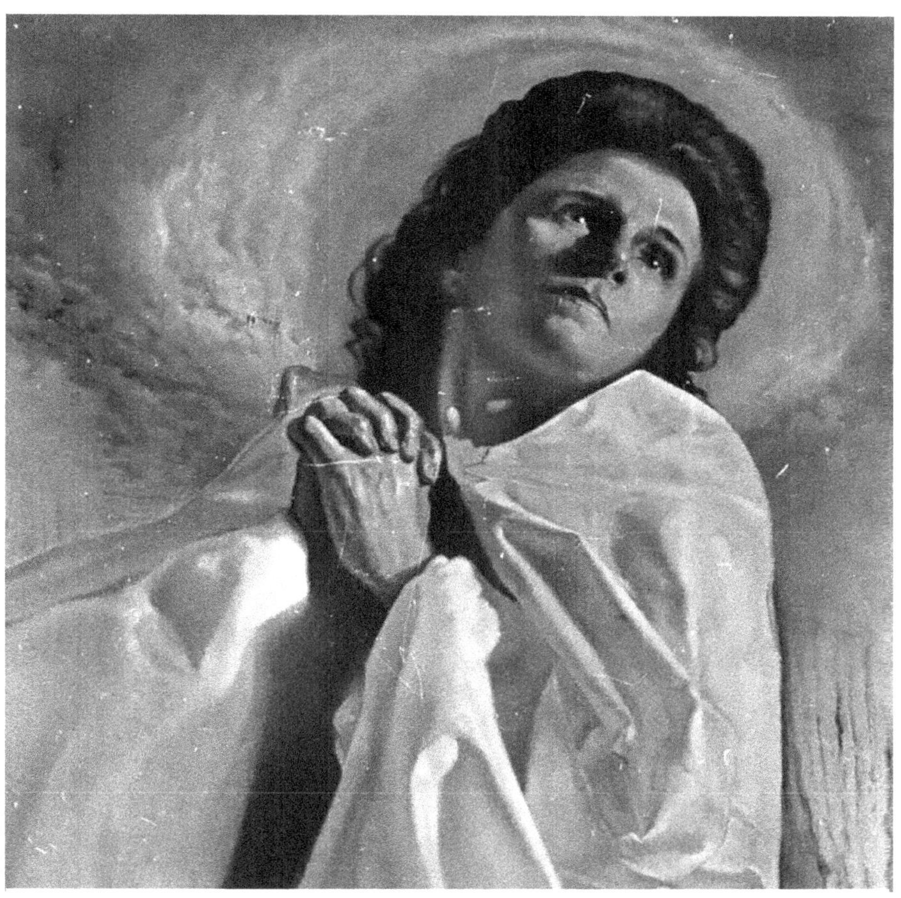

Detail from a photograph taken by Robert Decharnes of a depiction by Salvador Dalí of his Russian born Muse and wife Gala, as Our Lady the Blessed Virgin Mary. Gala was born Gala Helena Dekuvina Diakonoff in Kazan and consecrated by her mother to the Miraculous Icon Haffert would later ransom for the Blue Army. It was returned to the Russian people by Pope John Paul II in 2005 after having been kept in the Domus Pacis at Fátima since 1972.

18

Communicating Vision

Sister Lucia's refusal to cooperate was not something Haffert took personally, but it was something that surprised the charismatic layman. For one of the few times in his life, Haffert's charm had failed him. He had asked for intervention with Sister Lucia from some of the most influential clergy in Europe and when that failed he went directly to Sister Lucia himself through her close cousin who had also been a Carmelite. All of that prodding failed to arouse her. With no options left, he called to give Dalí the bad news.

He dialed the St. Regis Hotel and was transferred to the Dalí suite. Gala answered. Haffert reintroduced himself although it was doubtful that he needed to. Gala had an eye for good-looking men, especially well to do ones like Haffert. Given the chance, she was well known for offering herself to these wealthy gentlemen. Descriptions of her social behavior frequently allude to her flirting like an overly sexed young girl, sitting before the bewildered men with her legs tightly crossed and a bright comely smile gracing her face.

Gala was known to need frequent and intimate interaction from men, reassurance that she was attractive to the opposite sex. Yet, as related by those close to her, she received little if any intimacy from Dalí who was alleged by some to be bisexual, homosexual or even asexual.

Another explanation of Dalí's lack of sexual interests came from

Dalí himself, who told many people that his father left medical books around their house, opened to pages with photos of advanced cases of syphilis and other sexually transmitted infections. He did this to keep the young Dalí's sexual interests in check so as to avoid any unwanted pregnancies during his teenage years. It apparently worked, since there are no known Dalí heirs. But it was believed to have left a fear of sexual intimacy that scarred him for life.

Whatever the case, Gala had many male friends in New York and would often rendezvous with them for a romp in the hay. Reynolds Morse, perhaps Dalí's most avid U.S. collector, recalled to a biographer the time she offered herself to him amid a bed covered with surreal erotic drawings. Morse, a Cleveland, Ohio manufacturing magnate, blushed at her advances and said no. "She was old enough to be my mother," he said.

Such may have been Haffert's fate had he connected with her in person rather than over the phone. Nonetheless the two carried on a pleasant conversation about the grandeur of New York City and its beauty in Spring. Finally, Haffert broke the word to Gala that Sister Lucia would not make herself available to talk to Dalí about *The Vision of Hell.*

With that pronouncement, Gala quickly handed the phone to Dalí himself.

Dalí was a difficult man for Haffert to understand. With his rolling R's and deep Spanish accent, it was common for Dalí to carry on lengthy conversation in English in which the frustrated listener's head bobbed up and down as though he comprehended completely the wisdom coming from the famous Catalan's lips, yet in fact understood nothing. "It is like he is translating the muses," said one who struggled to comprehend Dalí on the phone. "What he says is only understood by him."

Haffert swallowed hard and revealed the dilemma of Sister Lucia to the great artist. As she had said to others, recounting The Vision of Hell was traumatic. So horrible were the images she stored in her mind that to bring them out and examine them was more than she was willing to bear. In the past she had refused the requests of even bishops who wanted to hear her eye-witness visit to Hell, so how could she reasonably be expected to recount the horror to one of the world's great artists?

Haffert said all of this to Dalí and then waited for a response. There was a lengthy silence that made him think the great artist was perhaps not listening or had maybe disconnected the call. Then Dalí's voice sprang to life.

"This is no problem," said Dalí, rolling the "R" in regal fashion. "I will study what she has said about the vision and then go into myself and put together my own vision."

Of course, said Haffert. How else could it work? Haffert knew enough about surrealism to know that its creation often took place on a sub-conscious level. In the case of Dalí, it meant going "into myself" through the use of hypnogogy, a half dream/half-awake state that allowed him to tap the dreamscape of his mind.

That is fine, he told Dalí, but he had one request: Would Dalí – as a courtesy to Sister Lucia, of course – consider making some sample drawings of the painting to show her, just to make sure his vision matched hers?

Once again there was silence, only much briefer this time. Haffert could hear Dalí quickly inhale a breath of air. Then his voice sprang to life.

"Absolutely not!" he declared. "I will paint what I see in my mind!"

Haffert could tell from the tone in Dalí's voice that he had gone too far. He apologized for making the request and wished Dalí both God's help and speed in making *The Vision of Hell* an accurate portrayal of the Hellish realm as seen by the Fátima visionaries.

"Your painting will be seen by millions and will be responsible for the saving of many souls," he assured Dalí.

"Thank you very much," said Dalí just before the phone hit the receiver.

Haffert hung up his own phone at The Blue Army headquarters in New Jersey. He looked out his window at the green fields and the rich blue sky. It was a sight to behold, a piece of heaven on earth in a world that Haffert felt had gone mad. If The Blue Army gathered enough members, and directed its efforts at defeating that Godless political system known as Communism, then perhaps the entire world would at least feel as good to be in as The Blue Army Apostolate's international headquarters.

Haffert took a deep breath and sat down. His mind wandered over many things – his decision to entertain the idea of Brother Michael to have Dalí paint *The Vision of Hell*, his communications with the clergy of his beloved church, some of whom didn't want him to waste resources on a Dalí painting, his meeting with Dalí and Gala at the St. Regis, and finally the conversation he had just had with the Great Master – until it finally settled on the question that had been in his mind since Sister Lucia refused to talk.

How can Dalí paint The Vision of Hell if no one tells him what it looks like? He thought.

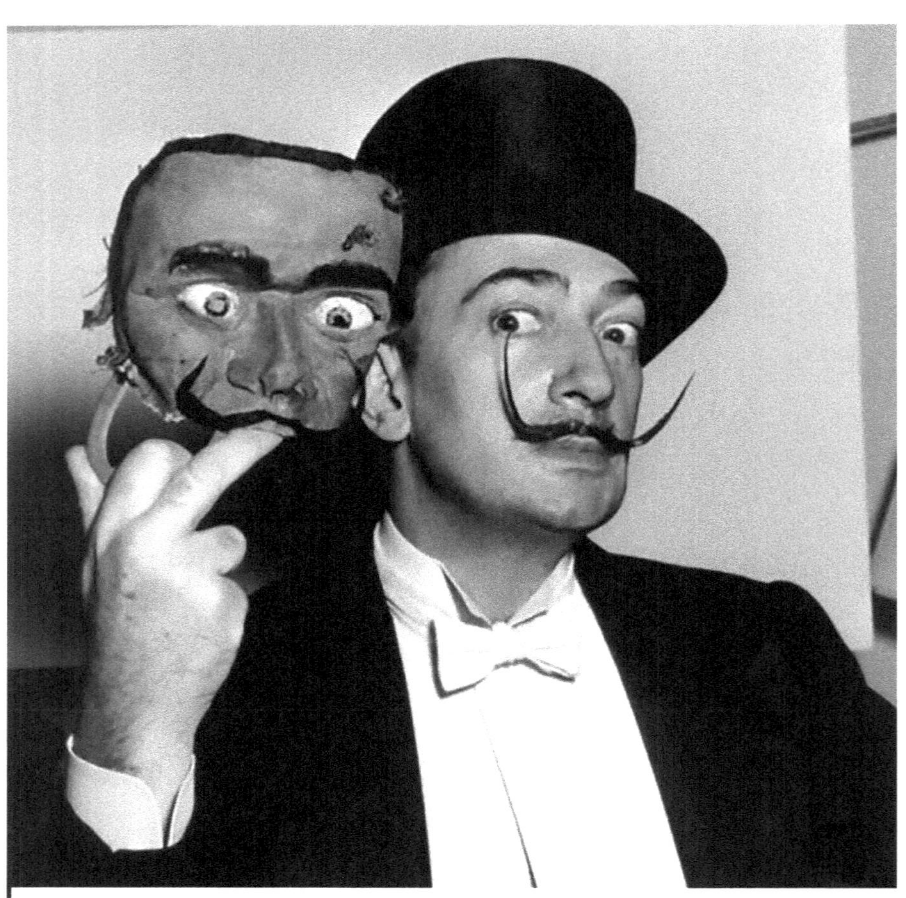

Salvador Dalí in white tie and top hat playfully posing with a papier-mâché
mask modeled after his own face.

19

Dalí's Fátima Secret

For almost two years there was no communication between Dalí and Haffert. Nor, for that matter, was there ever any written account from Dalí to explain how it was that he visualized the Hell of Sister Lucia. This is not a surprise, since most artist, Dalí included, rarely offer written explanations for the methods and meaning of their visual art.

Still there are many clues as to how Dalí produced Vision of Hell, and all of his surreal work, for that matter. It was a technique he used to plumb his subconscious called the "paranoic critical method."

Some historians have questioned that Dalí even knew the meaning of paranoia, which meant "disordered mind" in Classical Greek. The word was used in the 19th century by the new medical art of psychiatry to designate delusional insanity, which, ironically, was a diagnosis given to Dalí's grandfather. It was Freud's belief (most likely to Dalí's horror) that paranoia arose "as an attempt to fend off excessively strong homosexual impulses."

Was it possible, as some biographers have suggested, that Dalí's invention and use of the paranoic critical method was meant to be a defense against homosexual tendencies? Or was it just a method of capturing the unconscious so he could use it on his canvas? It is certain that madness as a creative tool was always of interest to Dalí. The painters and artist that he hung-out with in Paris described Dalí as a man who was either a bit mad or trying to reach that state to the best of his ability.

Andre Thirion, a Communist and surrealist in the Paris of the twenties, described Dalí as being afraid of everything in Paris and overcoming this fear by carrying an elaborate cane as well as a tiny piece of driftwood from his home in Spain, which he used to ward off evil spirits. Others described him as a young man who would launch into fits of laughter that didn't stop for several minutes. Filmmaker Luis Bunuel and painter Juan Miro both insisted that Dalí wasn't just pretending to be mad, he was trying with all of his might to actually go mad. As Dalí himself said, "My laughter was no frivolity; it was cataclysm, abyss and terror."

But it was not his real or imagined fits of madness that led to his greatest creative breakthrough, the paranoiac-critical method. Rather, it was hypnogogy, that twilight state between being asleep and awake, that gave him his most powerful images. In the hypnogogic state, a person sees what is being dished up by his subconscious. Sometimes it may just be bright flashes of color, or vivid dream sequences. Other times these clearer-than-life images have very powerful significance.

The first such image from the hypnogogic realm came for Dalí in 1931 with The Persistence of Memory, the painting with the melting clocks that defined the surrealist movement. Art critic John Canaday described this work best when he said,

> *"In its brilliant colour, its small size, its immaculate precision. It is in the technical tradition of early Flemish and early Venetian painting; also it is parasitic on their forms. The deep distance with its sea and its rocky promontories picked out in golden light is all but a steal from the early Venetian Giovanni Bellini, whose allegories would be Surrealist of their symbolism were morbid instead of poetic."*

With acclaim like this, Dalí felt it best to provide a name and theory for his method of surrealism. That was when he developed the name, "paranoiac-critical method," to describe the creativity that arose when his thoughts of camembert cheese turned to melting clocks as he fell into a state of semi-wakefulness.

One of the best descriptions of paranoiac-critical method comes from Carlton Lake, one of Dalí's biographers: "Basically, it involved setting down an obsessional idea suggested by the unconscious and then elaborating and reinforcing it by a perverse association of ideas and a seemingly irrefutable logic until it took on the conviction of inescapable truth. In dreams or waking fantasies, Dalí recorded the first image he saw and then filled in the space with the images this suggested. Just as a true paranoiac is constantly seeing countless persecutory forms in whatever object is presented to his view, so Dalí claimed that any given image suggested endless other images to him because of his 'paranoiac sensitivity.'"

The surrealist movement, led by Andre Breton, felt that Dalí had given them a great tool with the creation of paranoiac-critical method. It was a painter's version of automatism, where one image led to another image that led eventually to a chain of images that allowed one to plumb the depths of the psyche. Where Freud felt dreams to be the "royal road to the understanding of the unconscious," surrealist felt that Dalí had endowed surrealism with an instrument of primary importance, "capable of being applied equally to painting, poetry, cinema... to fashion to sculpture," even to the history of art, said Breton.

The paranoiac-critical method was essentially the hypnogogic state, that point between sleep and wakefulness in which the images of the subconscious could arise and often times be remembered. Many people throughout history have used hypnogogy, including Thomas Edison who would doze in a rocking chair with large dishpans on the floor by the arms and steel balls in his hands. When he dozed off, the balls would fall onto the pans and the noise would awaken the inventor. If anything of value came to him in that moment of dozing brilliance, Edison would write it down before picking up the steel balls and doing it all again.

This is precisely the method used by Dalí to conjure images from his unconscious mind. Dalí even went so far as to advise art students on how to "sleep without sleeping" using method he called "slumber with a key." He wrote a detailed how-to treatise for any who cared to try it themselves.

> **In order to make use of the slumber with a key you must seat yourself in a bony armchair, preferably of Spanish style, with your head tilted back and resting on the stretched leather back. Your two hands must hang beyond the arms of the chair, to which your**

own must be soldered in a supineness of complete relaxation. Your wrists must be held out in space and must have been previously lubricated with oil of aspic. This is intended to facilitate the benumbing of your hands at the moment when slumber approaches, inducing the tingling that is produced when one of your members goes to sleep – a tingling which is in reality a counterpitch, the physical ants, antidotes of the psychic ones of your redoubtable impatience to paint.

In this posture you must hold a heavy key which you will keep suspended, delicately pressed between the extremities of the thumb and forefinger of your left hand. Under the key you will previously have placed a plate upside down on the floor. Having made these preparations, you will have merely to let yourself be progressively invaded by a serene afternoon sleep, like the spiritual drop of anisette of your soul rising in the cube of sugar of your body. The moment the key drops from your fingers, you may be sure that the noise of its fall on the upside-down plate will awaken you, and you may be equally sure that this fugitive moment when you had barely lost consciousness and during which you cannot be assured of having really slept is totally sufficient, inasmuch as not a second more is needed for your whole physical and psychic being to be revivified by just the necessary amount of repose. For it is exactly, and neither more nor less, what you needed before undertaking your virtuous afternoon labors.

Dalí quoted Plato in calling this, "the sleep of truth," and said that through this dream state, "The quicksand of automatism and dreams vanish upon awakening. But the rocks of the imagination still remain."

It was in this dream state that Dalí did his best work. Exactly how he worked while using the paranoiac-critical method was described in The Secret Life, Dalí's first autobiography. In many ways this technique was similar to meditation.

I would awaken at sunrise, and without washing or dressing sit down before the easel, which stood right beside my bed. Thus the first image I saw on awakening was the painting I had begun, as it was the last I saw in the evening when I retired. And I tried to go to sleep while looking at it fixedly, as though by endeavoring to link it to my sleep I could succeed in not separating myself from it. Sometimes I would awake in the middle of the night and turn on the light to see my painting again for a moment. At times again between slumbers I would observe it in the solitary gay light of the waxing moon. Thus I spent the whole day seated before my easel, my eyes staring fixedly, trying to 'see,' like a medium (very much so indeed), the images that would spring up in my imagination. Often I saw these images exactly situated in the painting. Then, at the point commanded by them, I would paint, paint with the hot taste in my mouth that panting hunting dogs must have at the moment when they fasten their teeth into the game killed that very instant by a well-aimed shot.

At times I would wait whole hours without any such images occurring. Then, not painting, I would remain in suspense, holding up one paw, from which the brush hung motionless, ready to pounce again upon the oneiric landscape of my canvas the moment the next explosion of my brain brought a new victim of my imagination bleeding to the ground. Sometimes the explosion occurred and nothing fell. Sometimes I would dash off in a mad and fruitless chase, for what I had thought was a partridge turned out to be just a leaf that the shock of the bullet had shaken from the branch. To win forgiveness for my mistake I came back hanging my head and humiliated myself before my master. Then I would feel the protective fingers of my imagination scratch me reassuringly between my two eyebrows, and I would close my eyes with awing voluptuousness.

Dalí leaned so heavily upon unconscious images that arose from his mind that Sigmund Freud said of his paintings, "It is not the unconscious I seek in your pictures, but the conscious." And Dalí's "favorite psychiatrist," Dr. Roumeguere, said that at times in his life, Dalí "existed only in a bag full of holes, limp and shapeless, always on the lookout for a crutch."

It is clear at this point that Dalí lived on a planet of his own invented logic. It is also clear that no one, ever, has been more delighted with the workings of his own imagination than Salvador Dalì. Sure of his own genius and wearing it like a costume that included his wide, madness-filled eyes and a heavily waxed moustache, the great artist showed deliberate, prolific recklessness with words and images.

He wrote boldly of his own intellect in *50 Secrets of Magic Craftsmanship*, declaring,

> *" ... My intelligence has never ceased to grow in the course of my ambition which, as everyone knows, has been lofty and majestic since my tenderest childhood. I like to compare my ambition to a century-old oak tree, and my intelligence to a loving vine, which climbs round its bark to reach its top. And if this oak tree seems to me to be immemorial and immobile in its growth, so august and harmonious is its lofty height, the vine of my intelligence, on the contrary, appears to me to have a biological exuberance, to grow by leaps, inasmuch as each time I observe what is happening to me at the moment of beginning or of completing a work, I am always surprised at the bursting forth of vigorous new shoots."*

+++

If it was vigorous new shoots Dalí was looking for, then one must assume that he found them in *The Vision of Hell*. After entering his mystical period, Dalí's paintings became more serious. Gone were the leggy elephants and the voracious grasshoppers, the extravagantly sexy female being descended on by tigers, gone were the melting clocks and watches, glistening roses, and boiled beans. After decades of hopscotching from continent to continent, "scanDalízing" the masses, entertaining the rich, twisting his silly moustache and developing questionable relationships with dictators,

Dalì had entered a relatively serious phase. His religious art embraced formal constraints, bringing to it the fullness of his imagination, but giving more order to it than his earlier work. In essence, he created a new kind of religious painting by restraining his imagination to suit the subjects.

But with *The Vision of Hell*, Dalí had an opportunity to bring back some of the elements of surrealism that had made him the center of that world. In that sense alone, the painting is a transition piece – a missing link – between his surreal and religious work.

Dalí meditated on Lucia's description of The Vision of Hell day and night as he sat in his bony Spanish chair and dipped into his subconscious in search of inspiration and imagery. But still he was unable to paint that vision. He tried to put the vision to canvas and made several preliminary versions. But unsatisfied with the results, he destroyed the canvases and the sketches.

When he contacted Haffert to tell him of his frustrating dilemma, Haffert suggested that Dalí go to Fátima to seek inspiration. He arranged for him to go to Lisbon and had Fátima historian Canon José Galamba de Oliveira meet with him.

Dalí's biggest dilemma for the painting was not Hell per se but the depiction of the Blessed Virgin Mary. Haffert's concerns for his use of Gala as the model for the Mother of God seemed profane to Mr. Fátima. Hearing this, Dalí thought of leaving the face blank so that each person could imagine the Mother of God in his or her own way.

The small Painting by Dalí know as the Ecumenical Council that hangs today in the Vatican Museum is precisely the size of the painting Gala had proposed for the $15, 000 Dollar Vision of Hell. This painting, done in 1960, depicts a faceless Blessed Virgin Mary symbolizing the same struggle, one of putting an appropriate face to the Mother of God.

Canon Galamba was friendly and cordial to Dalí, but his deep, cavernous voice was supernaturally intimidating. To Dalí it seemed like the voice of God.

Dalí listened attentively as Galamba gave him the tour of Fátima indicating at the Capelinha the exact spot where Our Lady opened up the earth to reveal Hell. Dalí was nearly speechless as he stood on that spot.

"This is where the earth opened and they saw Hell," he finally said.

Traveling to the nearby Castle of Ourém, Dalí listened as Galamba explained the Legend of the Moorish Princess Fátima who allegedly converted from Islam at the castle and was baptized Oureana, giving her Christian name to Ourém and her Muslim name to Fátima.

Haffert had told Galamba that he wanted Gala to use her image and that of the Castle in the painting so as to symbolically depict the first Fátima Conversion. The appeal to Conversion, Galamba said to Dalí, was the key to understanding *The Vision of Hell* and the reason for showing the children the horror of eternal damnation.

Dalí was beginning to understand the concept that *The Vision of Hell* had with conversion. With the help of Galamba, he led to understand that once one was in Hell, it was too late to make a change through conversion. But somehow the Immaculate Heart of the Blessed Virgin Mary would shine through as beacon of hope for all who are attentive to her divine message, said Galamba.

Atheistic Communism, Galamba told Dalí, was the Devil's Militant Army. Dalí knew this well. Communists had killed friends and family during the Spanish Revolution for the simple crime of being Catholic. The prophecy of the rise of Communism in Russia and of the spread of the errors of the Soviet Union causing wars and persecution was also part of the July 13th Vision and the second part of the secret, said Galamba, who made it clear to Dalí that he had to depict it in the vision.

As a special treat, Galamba took Dalí to Coimbra, where the second oldest university in the world still operates. There they visited the Dead Poets Garden at Penedo da Saudade, where Galamba pointed to an 18th Century Cloistered Carmelite convent, Saint Teresa of Avila.

"That," he said, "is the home of Sister Lucia."

Galamba had surprised Dalí and at Haffert's request was bringing him along to a brief private meeting with the sister. No questions were to be asked regarding particulars of the apparitions. It was simply not allowed Canon Galamba explained. But at least Dalí would meet the sole surviving seer of Fátima face to face.

Galamba presented the World famous Master Artist to heaven's spokesperson, declaring she was the only person living at the time to have seen the Holy Trinity, the Blessed Virgin Mary, Saint Joseph and Saint Michael the Archangel, all of whom Dalí had painted several times yet had never seen with his own eyes. To be with Lucia, even with the iron bars of the parlor grill separating them, was still like being in a heavenly presence, said Dalí who later commented on how special it felt to breath the same air as a future saint.

Nothing was said by Lucia about The Vision of Hell she'd seen 43 years earlier, but she did promise that she would pray for the project and for Dalí and that he would be inspired to paint something that would be an instrument to convert souls.

Before leaving, Dalí asked Lucia to pray for Gala, revealing to Lucia that his wife was actually Russian from Kazan, her full name being Gala Helena Deluvina Diakonoff.

The unofficial meeting with the Fátima seer lasted no more than 15 minutes. But now, between the short meeting with Sister Lucia and his own surreal visions, Dalí had the inspiration to depict The Vision of Hell.

+++

On the drive back to Fátima from the convent, Galamba explained to Dalí that he thought it providential that Gala was born in Kazan. Our Lady of Kazan, he explained, was an icon venerated as Empress of all of Russia. It had had been carried by generals into battle since the 13th century and was a symbol of Russian victory and liberty. The miraculous image of the "Liberatrix of Russia," was considered the very soul of Russia, and was believed destroyed by the Bolshevists after Lenin had the Cathedral of Our Lady of Kazan in Moscow destroyed and replaced with Red Square, an act aimed at proving that God does not exist.

But in 1950, the icon re-emerged in the private collection of a British Aristocrat. Archaeologists found it to be authentic.

It was apparent that someone in the Communist Party had secretly sold the Icon to a western collector. John Haffert wanted it to be venerated and returned to the people of Russia.

In order to achieve that goal, Haffert started a fund drive to raise the millions needed to purchase the icon and enthrone it at his hotel in Fátima. Pope Pius XII was thrilled over the idea of the icon being rescued, said Galamba, because the world was waiting for the conversion of Russia and the fulfillment of the prophecies of Fátima.

Dalí was humbled by the task at hand, he told Galamba.

Before leaving Fátima, Dalí asked Canon Galamba to hear his confession, a penitential act that the priest later told Haffert was the most moving, sincere and profound confession he had ever heard in his many decades as a priest. Over the years Haffert tried to pry the confession out of Galamba, but the veteran priest would tell him nothing, only that Dalí had led a very interesting life.

Before Dalí left, he handed Galamba an envelope with what was later revealed to contain $15,000 in American Express Travelers Checks, the exact amount paid by Haffert and Brother Michael for the painting of *The Vision of Hell*.

When Haffert was told of the secret donation by Dalí, he had Galamba give the money to Father John Demarchi of the Consolata Missions to put it to use for the poor. In this way, said Haffert, *The Vision of Hell* would become a Work of God.

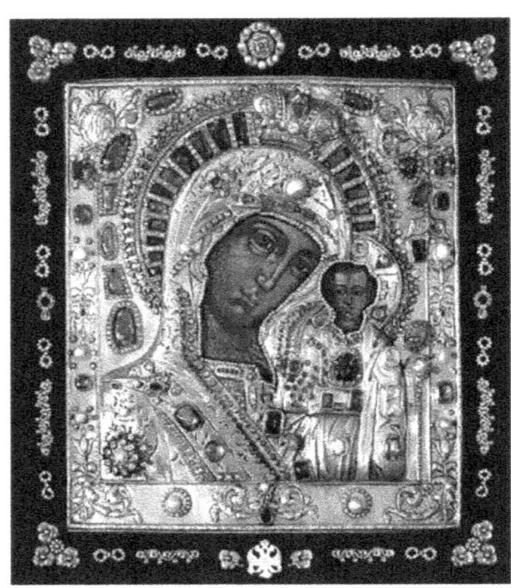

The Icon of Our Lady of Kazan, Empress and Patroness of all the Russians.

Gala Dalí who was born in Kazan Russia, kept a copy of this Icon in her bedroom.

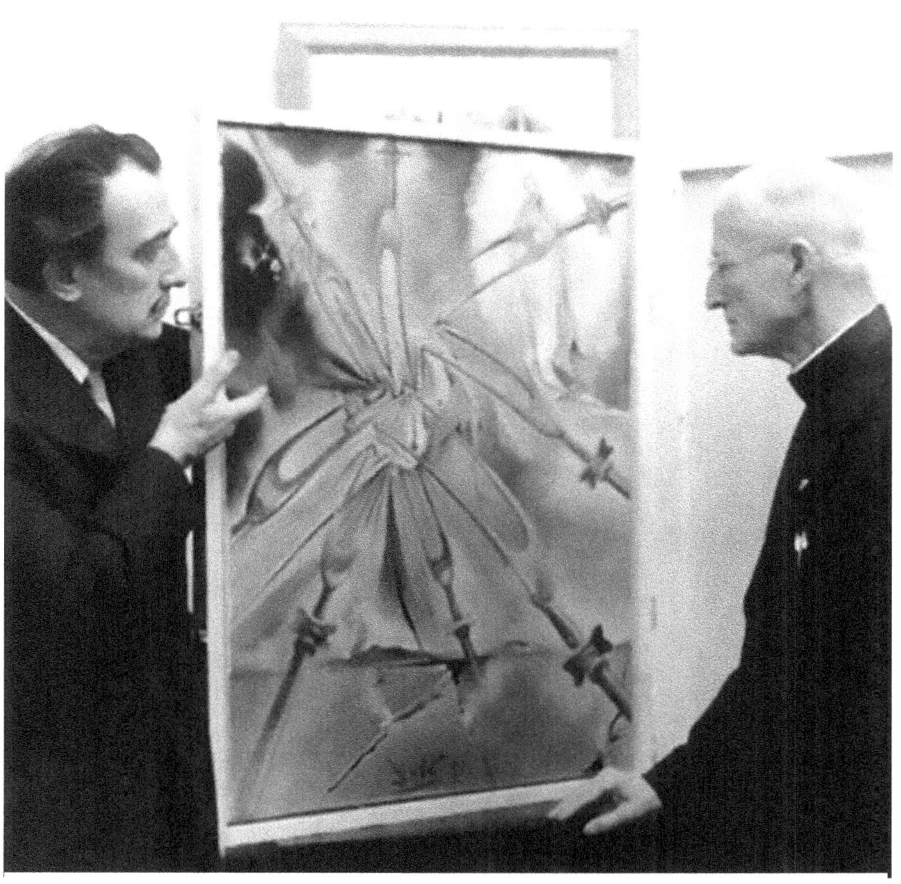

Recently rediscovered and never-before published photograph showing the initial reaction of Monsignor Harold Colgan, Founder of the Blue Army at the 1962 official presentation by Salvador Dalí of The Vision of Hell painting. Subsequent photographs were staged for publicity and depict the Monsignor smiling and shaking Dalí's hand. In reality Colgan confessed to Haffert that the painting was ridiculous and only represented "the Hell of money badly spent."

20

The Horror

Dalí was drawing on his unconscious mind and newly renewed "inner soul" to reproduce Sister Lucia's vision. He painted *The Vision of Hell* in utmost secrecy. No one, except possibly his wife Gala, saw him work on the painting. Even Robert Descharnes, Dalí's photographer and confidant whose job it was to paint the master at work, saw the painting before it was presented to The Blue Army.

Brother Michael, still in seminary school, was obsessed with the success of a painting he had never seen, and was trying to round up support for the painting from Don João Venâncio, the Bishop of Leiria in Portugal, and Cardinal Giacomo Lercaro of Bologna, Italy.

Brother Michael's letter to these powerful members of the Catholic hierarchy was a courageous effort at pre-publicity from a man who was still wending his way through seminary school. As you can see from the letter, Brother Michael did not know of Dalí's visit to Fátima nor his secret meeting with Sister Lucia.

Your Excellency,

You may recall that in February or March of 1960 you received a letter from me regarding a project that I proposed that a great artist be commissioned to paint the

Hell scene from the apparitions of Our Blessed Mother at Fátima. Also while in Washington, you kindly granted me an interview for a discussion of the painting.

I am happy to report that some months ago the great Spanish painter Salvador Dalí consented to accept our commission to reproduce the scene on canvas. No collaboration with Sister Lucia will be necessary. Mr. Dalí will fill in the details not included in her published description from his own creative genius.

The work will be completed in the autumn of 1961. It will be the property of The Blue Army and will eventually hang at the International Centre of that organization at Fátima.

Your Excellency, in making these arrangements with Mr. Dalí Our Blessed Mother was very evidently present. Her hand was so obviously in the entire procedure that there can be no doubt as to her will in this matter. Perhaps the best evidence of this was Mr. Dalí's great enthusiasm for the idea. The commission was possible only because he generously accepted it for less than he would normally receive for a work of this kind.

It is our fervent hope and prayer that the hierarchy and the clergy will recognize this painting as a great gift from Our Mother to the world and will use it to its full advantage by displaying prints in their churches and by directing the attention of the people to it in their sermons and in all other public communications.

If only the Priesthood can be convinced that this is not an ordinary painting by Salvador Dalí, if any work of this great artist can be called ordinary; but it is a message or warning so sorely needed by mankind that Jesus Himself sent it down from Heaven by His own Mother.

Why is to convince them? I a seminarian just beginning philosophy am in no position to present such a proposition to the Priesthood. Besides, I enter the novitiate of a religious order in July, the Graymoor Society, and will be confined there and in major seminary for the next seven years.

However, it seems to me that your Blessed Mother has been careful to give the project two distinguished friends in the hierarchy, Cardinal Giacomo Lercaro, archbishop of Bologna, Italy, who advised me and you yourself who is graciously encouraged and so correctly advised me in this matter. Surely Our Land would be pleased to have your Excellency and his Eminence, both of you prominent advocates of her Fátima messages, present this her gift to the Priesthood.

Brother Michael's letter went on to suggest that these powerful clergymen introduce the forthcoming painting with a display of prints in the churches of their dioceses and that they even go so far as to recommend to the Vatican that the prints of the painting go out to "the entire church."

"The painting would be a useful instrument and such indeed is our purpose, to produce a useful instrument for the salvation of souls," wrote Brother Michael. "The Priesthood must accept it as an instrument."

Brother Michael's hopeful letter was addressed to Bishop Venâncio and carbon copied to Cardinal Lercaro.

The response to Brother Michael's letter came from the Bishop of Leiria and was sent only to Haffert at The Blue Army headquarters in New Jersey and was the exact opposite of what was expected by Brother Michael. Coming from such a powerful bishop, it represented the official position of the Fátima shrine regarding Salvador Dalí and his art.

"It was a mistake to get mixed up with this fellow (Dalí) in the first place," wrote the Bishop. "The best thing you can do now is to forget he ever existed, and never mention his name again."

The bishop's letter continued:

If confusion is the hallmark of Hell, I have no doubt but that Mr. Dalí can do an adequate "Vision of Hell." I do not know what you propose to do with the painting. Just don't bring it into the diocese. Don't reproduce it in or on Soul (The Blue Army's magazine), and don't ask for any money to have it printed in any magazine that contains my name.

Such a response from a powerful Bishop would lead most seminarians to cower into prayer and meditation. Not Brother Michael. When he received the Bishop's testy response from Haffert, he immediately saw it as a public relations coupe.

"Too bad His Excellency takes this view," he wrote to Haffert in a July 14, 1951 letter. "However such controversy may be put to good use by Our Mother to attract attention to the painting."

In the same letter he revealed another path that had dried up.

Events have just about put an end to any possibility of effectively using the painting in Cuba (as Haffert had suggested.) There is practically no church left in which to display it. Perhaps next year after the picture has been introduced in the United States and in Europe such possibility will present itself.

Haffert too remained positive. "I believe that the Bishop will change his mind, too, when he sees the finished painting," wrote Haffert. "Our Blessed Mother is not to be outdone in her generosity, and your zeal for her cause is certain to bring great conversions."

+++

As the bishop suggested, Haffert very nearly did forget about Dalí, but it wasn't because he tried. Haffert became very busy with a new venture, the "Columbus Fleet" project.

Concerned that not enough young people were being drawn to Fátima, he decided to create a fleet of three sailing ships that would operate in the Bahamas during the winter months. As Haffert wrote in his biography, "(I) felt that a sail in the West Indies with daily Mass and a bringing home to young people of the almost miraculous nature of Columbus' original voyage and the subsequent apparition of our Lady of Guadalupe, would open the door to their minds and hearts."

Haffert considered it an act of God that he found the Santa Maria in Greenwich, NJ. Built in 1901 by radio magnate Atwater Kent, the ship was stored in a shipyard for several years until two carpenters bought it. They rebuilt the ship and after the war loaded up their families and set sail for Bora Bora. They were going there, they said, to escape the coming nuclear destruction.

Off the coast of New Jersey, they were caught in a terrible gale that drove the ship 300 miles off course and left them seasick and frightened. When they returned to port, one of the carpenters gave his share in the boat to the other, who sailed the sturdy ship to Florida where he left it tied up for several years in the Miami River.

Haffert reconditioned the ship and sailed it out of Miami headed for Bimini, 40 nautical miles away. Although three men accompanied Haffert, only one of them had any sailing experience at all. Shortly after leaving port, all three of the men became seasick, leaving Haffert to sail the ship through the dangerous Bimini reef alone.

It was a frightening and unexpected journey, but Haffert's navigational skill and luck brought them through it. After that event, Haffert and his new 110-ton schooner were almost inseparable.

So it was that he nearly forgot about Dalí and the painting by the summer of 1961. Then, that winter, an envelope arrived with a 4-cent stamp of Lincoln on the upper right side and the name "S. Dalí" written neatly above the return address for the St. Regis Hotel.

Haffert opened the envelope. It was from Gala, written in awkward English.

Dear Mr. Haffert,

We arrived very short time ago and will remain at Hotel St. Regis as usually.

Your painting, The Vision of Hell will come soon from Spain as it has been shipped only recently to give it time to dry – in order that will be no hurt.

Dalí is waiting the News about this shipping and as soon as any thing is in order and painting here we will announce it to you. Please accept our best wishes for New Year.

Sincerely,
Gala Dalí

Haffert felt a twinge of excitement as he closed the letter. His life had been one of religious accomplishments. He had started two important Catholic lay organizations, built a shrine in New Jersey and The Blue Army

International Headquarters at Fátima complete with a 300 room Guest House and a Byzantine Chapel. He had started the largest movement in the history of the church with over 80 million members. He had brought the Pilgrim Virgin he designed to almost every nation of the world. He had founded Fátima Travel, a large tour company with two Boeing 707s, and was now on the verge of returning the historic icon of Our Lady of Kazan, to the people of Russia.

His enterprise would send thousands of Pilgrims to the hallowed ground of the Fátima apparitions each year and it was, all aimed at having people experience "the Fátima reality." The Blue Army's magazine, *Soul*, had more than 200,000 readers, almost all of which donated significant amounts of money to keep the magazine financially healthy. His books were all Catholic bestsellers and autobiographical, giving readers insight into the thoughts and actions of this dedicated man. He was a religious luminary in the Northeastern United States and had so much power as a Catholic layman that he'd had several significant audiences with every pope since Pius XII, and was known to virtually all the Cardinals and bishops in the church as "Mr. Fátima."

And now as another crowning achievement there would be this Salvador Dalí painting, a major work of art illustrating one of the most dramatic and vivid of Fátima visions. As Haffert pondered the arrival of this precious cargo, he must have felt like a member of the Medici family, the great Italian art patrons of the 14th century responsible for the blossoming of religious art in their time. He most certainly realized that behind every great artist, stands a patron.

One month later on February 18th, a special delivery letter arrived at the St. Joseph's Friary in Saranac Lake, New York. It was addressed to Brother Michael at the Jordan Seminary in Milwaukee and was forwarded by one of the fathers to Brother Michael at his new seminary.

The letter was written in awkward English by Salvador Dalí, who spoke of himself (as always) in the third person:

> *As Dalí told you the shipping arrived in N.Y. Customs, etc.*
> *Did delayed some of delivery of the painting of The Vision*
> *of Hell. But could you be so kind and write now to Dalí*
> *telling him when you could come here in N.Y. around or*
> *soon after 10 – 12 March to see and take the painting of our*
> *Lady of Fátima.*

Dalí sorry about all this complications and hope see you
soon.

Please accept my respects.
Yours,
Salvador Dalí

Brother Michael felt a great stir of excitement. Finally, he thought. With the world in such great need of a religious revival, a vivid work of art showing Hell would certainly awaken the populace. There is nothing like fear to motivate people toward God. As Brother Michael had explained to Haffert, a man who carries with him an image of Hell will think twice before committing mortal sin. The painting, he hoped, would take the abstract nature of Hell out of the place, recreating the horror exactly as the three children had seen it.

With a great deal of excitement, Brother Michael wrote back to Dalí at the St. Regis Hotel. Explaining that he was a novice in a religious institute, Brother Michael said that it would be impossible for him to come to Manhattan and receive the painting. He gave Dalí the address and telephone number of Haffert and asked that he contact him since The Blue Army had commissioned the painting and he, Brother Michael, had only donated funds to help pay for it.

"May Our Lady of Fátima bless and keep you and yours," wrote Brother Michael.

Brother Michael took a deep breath as he posted this letter. He most likely didn't feel like a member of the Medici family, but he certainly felt like what he was, an art impresario who felt he would be the savior of souls.

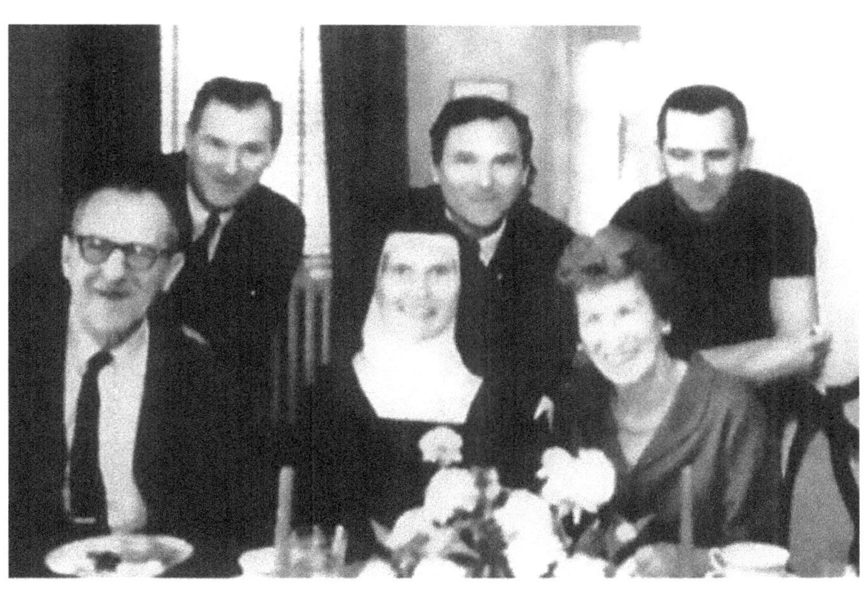

John Haffert (center) with his parents, brothers and Sister Betty, a Cloistered Carmelite Sister.

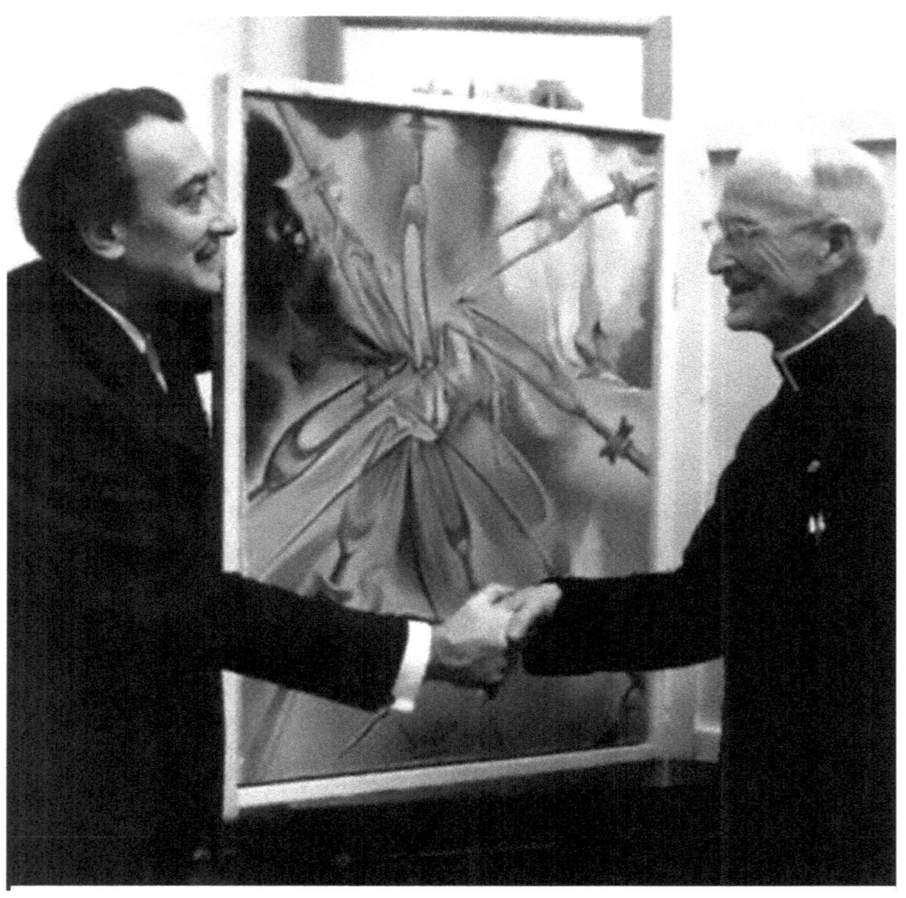

Monsignor Harold Colgan reluctantly smiles and shakes hands with Salvador Dalí for a promotional publicity shot taken during the presentation of the painting of The Vision of Hell at Fátima in 1962.

21

The Vision of Hell

When John Haffert received the letter from Dalí that the painting was completed and in New York, he sprang immediately into action. Although he was on a sailing venture in Nassau, and would be for another month, he hired Fred Joyce, one of the Hilton Corporation's top publicists, to begin a publicity campaign around Dalí's painting.

Joyce's immediate suggestion was to loan the painting to the Metropolitan Museum of Art. If they rejected it, he would offer it to the National Gallery in Washington, DC, where it could be shown in conjunction with other works by Dalí, including his modern masterpiece Sacrament of the Last Supper. If neither wanted to display it, Joyce suggested that it be loaned to other museums around the world.

Without waiting to see the painting, Haffert dictated a letter to his secretary Faith Bayley to be sent to the curator of modern art at the Metropolitan Museum of Art in New York City. The letter read:

> About a year ago we commissioned a painting by Salvador Dalí entitled "Inferno."
>
> ...Mr. Dalí was so deeply impressed by the concept, which has taken him more than a year and three months to materialize. However, the painting is finally completed and

we have just been informed that it is ready for delivery.

We would like to lend the painting first to the Metropolitan Museum in New York... We are sending a copy of this letter to Mr. Dalí at the Hotel St. Regis. We feel that the Museum will be able to give to this work a proper public reception, particularly proper during the season of Lent.

Haffert dictated a similar letter to be sent to the curator at the National Gallery in Washington, DC, and then he passed the duty of receiving the painting to Monsignor Colgan, the co-founder of The Blue Army.

Haffert wanted to be the first in The Blue Army to see the painting, but he was in the midst of a treasure hunting expedition on an island in the West Indies with three friends. They had found a Spanish galleon and were spending their days searching the clear sandy bottom for artifacts and gold coins. They had found many, but it wasn't the booty that kept Haffert interested in the expedition. He was intrigued by the conversations the four men had had in the evening about religion and the divinity of Christ.

It was from this adventure that Haffert wrote another Catholic bestseller, The World's Greatest Secret, a book about Christian unity. And it was because of this deep-sea adventure that he could not be the first to see the horror of Hell.

That duty was left to Monsignor Colgan.

+ + +

Monsignor Colgan had a weak heart. At one point it had become so weak that it stopped. When that happened the New Jersey priest found himself in the midst of what has become known as a near-death experience, bathed in divine light and standing before the Virgin Mary. That brief encounter with the other side was a powerful one for the priest. As he lay convalescing in the hospital, Colgan promised that – if spared – he would spend the rest of his life spreading devotion to Our Lady of Fátima.

Sometimes he didn't fully understand Haffert's methods and motivations, but he let the layman lead the way because he was usually right.

But Colgan, just like Bishop Venâncio, was not sure Haffert was right about Dalí. He had seen the Spanish painter's other works and found most of it to be incomprehensible and obscene. He understood Haffert's motivation to have Dalí paint *The Vision of Hell*. There was no question but what a painting by the likes of Dalí should have a strong impact with those lambs outside of the flock, the ones who mock the Holy Church and her strong belief in the punishments of Hell. But should a painter with the inclinations of Dalí be allowed to paint such an important religious moment without firm guidance from a church representative? Had Michelangelo himself not been guided by a pope?

Colgan didn't like the idea of Dalí being left alone to paint such a pivotal moment in church history. If the Vatican would not give such latitude to any artist, then why should The Blue Army?

Colgan didn't like the task he had been given now. He was preparing to leave for Fátima in two days and planned to have a relaxing evening at the New Yorker Hotel in Manhattan before flying out the next day. That all changed when, just before leaving Washington, NJ for the city, a note was delivered to him at his quarters. It was from Faith Bayley, Haffert's efficient and aptly named secretary.

Dear Monsignor:

Mr. Haffert just phoned from Nassau instructing us to send the enclosed check in the amount of $10,000 to be presented to Salvador Dalí in payment of the painting "Inferno" which he is to deliver to you in return.

Mr. Haffert asked that this be sent to you at the Hotel New Yorker for you arrival tomorrow.

...I just phoned Mrs. Dalí and 3 o'clock tomorrow afternoon (Wednesday) is the time she prefers for the presentation...

...Kindest regards from all here at the institute, and hope you are feeling fit and fine, and that your sojourn at Fátima will be the most rewarding in every way, as it certainly will be for those with whom you will be residing.

Sincerely yours,
(Mrs.) Faith Bayley

Colgan sighed and put the letter back into the envelope. Visiting Salvador Dalí was not high on his list before making a long transatlantic flight. He was a nervous flyer as it was, and he needed nothing to contribute to his anxiety. Still it should be interesting, he thought as he zipped closed his suitcase and headed for the car that would take him to the big city. How could Dalí possibly make Hell something easy to look at?

+ + +

There is no written record of Colgan's meeting with the Dalís, nor his first encounter with *The Vision of Hell* painting. But there is a verbal account that was told by Haffert to historian Carlos Evaristo years later in Fátima. There is also a photographic record of the unveiling, thanks to Haffert's foresight in sending his Blue Army photographer. For decades after the presentation Haffert claimed to have been there on the day of the presentation of the painting and to have taken photos. But that was false memory. In reality he was present institutionally, being represented by Colgan and having his photographer be his eyes at the event. Up until 2012 no photos of Haffert with Dalí or with the painting had ever been found and were believed to have been nonexistent. But it was the discovery of this photo that led to the authentication of the painting as being one by Salvador Dalí.

The photo shows Dalí on one side of the painting dressed regally in a black suit to match his slicked-back black hair. Dalí's most prominent feature in the photograph is his eyes. They are wide and filled with that Dalí madness, and are fixed keenly on Father Colgan's down-turned face. Dalí's look reveals a bit of insecurity about the painting in the box. Across his face is the look of a little boy who seems to know he has crossed the line.

Colgan, on the other hand, is not looking at Dalí at all. He is clenching his jaw and his right fist and looking down at what surely must be one of modern art's most horrifying works.

My God, it is a vision of Hell, is certainly one thought that passed through Colgan's mind.

In plain view between them is the painting itself. It is a horror. What Lúcia described matter-of-factly and with great care, Dalì erupted onto canvas in searing oranges, blues and reds; with gleaming escargot forks pressing into stretched flesh, bone and soul. What Lúcia managed to harbor for decades, Dalì released in a vivid and powerful image.

In a sentence, It's a portrait of thrilling and mighty tension – the tension wrought by fear and faith, perhaps the two most polar and poignant manners of dealing with uncertainty. But there was a secret to the composition that Dalí would later reveal to only one person. Mr. Fátima himself!

Although it didn't likely register in Father Colgan's mind right away (if at all) the painting that so obviously appalled him interprets what popes and laymen have believed to be one of the most seminal human events of the last century – the point at which the mysticism of the Roman Catholic Church was writ large across the sky.

The Church in those days was suffering a period of mass doubt and intensely focused persecution. There had been a rift in the constituency, a splitting in two: impassioned fundamentalists and more casual or non-literal believers. It did not have a healthy mainstream. The Roman Catholic Church was like a frustrated, aging, doddering old king in the Western world, with diverse enemies ascending to power. Anti-clerical regimes were on the rise throughout Latin America, Spain, and Portugal – all places with large Catholic populations.

In addition to governments, the scientific advancements of the Industrial age and the slew of eclectic, experimental art movements at the time (Cubism, Dadaism, Futurism, you name it) were inspiring doubt in the dogmatic foundation of the church. Throughout the Western world, communism as an ideology was just beginning to be considered, and no one quite understood then that it would be the focus of a lengthy Cold War.

It was also a time when information was a prized and highly controlled thing – although rumors could be passed from lip to lip with ease, the ability to mass-communicate was reserved for a rare few. Messages from the clergy were much more strictly watched and managed than they now are, and they could logically have been shifted or spun one way or another; articulated to fit the purposes and aims of the Church and its political allies.

And then came the three children of Fátima with their six Apparitions that linked people once again back into Catholic mysticism. Haffert like Sister Lucia believed that after reading the Third Secret in August of 1957 the Pope had assembled the Vatican II Council to try and help the Church adapt and better cope with the world situation. Dalí shared this opinion and tried to incorporate it in The Ecumenical Council the painting that now hangs in the Vatican Museum and was painted shortly before *The Vision of Hell*.

It is conversion and a return to faith that we see in the painting and is its underlying theme. Yet the intent of this painting is not the beauty of belief, but the Hell that awaits those who don't believe. Without the Virgin solemnly praying in the corner of the canvas, there would be no beauty in the painting. The horror portrayed by Dalí in this work of religious art classifies this work as being one of anti-beauty. A true Vision of Hell.

In the painting, eight fine, long-handled forks stab at a twisted and contorted soul, beneath which is a person carrying a crucifix, presumably a martyr, likely a pope or possibly the fabled Princess Oureana. Behind that figure is a castle, most likely the Castle of Ourém.

The forks are piercing the mysterious figure and causing drops of blood to fall from the folds of the skin. There is an almost playful clamor to their stabbing – as if each fork was trying to make off with the last savory bite of mashed potatoes at Thanksgiving supper. To the upper right, a slight woman draped in a river of powder blue cloth casts her eyes downward. She is a stylized icon of the Virgin Mary. Her face is blushing pink, her hair is parted in the center and covered with cascading silk, and her willowy shape is distorted. She is a pretty good replica of the image of Our Lady of Fátima, which, as mentioned, was instrumental in the effort to consecrate Russia to the Virgin Mary. She embodies love, mercy, wisdom and hope, but she's muddled at the edges and in her doll-like facial features. Her countenance emanates a subterranean glow that is dimmed by both sorrow and forbearance – an ownership of the sorrow. One of the forks appears to slide between the layers of her ethereal garments. And what is most evident for Dalí experts is that for the first time in Dalí's career the Virgin Mary Mother of God does not have Gala's Russian face!

The presence of the eight forks is a representation of his "mystical delirium," and a symbol of his transformation. When he first discussed his religious conversion at a conference in Barcelona, Dalí held up a two-pronged wooden fork, saying the object was the exact symbol of his philosophy in life. The left prong, said Dalí, represented the revolutionary and sacrilegious Dalí of the 1920s, a man struggling to realize himself as an artist. The right prong was the mystical Dalí of 1950, the painter of religious art. The fork's handle was the symbol of Dalí's unity, he said, his ecstasy.

A dried and violently cracked expanse of burnished red earth is at the bottom of the canvas and a fork pokes up through the cracks. To the upper left, a smoky group of dark figures – it is difficult to tell if they are animals, demons, or average souls – descend what looks to be a hill. Flatly decorative touches with yet more symbolism fill the space between these subjects – rolling hills, clouds, water and mountain air. The painting's essence is pure Dalí – devilish, divine, vivid with colors and imagery.

In the middle of the painting is a double image that reveals the profile of a man that is part of the tortured main figure. The upside-down figure holds his arms open and is crying blood onto the left fork. Some Dalí experts believe this to be a hidden self-portrait, a man tormented by death since his childhood, devastated by the monsters of Hell.

If that is the case, then Dalí experts who have examined this painting believe that Dalí reinterpreted the vision of the children and made it totally his: a portrayal of Dalí himself, tormented and crying about the inevitable approach of death. That is why, say some Dalí experts, he signed his name so prominently in the middle of the painting.

Whatever the case, Dalí truly connected with *The Vision of Hell.*

+ + +

It is unlikely, based on the bemused look on the face of Father Colgan in a second photo taken that day, that the monsignor considered any of these interpretations in forming his own opinion about the painting. Rather he took possession of the painting and then took his leave, giving Gala the $10,000 check before hustling the painting to the Dominican Convent in New York city and leaving for Fátima the next day. He'd had his brush with Hell for one day. Now Colgan wanted to get back to his personal heaven, the place in Portugal where his source of divinity – the Virgin Mary – touched the earth with her mystery.

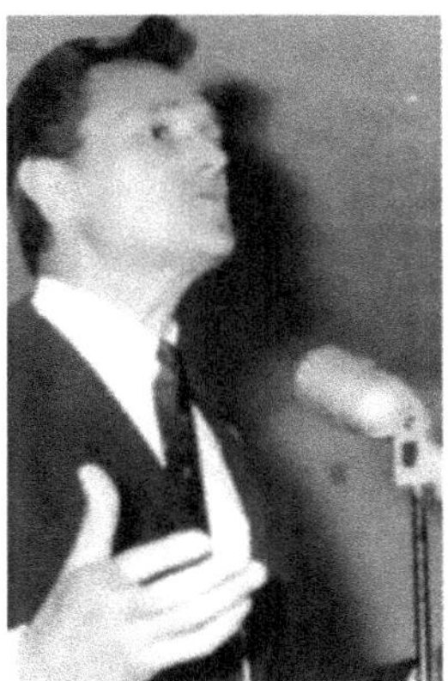
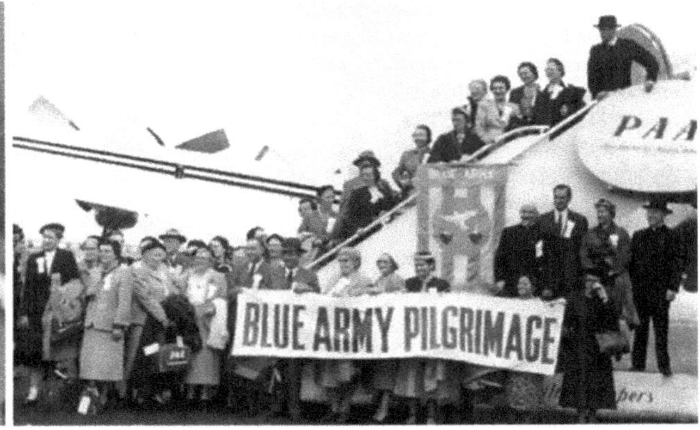

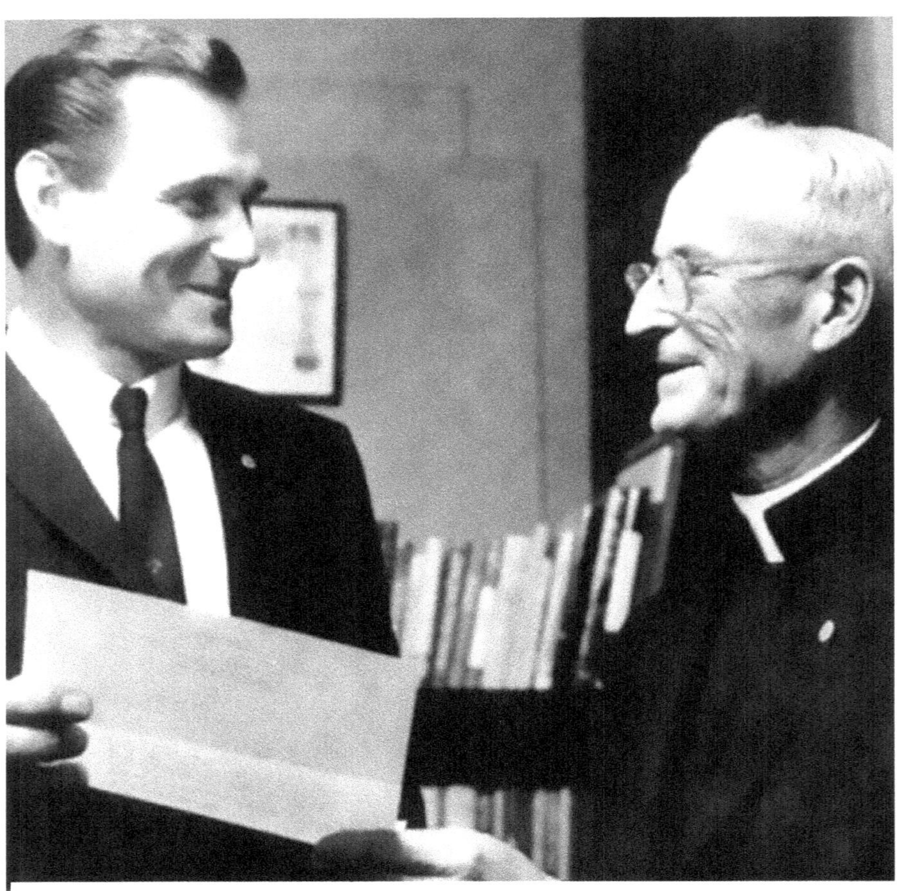

John Haffert presents Monsignor Harold Colgan with a letter. Haffert had informed Colgan that Salvador Dalí had given back to Our Lady the exact amount he had received for the Commission to paint The Vision of Hell. Contrary to usual practice, Dalí had relinquished to the Blue Army, in perpetuity, all rights to the intellectual property of the same.

Conclusion

A Hidden Work of Genius

When Haffert saw the painting, it was not what he had hoped for or expected. But, as he would explain later, he truly didn't know what to expect anyway. This was, after all, a Vision of Hell. For some reason he had expected something more appealing, work that made Hell a little, well, more attractive. Face to face with Dalí's creation, he was now adjusting his expectations.

"Dalí's handling of the subject is unique," he wrote in a letter to Brother Michael. "And while it was different than I expected, the more I have considered the painting the more it has appeared to me that it will serve the purpose intended."

Brother Michael was also surprised at what he saw, in part because it was a sophisticated image. "As you did, I expected a different treatment, but I am sure that the painting as it is done is a much greater work of art than anything I conceived. I was thinking of something for the ordinary people, the masses, whereas this is definitely directed to the sophisticate. I am convinced that Our Blessed Mother wants it this way and has produced what she needed."

Despite the notion of divine intervention from the Holy Mother in the production of the painting, Haffert had no success when it came to placing the painting in either the National Gallery or the Metropolitan Museum of Art.

For the Met, special exhibitions for living artists were forbidden. As Theodore Rousseau, curator of the Department of Painting, explained to Haffert: "The story connected with the commissioning of Mr. Dalí's painting. . . is most interesting. However, I am sorry to say that it will not be possible for this Museum to exhibit this work. It is a standing rule that we do not give special exhibitions to the work of a single living artist. I am sure that you will understand that to break this rule would start a very dangerous precedent."

The same rule applied to the National Gallery of Art. Although the museum director John Walker was interested in the painting, a glut of twentieth century paintings loaned to the museum by collector Chester Dale (a subject of a humorous portrait by Dalí in which he was made to look like his dog) prevented them from accepting further loans.

The lack of acceptance of the Dalí painting by the two major institutions in America was a blow to Haffert and Brother Michael. Still Brother Michael believed that the Virgin Mary would somehow intercede and there would be the soul-saving press he had hoped for. Haffert apparently believed the same.

For the next year and a half, Haffert retained the public relations firm of Bell & Stanton to publicize the painting, which now hung in the offices of Fátima Travel, the agency Haffert had founded to take pilgrims to Fátima.

Although hundreds came to see the painting in the travel agency's mid-town offices, Bell & Stanton was unable to place a single significant article about the existence and meaning of Dalí's painting.

Finally Haffert gave up. His frustration was clear in a letter he wrote to the Bell & Stanton account executive: "If you find that you cannot succeed in this venture with at least one important story by the end of the two month period since the account was placed with you, we will consider it a lost cause and on that basis consider the account closed as of that time."

Concerned that they may lose an account and embarrassed at their inability to place significant publicity, Bell & Stanton redoubled its efforts and was still unable to place stories about the painting. Surprised at the lack of response to the painting, Alan Bell suggested that Dalí's Hell was maybe a bit too Hellish for a media that was increasingly focused on beauty. Haffert agreed but insisted that somewhere, there was an editor who was interested in saving souls and gaining converts through the message of Fátima painted by a famous artist.

Alan Bell agreed and decided to work free of charge on behalf of

The Blue Army in getting the word out about *The Vision of Hell.*

Brother Michael was pushing hard, too. He expressed to Haffert and others that the painting would be a useful instrument for reminding men of a "truth that is certain and potent," and for that reason he felt that the power in the painting was the fact that it was difficult to look at. Yet despite all of his focus on Hell, Brother Michael could never come to grip with the Catholic doctrine of Hell, in which Hell is material and eternal. His constant questions about the doctrine as a seminarian finally led to doubt by his superiors at the Graymoor Seminary that he could become an effective priest. After nearly a decade of study, Brother Michael was asked to leave the seminary.

Still, in his last letter written on seminary stationery, Brother Michael said that he trusted "Our Blessed Mother" to guide Haffert's hand in handling the Dalí painting and made a suggestion: "Perhaps it could be displayed in a European museum, perhaps even the Louvre in Paris. If it attracted attention in Europe then maybe it would be at least as well received in the United States. The question is, will it attract attention in either Europe or in the United States at the present time. People are pretty comfortable with any kind of art these days. Perhaps the time just is not right for an awakening to the doctrine of Hell."

Six months later, on January 28, 1964, Haffert received a copy of a letter that Brother Michael wrote to Clare Boothe Luce, the writer, congresswoman and wife of Henry Luce, whose company Time Inc., published both Time and Life magazines.

The letter is a lengthy one and relates the story of Fátima, The Blue Army and Dalí's painting in concise terms, so as not to "bog down in unessentials" yet to relate "my own hope, fears and indecisions that ended in the triumphant realization of a dream, Mr. Dalí's acceptance of our commission to paint *The Vision of Hell.*"

The former seminarian told Mrs. Luce of his conversion to Catholicism followed by "intense meditations on the horrors of eternal damnation," as a result of Lucia's description of Hell as seen at Fátima.

"God permitted me to experience something of the hopelessness of the damned," he wrote to Luce. "I cannot put this experience into words; I have tried. I can only say that I knew something of the terror and pain of the lost soul. But it was more than this. I had a concept or an understanding of hopelessness and everlasting regret with no end, no relief, no resignation. I did not fear for myself but I began to see friends and loved ones in Hell. From this developed the clearest concept of God that I had known," namely that he was a tyrant.

Then, said Brother Michael, he prayed for help and had an epiphany, "our dear Lord does not want the souls he died for to fall into Hell. But for some reason I cannot clearly see, those who offend God and do not repent must perish."

He was pouring his heart out to Luce, he wrote, because he wanted her to understand why Salvador Dalí's *Vision of Hell* was so important.

"Though Hell is an unpopular doctrine, a fear of it can save souls," he wrote. "The vision had its origin not on earth and in the minds of fallible men, but in Heaven and in the mind of the infallible God. God gave man this extraordinary reminder of the penalty for sin; therefore, we know that man needs it. The vision was not merely for the benefit of the three children... If man so needs a reminder of the penalty for sin that Heaven itself is moved to send the Mother of God that she might open the earth and reveal the very horrors of Hell, should we not. . . show this vision to all the people?"

Brother Michael pleaded with Luce to "help us to bring this reminder of the wages of sin to the people," ostensibly by publishing a story of it in Life magazine.

He ended his letter with a call for her "prayerful consideration."

"The existence of Hell is a truth that we cannot alter or deny," he declared. "However, by cooperation with God's graces, we can save our own souls, and we can help others. A tried and proven way of doing this is to remind ourselves and to warn our neighbors."

Brother Michael never received a response from Luce.

+ + +

When Sister Lucia finally saw a photo of the painting in 1997, she stared at it for a long time and then nodded in agreement with what she saw. The Sister, according to her interpreter Carlos Evaristo, said that Hell is spiritual and not physical and it is impossible for anyone to make an image of Hell. The painting, she said, comes as close as humanly possible to representing Hell.

She had no more to say about it.

She died in 2005.

+ + +

A couple of years after painting *The Vision of Hell*, Haffert said that Dalí went to Fátima. He was deeply moved by the experience, says Haffert. So moved, that he went to confession and returned to the sacraments. No dates were given for this visit and Haffert himself did not witness Dalí at the shrine, but said he only heard the details of the visit from Canon Galamba and Camile Paul Berg, who managed the Blue Army hotel. Dalí later confessed to John Haffert that he had painted his own conversion and spiritual rebirth into *The Vision of Hell*.

+ + +

Ultimately it was Haffert who gave the most publicity to *The Vision of Hell*. In the July, 1965 and in the March - April 1974 Issues of Soul, the official publication of The Blue Army, Haffert ran a full-page photo of *The Vision of Hell* along with a brief story about its inception.

Then he wrote his own review of the painting. Almost four years of of observing the painting and thinking about Dalí's motivations gave him a different perspective on the work of art than the one he had when he first looked at the startling canvas. He wrote:

> *"If Dalí had painted just an ordinary picture, showing bodies in fiery torment, it is not likely that the horror of Hell would even have been conveyed. Dalí had to paint something so terrible that it would make the person looking at it feel like the child having the vision, cried out: "NO, IF OUR LADY HAD NOT BEEN THERE I WOULD HAVE DIED OF FRIGHT!"*

This may be one of Dalí's greatest masterpieces. In any event, it certainly causes us to recoil in horror before the three elements starkly conveyed in that dramatic vision on July 13, 1917:

Our Lady herself, <u>anxious to open the grace of her Immaculate</u>

<u>Heart</u> (Dalí shows heart of Mary in light) <u>upon the world</u>, in motherly anguish (this does not show so effectively in this small reproduction, but is extraordinary on the original painting, which is about three feet high);

The terrible horror of a soul <u>suddenly dismembered by death</u> and realized that it has been <u>damned forever</u>. To the left we see the damned soul, fiery red, emerging from the dismembered body;

Below, on the whole earth there is only one figure, because Our Lady is saying: "You see Hell where the souls of poor sinners go, so many souls are lost because THERE IS NO ONE TO PRAY AND TO MAKE SACRIFICE FOR THEM, wrote Haffert."

"It is the purpose of this painting to awaken us to the horrible reality of Hell not only because we ourselves deserve to go there because of our sins, but because the one thing Our Lady has asked us not only at Fátima but in every one of her apparitions is that WE PRAY FOR THE CONVERSION OF SINNERS.

"Each of us, as we witness The Vision of Hell given by Our Lady at Fátima should ask himself: When did I last think to pray for the conversion of sinners? How many sacrifices did I make today that a soul about to die in mortal sin might receive the grace of final contrition?

"If I have not done this, then I have not fulfilled the main, essential request which Our Lady made at La Salette, at Lourdes, and finally at Fátima. Is it because I do not REALIZE that Hell exists? Will I continue to permit many souls to be lost because there is no one to pray for them?"

And with that, John Haffert wrote no more about *The Vision of Hell* and said little about the subject. The article from which the material above was quoted was run again in the magazine in 1988. Other than that, Haffert's pen was silent on the subject of Dalí and the painting.

And with his silence came the nearly total disappearance of the painting.

At first it hung on the wall of the office of The Blue Army in New Jersey, where most of the staffers developed a deep fear of Hell from what they saw on the canvas. Somehow it was then moved back to the offices of the Catholic Traveler in downtown Manhattan, where it hung in a corner close to the office coffee machine.

When someone splashed coffee on it (there is a slight coffee stain in the lower right-hand corner of the canvas) the painting was moved back to The Blue Army headquarters and hung once again in the administrative offices.

It was after some playful Fátima Travel secretaries used the painting as a coffee tray and a cup stain left visible on the canvas that John Haffert took measures to preserve the valuable masterpiece.

The Vision of Hell simply vanished and no one seemed to know that it was gone or where it had gone. No one in fact cared. Haffert, was already focusing on his book writing and a myriad of other things and confided its whereabouts to only one other person, a member of his competent staff who had stored it exactly where Haffert ordered for safe-keeping.

In essence, what happened was Haffert confided the custody of the painting to the Prioress of the Handmaids of Mary Immaculate, the nuns of the Order he had founded who resided at the Blue Army headquarters in New Jersey.

Haffert, who believed in crime prevention did not invest in any crime prevention measures at all at the shrine. These were not only costly but involved sharing precious knowledge with others. By the 1950's he had devised methods for keeping valuables safe, safer than the biggest and strongest vaults.

He hid them underneath the beds of nuns.

Haffert now commanded the Mother Prioress to hide the Dalí painting underneath her bed in the convent at the Blue Army Shrine in Washington, New Jersey. The nun died without revealing the hiding place of the painting to anyone after John Haffert retired from the Blue Army Leadership in the late 1980's.

And so it remained undetected, under the bed of a deceased Nun for 30 years. Subsequent photos of the painting were published throughout the 1970's and 80's by the Blue Army in articles run on Hell published in *Soul* Magazine. The painting secretly toured several Japanese cities for an exhibition marking the memorial of the atomic bomb first dropped on Hiroshima.

According to studies by a psychoanalyst, people usually changed opinion regarding paintings and photographs once the subject matter is inverted. In keeping with this idea, the Blue Army tried to make the painting more appealing to Catholics by publishing a mirror image photograph in *Soul* Magazine in 1974 and then by distributing mirror image prints during a Hell awareness campaign organized by John Haffert in 1979.

Then in 1997 the painting was found by a cleaning crew and shown to Sister Mary Ann Sullivan, a nun with an art background. She believed it to be authentic and reported its existence immediately to Executive Director William Sockey III.

"Do you know that the Blue Army owns a Dalí painting?"
the Sister asked Sockey.

"A what?"

"A Salvador Dalí painting."

"You're kidding! Where is it?"

"Under the bed of the late Mother Prioress."

One of the oldest staff members was asked about the painting and within minutes she produced a dusty accordion file from storage that contained letters from Salvador Dalí, Haffert, Brother Michael, and others.

When the new Director asked Haffert about it, a smile came over his face and he recalled the entire story, from his first contact with young seminarian Brother Michael to his last contact with the bizarre work of art and the artist. But still disgruntled over the way he had been treated by the Blue Army in his last years at the helm, he kept silent on the subject and refused to give any further information. Unbeknownst to everyone there was still one major secret associated with the painting and Salvador Dalí.

Sockey considered the rediscovery of the painting providential. 1997 was the 80th Anniversary of the Fátima Apparitions and so he decided to send it for display to the Fátima Shrine in Portugal as part of the Blue Army's 50th Anniversary celebrations. But things had not changed in Fátima since Bishop Venâncio wrote the discouraging letter to John Haffert.

The painting was given a cold reception by the shrine's administration who instead of placing it in a prominent place for exhibit, placed it instead on an easel in a corner of the lobby of the Shrine's rectory building. Few came to see it despite the $10,000 expense it cost to fly it to and from the U.S. and insure it. Little publicity was given and no special protective measures were in place.

But after returning from Portugal, Blue Army Treasurer John Labradore came up with the perfect temporary home for the painting. He approached the Las Vegas Art Museum and asked if they wanted to exhibit this unique and relatively unknown masterpiece. The museum trustees were ecstatic with the offer.

In 1998, *The Vision of Hell*, commissioned to depict and warn against the penalties of sin, found a home in Sin City, where it spent six months as the main art attraction in a town that some would say is dedicated to its subject matter. Afterwards it was featured in a Dalí Exhibition in Japan.

After the successful Japanese tour, Blue Army Director William Sockey and Blue Army President Bishop James Sullivan decided to ask John Haffert what he thought should be done with the painting. Haffert suggested it be permanently displayed in the lobby of the Domus Pacis, the organization's Fátima hotel.

After meeting with Haffert and his new Fátima Foundation Director Carlos Evaristo who was also Sister Lucia's interpreter and confidant, Sullivan and Sockey decided to have a bullet proof case made for the painting in Fátima. It was at that time that Evaristo accompanied the Blue Army administrators to the convent in Coimbra where Sister Lucia was shown a copy of the painting for the first time. She agreed that the ideal place for the painting was the Domus Pacis.

Although Dalí's painting is about the curse of Hell and was considered a curse for The Blue Army for many years, it eventually came to be seen as a blessing for the apostolate. The organization's main objective had been the defeat of Communism and the return of Christianity to Russia and her neighboring countries. With the demise of the Soviet Union in 1991 and the death of John Haffert in 2001, The Blue Army went into a decline in both membership and funding.

Bishop Sullivan had died and William Sockey was retired before Salvador Dalí's painting could be transferred to Fátima. The costly bullet proof display case for its permanent display at the Domus Pacis was completed on the site of a previous lobby telephone booth.

Then plans for the painting changed again.

The new Executive Director Michael LaCorte assessed the assets of The Blue Army and did the unthinkable. He decided to put *The Vision of Hell* up for sale. Haffert's widow Patricia was shocked. How could the Blue Army sell one of its most priceless treasures?

In the early 1990's the apostolate had lost the Icon of Kazan after Pope John Paul II had it retrieved from the Domus Pacis by the Bishop of Fátima D. Serafim Ferreira e Silva and brought to the Vatican to schedule its return to Russia. The Pope was photographed with Russia's President Vladimir Putin, the icon symbolically displayed on a table between, and then returned to the Russian Orthodox Church. The return of the holy icon took place shortly the pope's death in 2005 and was done as a symbol of the fulfillment of the Fátima prophecy regarding the conversion of Russia.

The Blue Army had also donated to the Spanish Blue Army relics from the "mighty vision" of the Holy Trinity at Tuy. These were to be kept at the convent in Pontevedra, Spain where Sister Lucia once lived.

Now the Blue Army was also contemplating the sale of the valuable properties in Fátima including the Domus Pacis Hotel.

Mrs. Haffert considered all of this scandalous and deeply disrespectful to her husband's memory, especially since proceeds from the sales were going to pay the back salaries of executives when her husband had never taken a penny from the apostolate.

Eventually it was decided to sell part of a lot behind the Domus Pacis and the Dalí painting to pay the debt. A copy was made, framed and placed in the protective display case in the Lobby of the Domus Pacis in Fátima. This copy is believed by many to be the original painting.

In reality The Blue Army had the painting examined by a Dalí expert who gave the painting a replacement value of $2-million and high marks as a painting. He wrote in the appraisal:

> *"While the subject matter of "Vision of Hell" and its treatment are intentionally disturbing, I believe that if offered for sale, the painting would sell for a substantial sum, especially as the recent and current art markets are characterized by more and more money chasing fewer and fewer good artworks. This is especially true of the limited supply of good oil paintings by Salvador Dalí which have not yet been taken into museum and foundation collections from which they will not re-emerge onto the market."*

A private art collector purchased the painting in 2007. It hangs at his home in Connecticut, surrounded by two other Dalís and the works of a number of great 20th century artists, painters who both admired and were puzzled by the genius from Spain.

+ + +

At the end of all of this is a story about Salvador Dalí that seems almost too ironic to be true. Five years before his death in 1989, Dalí was lying in his sickbed trying to summon one of his attending nurses with an electric buzzer that was cabled to his bed. Angered that no one came within the first few rings, Dalí held the button down for a long time. At that point, sparks from a short in the buzzer's electric cable started his bed on fire.

Now the ringing began in earnest, yet still no one came. Before long the room was filled with black smoke and the skin on Dalí's right leg was melting in a lake of fire.

The painter was in Hell, all right, a living Hell that was strangely akin to the one he had painted for the Blue Army. Dalí rolled from the bed and began crawling across the floor until the thick black smoke from the fire suffocated him into unconsciousness.

The next thing Dalí knew, three assistants were carrying him to the library where they proceeded to administer mouth-to-mouth respiration and heart massage. Dalí apparently needed neither. He was in good enough condition to shake off one of the assistants and yell, "Bitch! Criminal! Assassin! I called you and you didn't come." Still protesting, he was carried from the Castle and moved into the backseat of a car where he watched flames spitting out the window of his upstairs bedroom and into the dark of the Spanish sky.

Pain emanated from his burned leg, which was scorched so badly that it would require extensive grafting surgery within the week. Firemen rushed up the street as did policemen and eventually curious pedestrians and the media. For several hours Dalí had lost control of his well-controlled world as he was surrounded by pain and death, the elements he feared the most.

Up until this point Salvador Dalí convinced himself that he could face death dispassionately. But for those sick moments of flame and fear, Salvador Dalí, the father of surrealistic art, realized that the Doctrine of Hell was anything but surreal. He was living in his own painting. To his horror, he was in the Vision of Hell.

Dalí never truly recovered from the hellish fire. He died five years later in 1989.

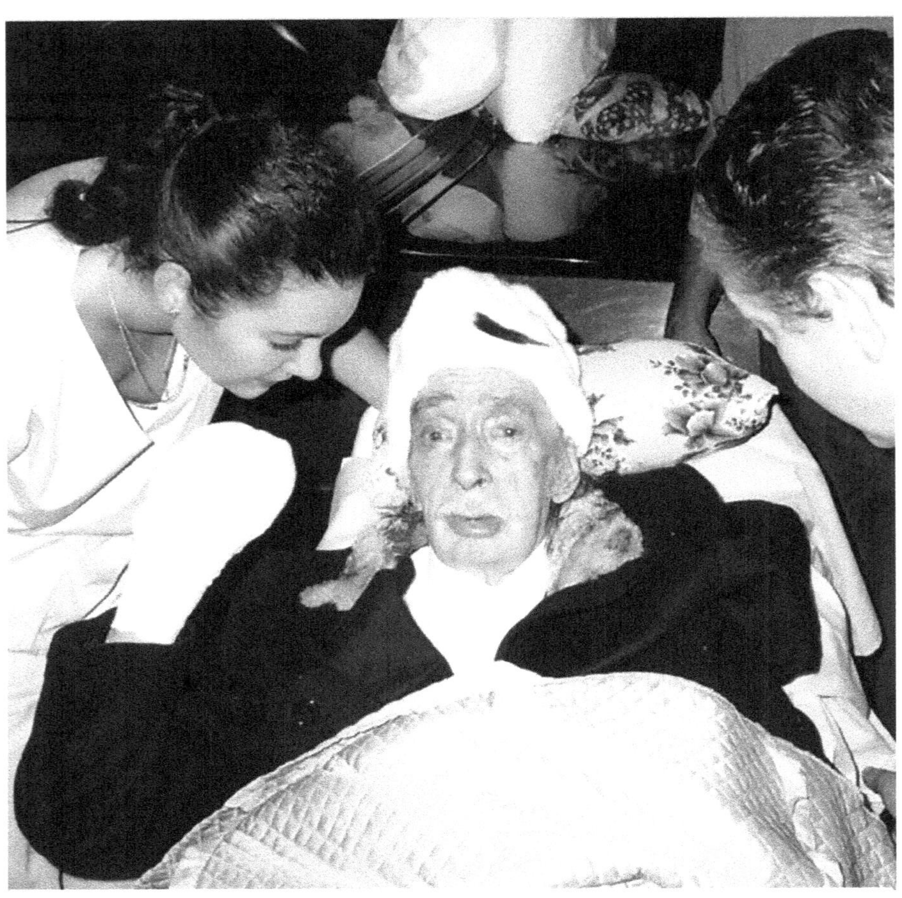

Salvador Dalí waves with bandaged hand after suffering serious burns during a fire that broke out in his bedroom at his Castle in Pubol, Spain. Saved by Robert Descharnes, Dalí compared his ordeal to a Hellish torment. One of the few items spared destruction in the bedroom was his late wife Gala's replica of the Icon of Our Lady of Kazan.

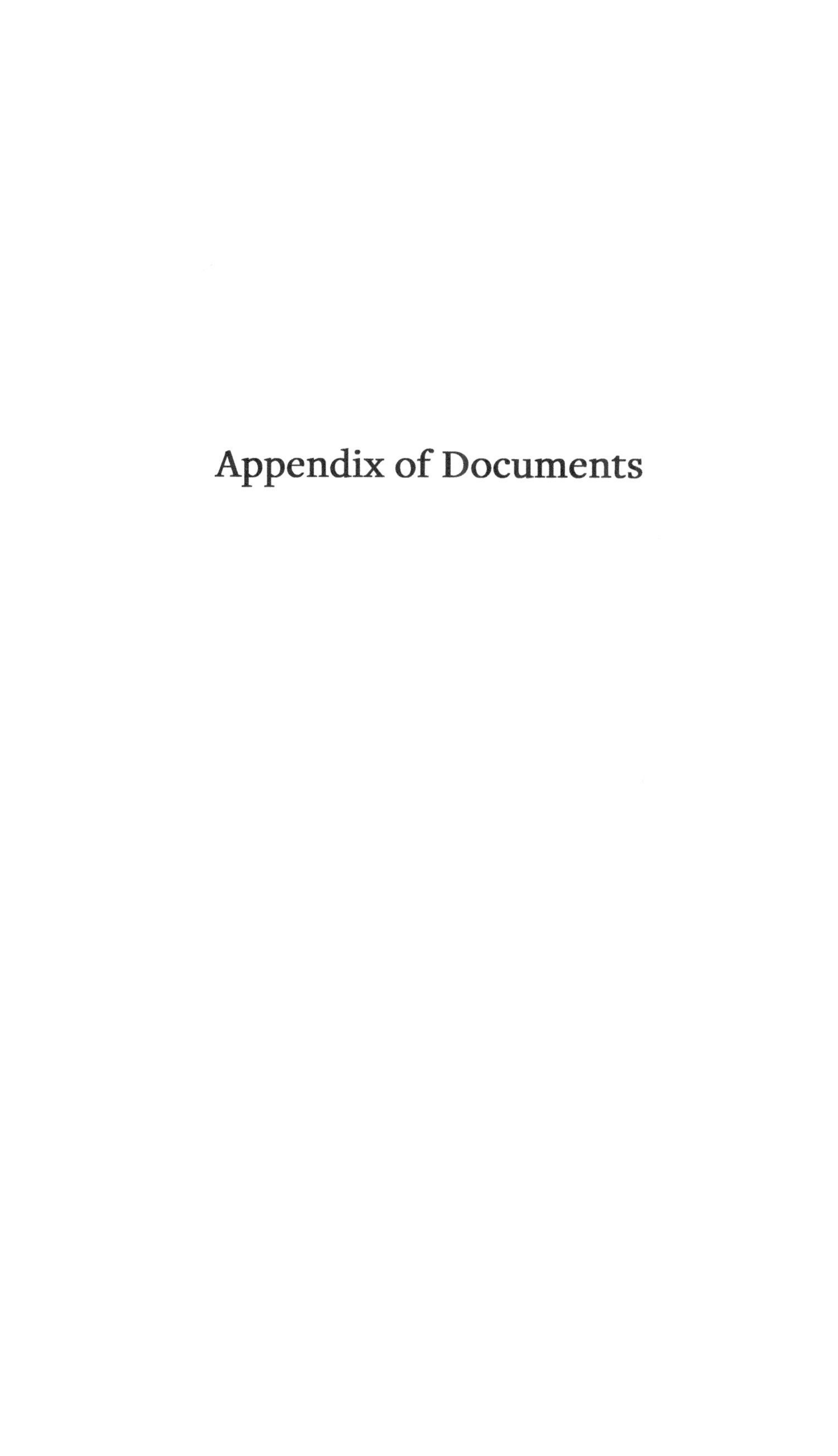

Appendix of Documents

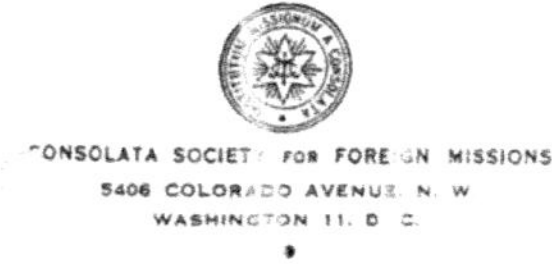

January 9, 1960

Thank you for your letter of December 23.
I do not like to discourage you in your project,
but I think it wouldbe extremely difficult if not
impossible to get Sister Lucy to give any description
of hell to an artist. Of course, you can always try.

As to my own part in your project, I must say
that my obligations make it impossible for me to
take on any additional work now or for quite a while
to come. You had better not depend on me.

With all good wishes for the New Year, I remain

Sincerely yours in Christ,

Rev. John De Marchi, I.M.C.

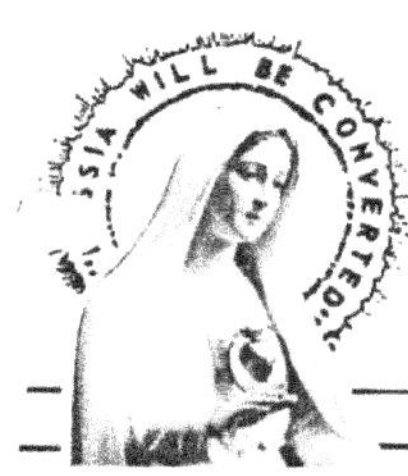

THE BLUE ARMY

of

Our Lady of Fatima

Ave Maria Institute
Washington, New Jersey

Telephone: MUrray 9—1700

"I gladly give my blessing to . . . the leaders and members of the Blue Army." — POPE PIUS XII

January 15, 1960

I agree with you completely on your idea.

I have often thought of that vision of hell, and its importance to the world.

However, I hold little hope that Sister Lucia could give us a very adequate description, and even less hope that it could be translated onto canvas.

You see, during an interview with her, I asked her about this apparition and she was terrified by the very memory of it. The best she could say was the souls looked as if they were burning from within and from without.

I also recall that when a sculptor was commissioned to do the vision of Our Lady according to Sister Lucia's description, the sculptor worked day in and day out, but Sister Lucia always made changes. Finally in desperation, on the very last day she squeezed the whole face as though desperately trying to change it into what she had seen, and then gave up.

It was impossible to transfer into clay and into physical colors the tremendous light and mystery of what she had seen.

Nevertheless your idea is certainly worth a try. And if anyone in the world could do it, and I think even get the opportunity to interview Lucia on the subject, it would be Mr. Dali. By all means try, and my suggestion is to write directly to the Bishop of Fatima, and tell him of your desire and purpose.

Wishing you every success, and with every best personal wish, I remain.

Sincerely yours,

John M. Haffert

Jordan Seminary
Menominee, Mich.
Dec. 1, 1960

Mr. Salvador Dahli
Port LLIGAT prov de
Gerona, Spain

Dear Mr. Dahli:

As you may know in 1917 Mary the Virgin mother of Our Lord and Savior Jesus Christ appeared six times to three shepherd children near Fatima, Portugal. During the third apparation the children were privileged to witness a scene of hell.

There is only one surviving member of this trio, Lucia dos Santos. She is now a member of a religious community of the Order of Discalced Carmelites. Sister Lucia's description of the scene has been widely publicized. The following is a translation taken from a popular book on the apparations, Our Lady of Fatima by William Thomas Walsh, published by the Macmillan Company, New York, 1954.

" As the Lady spoke the last words she opened her lovely hands as before, and poured down from them the revealing and penetrating radiance that had warmed the hearts of the children

December 21, 1960

        Enclosed is a copy of my letter to Mr. Dali, and I hope to have
the material for the next issue of our magazine, which we will put
together during the first week in January.

        In the magazine we will start the special fund for the painting,
and I am sure that Our Blessed Mother, who is not outdone in generosity,
will make it possible for both of us to recover in large part the large
sums which we are creating for this project in Her honor.

        Words are feeble in trying to tell you how deeply we appreciate
your concept of this wonderful idea and your perseverance in its
realization.

        Taking this occasion once again to wish you a joyous Christmas
and a blessed New Year, I remain

                              Sincerely yours,

                              John M. Haffert

JMH:B

December 21,1960

Mr. Salvador Dali
Hotel St. Regis
New York, N. Y.

Dear Mr. Dali:

We are very pleased that you have accepted the commission to paint the "Vision of hell", which will be given to the Church at Fatima.

It is our understanding that we will pay $5000 now and a balance of $10,000 when the painting is delivered in the fall of 1961 - the painting to be approximately thirty inches.

Our purpose in commissioning this painting is to attract attention to this very important aspect of the message of Fatima; and the painting will be widely publicized and exhibited throughout the world before it is finally hung in the main hall of the International Centre at Fatima, which receives millions of visitors a year.

To prepare advance publicity may we arrange a photograph with you? If Friday, January 6th will be agreeable, this will be an opportune time for us. Also at this time we will present our deposit check of $5000.00.

Secondly, could you loan us a transparency of your painting of the Crucifixion for reproduction in color on the cover of our magazine, together with a biography of yourself and some publicity photographs?

I am enclosing a sample issue of our magazine.

Taking this occasion to wish you a Holy and blessed Christmas, I remain

Sincerely yours,

John M. Haffert

JMH:B
Enc.

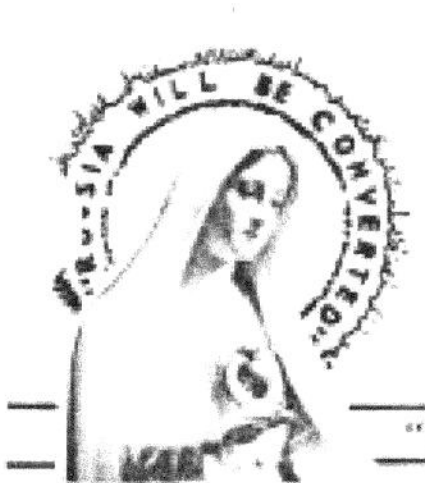

THE BLUE ARMY
of
Our Lady of Fatima

Ave Maria Institute
Washington, New Jersey

Telephone: MUrray 9–1700

"I gladly give my blessing to . . . the leaders and members of the Blue Army." — POPE PIUS XII

June 23, 1961

Anything whatever you do concerning the picture has my complete approval. Unfortunately my own hands are tied because of the enclosed excerpts from letters from our Bishop. Apparently he does not like Salvador Dali's art. However, I believe that the Bishop will change his mind, too, when he sees the finished painting.

I have thought of you often and will remember you particularly at Mass on the occasion of your entering the Novitiate.

Our Blessed Mother is not to be outdone in her generosity, And your zeal for her cause is certain to bring great conversions.

With every best personal wish, I remain

Sincerely yours,

John M. Haffert

S. DALI
The St. Regis
Fifth Avenue and Fifty-Fifth Street
New York

Yan. 9 - 62

Dear Mr Haffert,
We arrived very short
time ago and will
remain at Hotel St Regis
as usualy.
Your painting The Vision
of Hell will came soon
from Spain as it
been shiped only
resently for leave it
dray — in order that
will be no hurt.
Dali is waiting the
News about this shiping
and as soon as every
thing is in order and
painting here we will
announce it to you
Please accepte ours best a your
wishes for new year Sincerely yours DALI

C O P Y   C O P Y

THE ST. REGIS
FIFTH AVENUE AND FIFTY-FIFTH STREET
NEW YORK

Febr. 18, 62

As Dali told you the shipping arrived in N.Y. Customs ect. did
delayed some of delivery of the painting of the Vision of Hell. But
could you be so kind and write now to Dali telling him when you could
come here in N.Y. around or soon after 10 - 12 March to see and take
the painting of Our Lady of Fatima.

Dali sorry about all this complications and hope see you soon.
Please accept my respects.

Yours

Signed: Salvador Dali in same handwriting.

MEMO   **Blue Army Headquarters**
                  Ave Maria Institute
                  Washington, New Jersey

To:

From:

Mrs. Dali called Monday morning, March 5, 1962
and said that Mr. Dali would like to meet you
at 5 PM on Tuesday, March 13, at the St. Regis
to give you the picture etc.etc.

Please call him at the St.Regis, preferably in the
morning, as soon as you can.

Phone: Code #212, PL(aza) 3-4500

THE METROPOLITAN MUSEUM OF ART
NEW YORK 28, N. Y.

May 15, 1962

Mrs. Faith Bayley
Secretary
The Blue Army of Our Lady of Fatima
Ave Maria Institute
Washington, New Jersey

Dear Mrs. Bayley:

I must apologize for having taken so long to answer your letter. The delay is due to my having been absent from the city.

The story connected with the commissioning of Mr. Dali's painting entitled "Inferno" is most interesting. However, I am sorry to say that it will not be possible for this Museum to exhibit this work. It is a standing rule that we do not give special exhibitions to the work of a single living artist. I am sure that you will understand that to break this rule would start a very dangerous precedent.

With kind regards,

Yours sincerely,

Theodore Rousseau
Curator
Department of Paintings

TR:EW

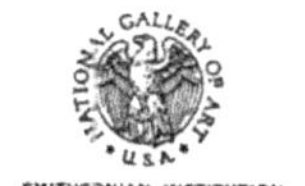

NATIONAL GALLERY OF ART
WASHINGTON 25, D. C.

SMITHSONIAN INSTITUTION

TELEPHONE: REPUBLIC 7-4215
CABLE ADDRESS: NATGAL

May 29, 1962

Dear Mrs. Bayley:

Thank you very much for your letter of May 18th.

I am interested to know about the painting by Salvador Dali, entitled the _Inferno_. It is also most generous of you to offer this painting as a loan to the National Gallery of Art. We have on view the _Sacrament of the Last Supper_ by Dali, which has been lent to us by Mr. Chester Dale as a part of his larger loan of twentieth century painting of the School of Paris. In recent years, however, the number of gifts to the Gallery have caused the Trustees to decide against accepting further loans. We do not like to crowd our paintings, and, consequently, a certain number of pictures belonging to us are shown only inter-mittently.

I appreciate greatly your interest in the Gallery, and I am sorry that we cannot take advantage of your offer.

Very sincerely yours,

John Walker
Director

Mrs. Faith Bayley, Secretary
The Blue Army
Ave Maria Institute
Washington, New Jersey

■BELL & STANTON INC., *public relations*
■ 757 THIRD AVENUE, NEW YORK 17, N.Y. PLAZA 9-4800

September 16, 1963

Mr. John M. Haffert
Hotel Napoleon
Piazza Vittorio Emanuele, 105
Rome, Italy

Dear Mr. Haffert:

Your letter of August 22 to Jack Drury has been forwarded to Alan Bell who asked me to look into the matter of the Salvador Dali painting, "Vision of Hell."

After viewing the painting at the <u>Catholic Traveler</u> office, we will have to have some background information before we can start the publicity, to wit:

1. Why was Dali selected to do this painting? Who chose him and when? How much time elapsed between the commission and the completion of the painting?

2. Regarding the subject of the painting: Is the subject matter Dali's or was it suggested by the person who commissioned him? Did Dali's watercolors on the "Divine Comedy" have anything to do with this commission?

3. Why the carving forks, what are they symbolic of?

4. You mention in your letter that there is a description of the painting in your book "Russia Will Be Converted." I have this book but cannot find this reference.

I am writing to both Salvador Dali and to   in order to get information. However, anything you can tell me about the painting and how it came into being will be most helpful.

Cordially,

Marion Cook

ccs: Messrs. Jack Drury
     Alan Bell

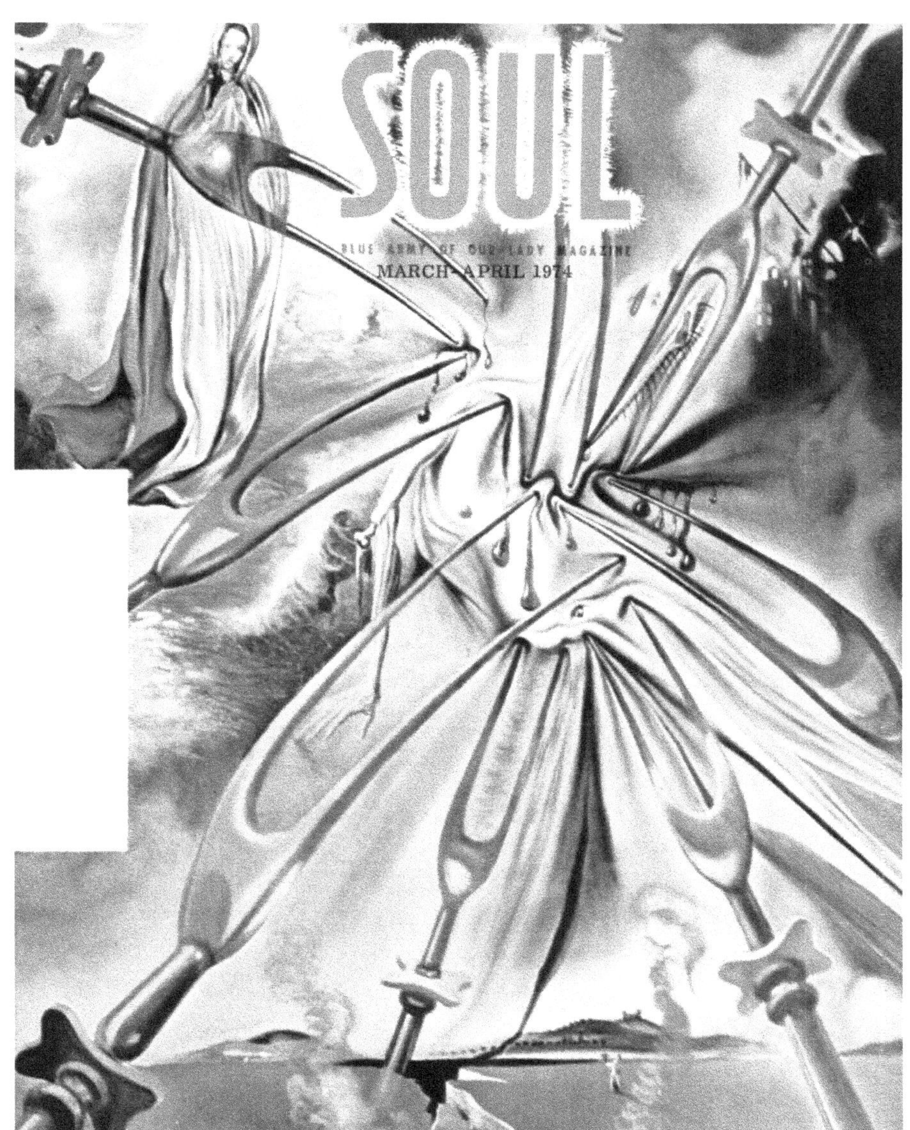
SOUL
BLUE ARMY OF OUR LADY MAGAZINE
MARCH-APRIL 1974

HELL is "FOR REAL!"

by GERARD E. MAYERS

The present interest and rise in Satanic worship was anticipated by Our Lady of Fatima in the famous July, 1917, vision. This same vision stressed and affirmed the existence of hell, a topic which today is too little mentioned.

"A Reality So Terrifying..."

Seven years ago, the late Pope Paul VI himself told us of the reality of "the evil which we call the devil," calling him "the occult enemy who spreads errors and darkness in human history. He is the evil and crafty deceiver who knows how to creep into us."

An attempt in today's world to convince people of the existence of a being totally evil usually brings a snide remark, a chuckle, or a comment that he "doesn't exist." The devil has scored a victory when he "persuades" people to believe he doesn't exist, thereby making his work easier. Yet, three children aged seven, nine and ten saw a glimpse of a reality so terrifying that if Our Lady *had not been there with them*, they would have died of fright!

Years later, Lucia recalled one incident which involved her little cousin Jacinta and which took place after the July vision:

"'Hell! Hell! How sorry I am for the souls that go there! And people burn there alive, like wood in a fire!'"

Trembled with Fear

Lucia then notes that Jacinta would shake with fear and kneel down to say the pardon prayer Our Lady had taught them.

What did these shepherd children see that so terrified them? What made Jacinta especially tireless in offering sacrifices of reparation? We have the answer in Lucia's own words:

What Did They See?

"...She opened her hands as she had in the two months before. The rays seemed to penetrate the ground and we saw what looked like a sea of fire. Plunged in this fire were the demons and the souls, almost like coals, transparent and black or bronze-colored, with human forms, which floated about in the conflagration, borne by the flames which issued from it with clouds of smoke falling on all sides as sparks fall in great fires as without weight or equilibrium, among shrieks and groans of sorrow and despair that horrify and cause people to shudder with fear....

"The devils were distinguished by horrible and loathsome forms of animals, frightful and unknown, but transparent like black coals that have become red-hot."

The children turned to Our Lady, who then told them that they had just seen hell *"where the souls of poor sinners go."* She said that God wishes to establish the devotion *to Her Immaculate Heart in the world in order to save them.*

First-Hand Experience

We have seen at first-hand what the powers of darkness can do to men. The current waves of immorality, improper sex education and

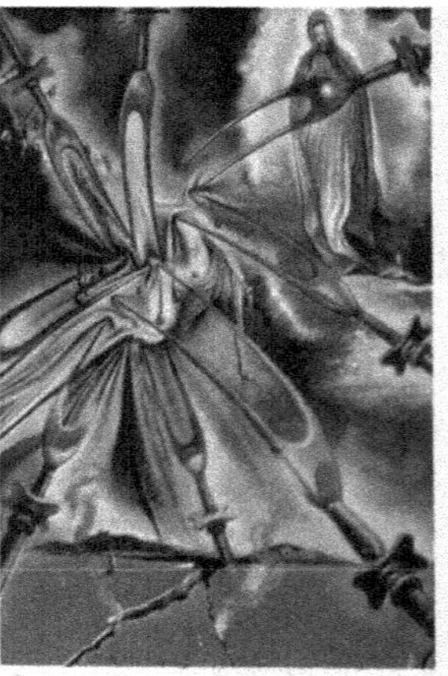

Above: The vision of hell, July 13, 1917, as painted by Salvador Dali.

pornography, occultism and Satanism, and anti-life forces can be traced to him whom Pope Paul VI called "the occult enemy."

And if the forces of evil can operate with such power in the world today, can they not also hinder the effective spreading of the very message which would insure their final defeat?

Commissioned Painting

Upon reading an account of the July apparition of Hell some years ago, a Protestant in Mississippi was so shaken that he converted and afterwards entered the seminary. At the same time he gave his entire life savings to commission a special painting of the vision of Hell by the famous surrealist artist, Salvador Dali. Upon completing this painting, Dali himself went to Fatima. There he made a general confession, returned to the Sacraments, and rejoined the Church! (This painting by Dali is now at the National Center of the Blue Army in Washington, N.J.)

The devil knows his ultimate defeat through the instrument of Mary (*"and she will crush your* head..." (Gn. 3:15) will happen soon and that the time for him to be "prince of this world" is growing short. Therefore, should we be surprised or alarmed when we realize that the waves of evil which have been erupting over the past few decades or the attempts to confuse or falsify the *authentic* Message of Fatima are but the attempts to draw as many souls as possible away from Christ?

We CAN Help!

Knowing this, we can personally help defeat Satan and his plan for the domination of men and their souls. We can defeat our "occult enemy" by doing three things:

Using our weapons of the Rosary and the Scapular; believing in the Message of Fatima and all that it contains; redoubling our efforts at the promotion of this message through every medium open to us, including television.

May It Reach Them!

For a timely reminder, why not order several copies of our leaflet L66 ("Would YOU Like to See a Vision of Hell?") and pass them out among your friends and acquaintances? (See pg. 31.)

It took only the account of the vision of hell to convert a sincere Protestant in Mississippi. A copy of

the "Vision of Hell" leaflet in the right hands may cause the conversion of the last person Our Lady needs to fulfill Her promise of the conversion of Russia, the triumph of Her Immaculate Heart, and the granting of the era of true peace.

And let's all remember, the peace and safety of the world as we face these troubled times depends on EACH one of us doing what we can to make Our Lady's message...and the vision of hell...known.

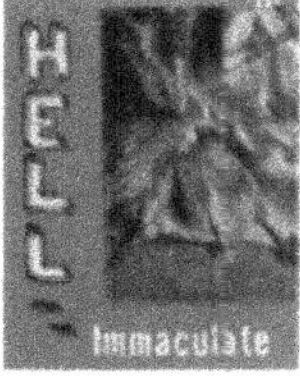

JULY VISION OFFER

July is the month of the major Secret of Fatima and also the anniversary of the famous vision of Hell. In connection with the article *HELL is "FOR REAL"* on page 13, we are offering the following items:

Vision of Hell poster (Dali painting)

50c

Would YOU Like to See a Vision of Hell?

3c each

Hell and the Immaculate

25c

(For ordering and price information, see right.)

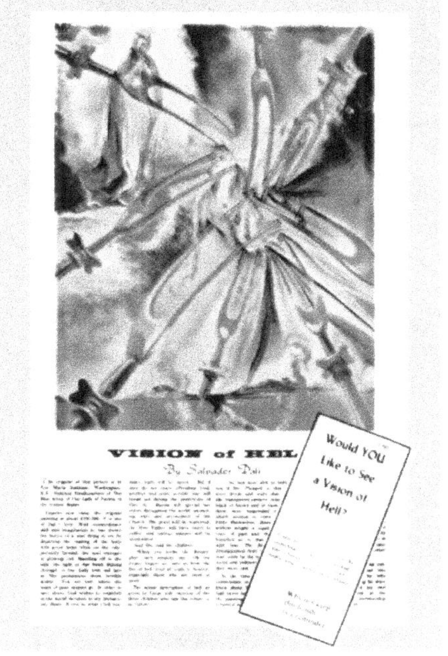

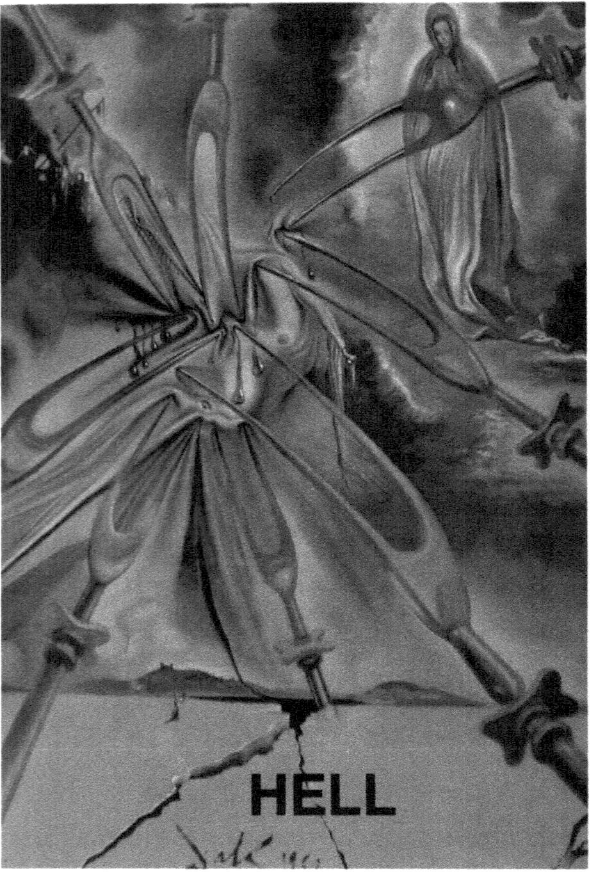

Above is a copy of the original painting by Salvador Dali of the Vision of Hell.

The celebrated artist wanted to show the horror and disfigurement of man by the sins which cause souls to be lost in the eternal flames.

To the left, as though floating from the body dismembered by sin, is the perfect form of the damned soul glowing like a red coal.

Lucia, the visionary of Fatima who described the Vision of Hell, stands on the fissured ground. The locale is identified by the Castle of Ourem in the background, a castle which witnessed some 2000 years of history leading up to the great Message and miracle of Fatima.

In 1982, paintings of Dali, from museums and private collectors all over the world, were brought together in four major cities of Japan. This Vision of Hell (described in the accompanying article) was one of the few of the major works of Dali reproduced for these Japanese exhibits in full color in a commemorative book of the exhibition.

On July 13, 1917, Our Lady of Fatima showed the children a vision of hell.

It was so terrible little Jacinta cried afterward that if Our Lady had not been there she (Jacinta) would have died of fright!

"You have seen hell," Our Lady said, *"where the souls of poor sinners go. In order to save them, God wishes to establish in the world devotion to my Immaculate Heart."*

When the Collegial Consecration of Russia to the Immaculate Heart of Mary was at first not made, the sole survivor of the three children who saw this vision of hell said she was very sad that the consecration had not been completed because so many souls would continue to go to hell.

It would therefore seem that following the completion of the Collegial Consecration, a first phase of which was completed by the Pope in Fatima on May 13, 1982, there will be not only a conversion of Russia but a great spiritual awakening in the world as a result of which many souls, now being lost, will be saved.

The Picture

A Southern Baptist, on reading of the vision of hell at Fatima changed his life, became a Catholic and later a Franciscan brother.

Before entering the Franciscans, this extraordinary convert wanted to use his life savings to have a painting done by Dali, a famous artist, so that many more people would become aware of this important vision of hell.

The original painting is at the National Center of the Blue Army in Washington, N.J. Recently it was loaned to Japan for exhibitions in Tokyo, Osaka, Kitakyusu and Hiroshima.

It is interesting that the exhibition took place in Hiroshima from June 11 to July 11, 1982, and closed in that city which was the first in the world to be destroyed by the atomic bomb.

Urgency

Consecration to the Immaculate Heart of Mary and the devotions of reparation on the First Saturday of the month are urgently needed to bring about the great triumph of Mary's Immaculate Heart through which many souls will be saved from hell.

Dali Painted His Own Conversion

How much is it worth?

Last August 1, it was reported that a Japanese buyer had purchased a Salvador Dali painting for a record $2.3 million.

It is reputed that the previous highest price paid for a Dali painting was $1 million.

These astronomical figures bring to mind what is probably the most meaningful painting in the life of Dali: A painting of Hell.

A good Protestant in Mississippi read of the vision of Hell which Our Lady showed to the three little children at Fatima. This was the cause of his becoming a Catholic and eventually entering a monastery. Before he entered he wondered how he could get others to know about this vision. He decided to ask Salvador Dali to paint a picture of it. After Dali painted the picture, he himself went to Fatima, went to confession, and returned to the Sacraments.

Dali's "Vision of Hell" may well be one of his greatest works. It shows Mary in motherly anguish, revealing Her sorrowful and loving heart before the terrible horror of a soul suddenly dismembered by prodding forks.

Would Have Died of Fright

On July 13, 1917, the ground opened at Fatima to reveal to three children a vision of Hell. Afterwards one of them cried, "Oh, if Our Lady had not been there, I would have died of fright!"

Our Lady told them, *"You have seen Hell where the souls of sinners go. It is to save them that God wants to establish in the world devotion to my Immaculate Heart."*

Dali's "Vision of Hell"

Dali's painting shows:

1. The body torn by painful prodding forks.

2. The soul, translucent red, separated forever from the God Who created it.

3. The fissured earth. The ground opened before the children at Fatima.

Dali did not try to picture Hell as Lucia described it: "... we were now able to behold a sea of fire. Plunged in the flames were devils and souls that looked like transparent embers; other were black or bronze and in human form, these were suspended in flames which seemed to come from the forms themselves—there

to remain without weight or equilibrium amid cries of pain and despair which horrified us so that we trembled with fear. The devils could be distinguished from the damned human souls by the terrifying forms of weird and unknown animals in which they were cast."

4. War. Our Lady said, *"You have seen hell where the souls of poor sinners go.... If you do what I tell you, many souls will be saved, there will be peace. The war will end, but if men do not cease offending God, another and more terrible war will break out."*

5. Our Lady with Her Immaculate Heart. She taught the children, "When you pray the rosary, after each mystery say: *'O my Jesus, forgive us our sins, save us from the fires of hell; lead all souls to Heaven, especially those most in need of Thy mercy.'"*

6. The lone figure. This is the most tragic part of the picture. Dali has painted a lone figure holding up a crucifix to Heaven in prayer. Our Lady had told the children in August: *"Pray, pray very much and make sacrifices for sinners, for many souls go to hell because they have nobody to pray and make sacrifices for them."*

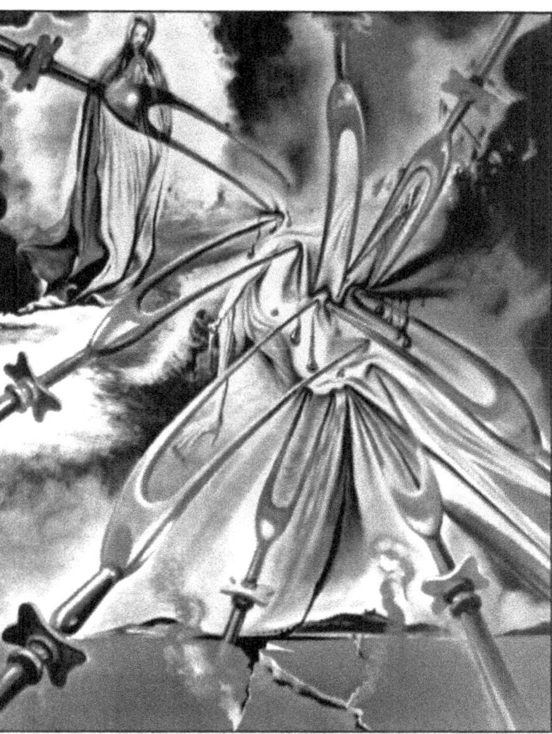

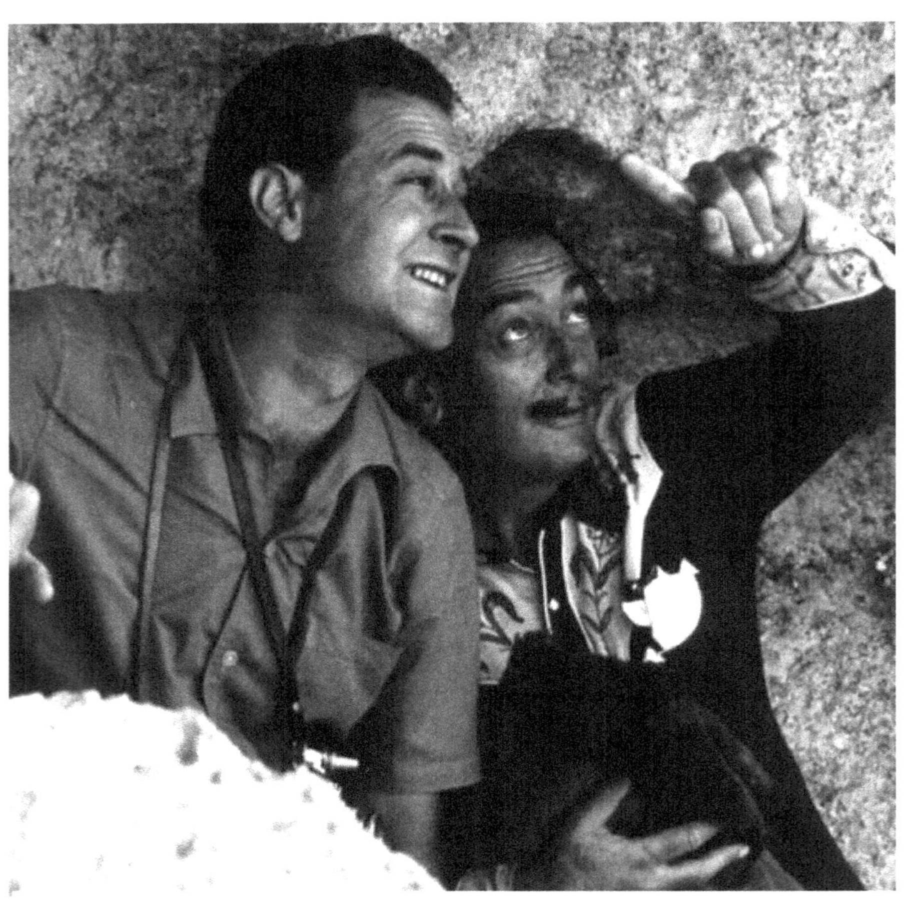

Salvador Dalí with his friend, personal aide and photographer of 40 years Robert Decharnes.

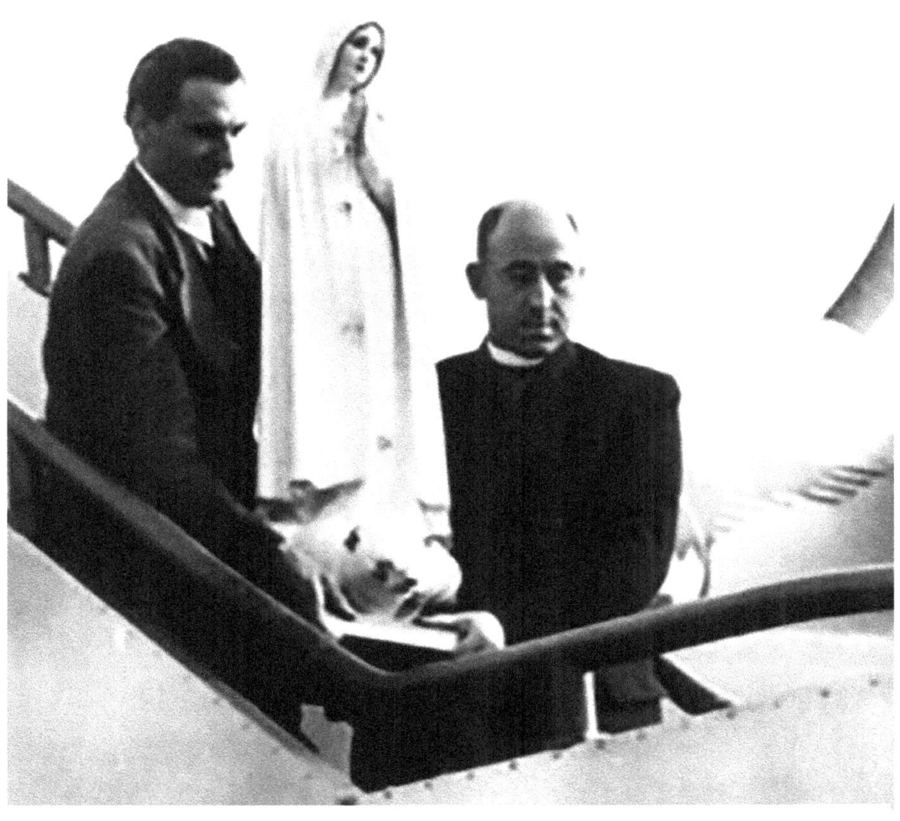

John Haffert and Canon José Galamba de Oliveira carry the image of the Pilgrim Virgin of Our Lady of Fátima off the plane in 1947 following her arrival in the United States.